65
E

MANAGERIAL AND
ORGANIZATIONAL COGNITION

MANAGERIAL AND ORGANIZATIONAL COGNITION

Theory, Methods and Research

edited by
COLIN EDEN AND J.-C. SPENDER

SAGE Publications
London • Thousand Oaks • New Delhi

Editorial arrangement and Chapter 1 © J.-C. Spender and
    Colin Eden 1998
Chapter 2 © J.-C. Spender 1998
Chapter 3 © Bo Hellgren and Jan Löwstedt 1998
Chapter 4 © Kees van der Heijden and Colin Eden 1998
Chapter 5 © Pia Lindell, Leif Melin, Henrik J. Gahmberg,
    Anders Hellqvist and Anders Melander 1998
Chapter 6 © Kjell Grønhaug and Joyce S. Falkenberg 1998
Chapter 7 © Jacky Swan and Sue Newell 1998
Chapter 8 © Phyllis Johnson, Kevin Daniels and
    Rachel Asch 1998
Chapter 9 © Roland Calori, Michael Lubatkin and
    Philippe Very 1998
Chapter 10 © Mauri Laukkanen 1998
Chapter 11 © Colin Eden and Fran Ackermann 1998
Chapter 12 © Robert P. Bood 1998
Chapter 13 © Mark Jenkins 1998

First published 1998

SAGE Publications Ltd
6 Bonhill Street
London EC2A 4PU

SAGE Publications Inc
2455 Teller Road
Thousand Oaks, California 91320

SAGE Publications India Pvt Ltd
32, M-Block Market
Greater Kailash – I
New Delhi 110 048

British Library Cataloguing in Publication data

A catalogue record for this book is
available from the British Library.

ISBN 0 7619 5194 6
ISBN 0 7619 5195 4 (pbk)

Library of Congress catalog card number 97-062468

Typeset by M Rules
Printed in Great Britain by The Cromwell Press Ltd,
Trowbridge, Wiltshire

CONTENTS

NOTES ON EDITORS AND CONTRIBUTORS

The editors

Colin Eden is Professor of Management Science at the University of Strathclyde. His interest in managerial and organizational cognition stems from his work in industry before he moved to the University of Bath. Initial experiments in the 1970s using repertory and implications grids for problem structuring led to a dissatisfaction with their representation of personal construct theory and their efficacy in a managerial environment. He consequently developed his own version of cognitive mapping, reported in two books, *Thinking in Organisations* (1979) and *Messing About in Problems* (1983). His interest in MOC has always been from the standpoint of its use in helping individuals and teams resolve complex problems, and for working with idiographic research data. Over the last decade he has extended the use to helping management teams resolve major strategic issues and develop strategy.

J.-C. Spender is the Dean of the School of Management, New York Institute of Technology. He spent fifteen years in the nuclear engineering, MIS consulting, and computer software industries. Since becoming an academic he has been on the faculties of Rutgers University (Newark), University of Glasgow, UCLA, York University in Toronto, and City University in London. His most recent publication is *Scientific Management: F. W. Taylor's Gift to the World?* (1996), and he also publishes in many journals. He serves on the Editorial Boards of the *Strategic Management Journal*, *Organization Studies*, the *British Journal of Management*, and the *Journal of Business Research*, and on the Review Board of *Organization Science*. His current research projects cover theories of organizations as technologically constrained activity systems, the nature of workplace knowledge, and the teaching of technology, and the analysis of technological systems, to managers.

The contributors

Fran Ackermann is a Senior Lecturer in the Department of Management Science, Strathclyde University. Her main research interest encompasses exploring how systems can be designed and used to support groups working on messy, complex problems – an interest identified during her PhD studies. She has been actively investigating how groups of managers structure, negotiate and resolve problems/issues, particularly in the arena of strategy making. To inform this research she has worked widely with organizations in both the public and private sector at senior and junior levels. Other research interests include inquiring into the link between group and individual decision-making, and between operational and strategic decisions as well as furthering understanding about the role of the facilitator.

Rachel Asch is a Chartered Psychologist who currently works in the Human Factors Group at Cranfield University where she is a lecturer in Applied Psychology. Her main teaching areas are in organisational behaviour, research methods and statistics. Rachel's research interests encompass many aspects of organisational behaviour, but her primary interests relate to well-being at work and equal opportunities issues.

Robert P. Bood is currently an Assistant Professor of Strategic Management at the University of Nijrode, Faculty of Economics, the Netherlands. He is preparing a PhD thesis in which he studies the process of diversification in small and medium-sized enterprises from a cognitive perspective. His research interests include topics such as diversification and growth strategies, organizational learning and scenario analysis.

Roland Calori is Professor of Business Policy at the Groupe ESC Lyon, France and a business consultant in strategy. He is the author or co-author of several books and articles on strategic change and comparative management among which is *A European management model beyond diversity* (1994). His recent research is focused on managerial cognition in complex international settings. He is a founding member of the Association Internationale de Management Stratégique and co-editor of *Organization Studies*.

Kevin Daniels is a Lecturer in Organizational Behaviour at Sheffield University Management School. He received his PhD in applied psychology from Cranfield University. He has published research in the areas of stress management and psychological well-being at work; cognitive mapping methodology; and the role of cognition in strategic management. His current research interests include the influence of emotion on cognition in organizational contexts; methodological issues in assessing emotion at work; organizational and cognitive factors promoting or inhibiting effective coping with work stress; and teleworking.

Joyce S. Falkenberg is Associate Professor at the Norwegian School of Economics and Business Administration. She received her PhD from the University of Oregon. Her research interests include strategic change and adaptation. She has recently published an edited book (co-authored with Sven Haugland) *Rethinking the Boundaries of Strategy*, and is editor of a practitioner's journal, *Statoil Forum*.

Henrik Gahmberg, DBA, is Professor of Management and Organization in the Department of Management, Faculty of Business Administration at the University of Vaasa, Finland. He has taught in the Swedish Business School in Finland, both in Helsinki and Vaasa, as well as in the Helsinki School of Economics, where he also gained his academic degrees. Henrik Gahmberg's research interest is in organizations and leadership from a cultural perspective. His speciality is the application of narrative semiotic methodology in this field. In his work he is also using newly developed software for text analysis.

Kjell Grønhaug is Professor of Business Administration at the Norwegian School of Economics and Business Administration, Bergen-Sandviken. He holds an MBA and PhD in marketing from the School, an MS in sociology from the University of Bergen and did his postgraduate studies in quantitative methods at the University of Washington. He has been Visiting Professor at the universities of Pittsburgh, Illinois at Urbana-Champaign, California, Kiel and Innsbruck. He is also an Adjunct Professor at the Helsinki School of Economics and Business Administration. His publications include 15 books and over 200 articles in leading European and American journals related to marketing problems, corporate strategy, managerial cognition and methodological problems.

Bo Hellgren is a Professor of Management in the Department of Management and Economics, Linköping University. His current research interest concerns strategic change in the industrial field. Another research interest is decision processes in networks of organizations. His recent publications include 'The Role of Strategist's Way of Thinking in Strategic Change Processes' (with L. Melin) in Hendry et al., 1994 and 'Design and Implementation in Major Investments – A Project Network Approach' (with T. Stjernberg), *Scandanavian Journal of Management*, 1995.

Anders Hellqvist, PhD, is a Lecturer in Business Administration at Linköping University. His main research interest is concerned with organizational routines and strategic change. In 1997 he concluded his dissertation in which he studied changes in a large hospital from the perspective of organizational routines, and where one of his findings was a rather strong decoupling between strategic change ideas and the everyday practice.

Mark Jenkins is a Senior Lecturer in Strategic Management at Cranfield School of Management. Prior to joining Cranfield he worked for the Lex Service Group and in the marketing and sales functions of Massey Ferguson Tractors Ltd. In his current role he teaches on both the MBA and senior management short courses, specializing in the areas of competitive strategy, strategic capabilities and customer facing organizations. His consulting activities reflect these teaching specializations where he has worked throughout Europe, the USA and in parts of the Far East and Middle East. In addition to his work at Cranfield he has contributed to programmes at the University of Colorado and Warwick Business School. He has published and presented a wide range of work in the areas of strategy and marketing. He is a founding editor of the *Journal of Marketing Practice* and is author of *The Customer Centred Strategy* (1997).

Phyllis Johnson completed her first degree in psychology and business management at Leeds University and went on to gain her Masters degree in applied psychology from Cranfield University in 1993. Since that time she has been based in Cranfield School of Management working on her PhD, studying part-time with the Institute of Counselling and is conditionally registered as a chartered psychologist. Her research interests focus on collective cognition and the social psychology of the board room.

Mauri Laukkanen is Professor and Head of the Department of Entrepreneurship and Management at the University of Kuopio. Before his academic career, he worked for several years as the owner-manager of a family firm. He received his PhD at the Helsinki School of Economics in 1989, where he currently serves as a Docent of Management and Organization Cognition. His research interests include management of small and medium-size enterprises (SMEs), cognitive mapping, and proactive SME development.

Pia Lindell, MSc, PhD, is Assistant Professor in Industrial Marketing at Linköping University. Her research is focused on strategic change processes in both private business firms and public organizations and on the role of cognition in these processes. In addition to teaching in regular university courses in strategic management she also takes part in management education programmes on leadership and strategic management.

Jan Löwstedt is an Associate Professor in Organization Theory at the Stockholm School of Economics. During the academic year of 1990–91 he was a visiting professor at the Templeton College, Oxford University. He is active in the programme committee for the annual International Workshop on Managerial and Organizational Cognition and was the chairman of the fourth workshop held in Stockholm in 1996. He has published books and articles on organizational change, technology and change and managerial and organizational cognition. He is currently researching the role of management and management tools in the transformation of state schools.

Michael Lubatkin is a Professor of Management at the Groupe ESC Lyon and the University of Connecticut. He is also the elected chair of the

Business Policy and Strategy Division of the Academy of Management. He has published over 45 papers specializing in corporate diversification issues as they pertain to problems of core competency transfer between divisions and across national boundaries. His research has been honoured with two international awards and three US-based regional awards by the Academy of Management.

Anders Melander, MSc, is a Research Fellow in Business Administration at Jönköping International Business School, Jönköping University. His research interests concern social cognition and strategic change. He has recently completed his dissertation on industrial wisdom where the complex relationship between collective cognitions and strategic change within an industrial sector was dealt with in a processual and longitudinal manner.

Leif Melin is Professor of Management and Director of the PhD programme at Jönköping International Business School, Jönköping University. His current research interests concern the ways of thinking and rhetorics of leaders, change and renewal processes in mature firms, networking principles of organizing, and governance and cultural issues in family businesses. He has published widely in edited books and international journals in his field. He serves on the editorial boards of many journals, such as *Strategic Management Journal* and *Organization*.

Sue Newell is a Lecturer in the Organization Behaviour Group at the Warwick Business School, University of Warwick. She graduated in psychology and has subsequently been involved in the applied occupational and organizational area. Her main research interest is concerned with inter-organizational networks and the diffusion of new ideas to business firms. Her most recent research has focused on the role of professional associations in this diffusion process. Other research interests include the process of organizational learning and management development.

Jacky Swan is Senior Lecturer in Organizational Behaviour at Warwick Business School, University of Warwick. She was the principal researcher on a three-year project investigating the roles of professional associations and technology suppliers in the diffusion of knowledge needed for IT development. She is commencing work on a new project exploring knowledge articulation and the creation of expertise in processes of innovation.

Kees van der Heijden joined the faculty of the Strathclyde Business School as Professor of General and Strategic Management from industry where he was engaged for many years in developing methodology in strategic management in a practical setting. He developed his 'four-box' approach to strategy, which concentrates on the ongoing process of institutional strategic thinking and learning. His research interests include the evolution of the business process and the managerial role, in the light of current societal and technological change. Before joining the SGBS faculty in April 1991 he was in charge of Shell's internationally renowned scenario planning group. He has consulted widely in the areas of scenario planning and strategy. He is the author of *Scenarios, the Art of Strategic Conversation* (1996).

Philippe Very is Professor of Business Policy at the Groupe ESC Lyon, France, and business consultant in strategy. He is the author of *Diversification Strategies* (1991) and co-editor of *Perspectives in Strategic Management*, vol. 3 (1995). He is also the author or co-author of several articles dealing with diversification strategies and international mergers and acquisitions. His current research is focused on core competencies and the management of mergers and acquisitions.

1

INTRODUCTION

J.-C. Spender and Colin Eden

When the US Academy of Management established an Interest Group in Managerial and Organizational Cognition in 1991 it publicly recognized it as a new area of study. The subsequent growth of interest and of scholarly activity has been explosive, and the number of publications claiming to address managerial and organizational cognition has grown by leaps and bounds. In the past few years we have seen, for example, *Organization Science*'s special issue (1994), *Mapping Strategic Thought* (Huff, 1990) and a new JAI series, Advances in Managerial Cognition and Organizational Information Processing. Along with this burst of interest and activity have come the concomitant questions that arise whenever any new line of study is opened up: is the field distinctive, necessary or appropriate? The present volume explores these questions, but unlike the work cited above, reflects a more European view – even though one European author appears in both places. This book is based on work initially presented at a Managerial and Organizational Cognition research workshop held in Brussels 1994. Its value is that it will give readers some additional insights into the assumptions, thinking, research activities, and methodologies that demarcate the field, and help illustrate how the field is both theoretically distinct, researchable and yet also of considerable relevance to practicing managers and consultants.

In the introduction to the 1994 special issue of *Organization Science*, Meindl et al. pose five key questions:

1   What is an appropriate construct system for describing managerial and organizational cognition?
2   What is an appropriate way to treat level-of-analysis issues?
3   What is the relationship between cognitive structure and cognitive process?
4   What is the relationship between managerial cognition and organizational outcomes?
5   What role do 'cognitive aids' have in shaping managerial and organizational cognition?

For those of us who have helped shape this field, these kinds of question are important. While they may seem pedantic and of little relevance to practitioners, they help theorists understand how the study of managerial cognition is distinctive and why it needs to be separated from the large body of work that is already familiar to organizational analysts. Why is it a field that warrants its own Academy of Management track?

The editorial ideas shaping this volume were similar to those behind the questions of Meindl et al., but we approach them in a rather different way. If managerial and organizational cognition is to be a distinct field, the first question must be: Why is the vast body of completed research into managerial decision-making inadequate? Theories of rational expectations and managerial choice continue to dominate the syllabi of business schools and they obviously imply very specific notions of managerial cognition and organizational rationality. So what do we have to say that is new about managerial and organizational cognition? As is well appreciated, our field actually grows out of a rejection of the presupposition that managerial decisions can be analysed adequately by using these hyper-rational notions of complete data, well-defined objective functions and rigorously logical choice processes. We argue that managers form personal models of the focal situation, personal in the sense that they differ significantly from the abstract models which formal choice theories presuppose. Hence one way in which our field is defined is by the nature and sources of the differences between 'real managers' models' and the abstract and hyper-rational models of the various manifestations of utility theory. The challenge is to give this statement some meaning.

One dimension of difference deals with the apparent boundaries around or 'boundedness' of the manager's decision-making model. The classic argument is that the manager's choice process will be limited by the fact that she/he has neither full information nor the unlimited capacity to process the information that is available. The problem facing those wanting to do empirical research into bounded rationality is to find a workable research framework. One approach is to examine the determinants and invariants of managerial boundedness by using, for instance, the concepts of decision-making 'bias' which Kahneman et al., 1982 introduced into our field. The heuristics they reveal, representativeness, availability, and anchoring and adjustment (Kahneman et al., 1982: 4), help us see how we can research the systematic and invariate differences between humans' choice behaviours and the abstract models of the decision-making theorists. But their work is of only limited interest to us because it is profoundly behavioural, in the sense of being non-cognitive, and comparative, in the sense that it means little unless we also know the purely logical approach against which the bias can be measured. For us, managerial and organizational cognition must go well beyond what can be deduced from such observations because neither managers nor those who research their behaviours have the logical answers available as reference points. In practice managers make their decisions under conditions of information inadequacy and other forms of uncertainty.

Uncertainty and the managerial response

Ultimately it is this concern with uncertainty, and with managers' responses to this fact of their activity, that demarcates our field. It is here that we separate from the traditional literature on managerial decision-making, which, if it treats uncertainty at all, is actually discussing computable risks. Thus instead of defining the manager as a computing device, we define her or him as a key actor who invents or creates a bounded field of decision possibilities which is then navigated in the process of choice. Our inquiry must cover both the boundary of this field and the terrain to be navigated. By definition, we are not able to assume the nature of the manager's answers a priori. We do, on the other hand, assume that we are able to gain access to the personal model which the manager has created, and which, we assume, she/he uses when making decisions. We are interested in the boundaries and structure of the model created, and in the process through which its creator navigates its terrain. It is these interests which place our inquiry within the body of cognitive science rather than within the behavioural sciences – which would include the newly popular field of behavioural economics.

Discussing the foundations of cognitive science, Simon and Kaplan (1989: 2) argue that it has three threads, the study of intelligence and intelligence's processes (a) in the abstract; (b) in computers; and (c) in humans. Many academic battles revolve around the distinctions between these domains. Godel's theorem argues for the first distinction, that computers are fundamentally limited, and much recent theorizing revolves around non-computable problems and processes. The hard and soft approaches to artificial intelligence reflect different attitudes to the second distinction. While philosophers such as Searle and Dreyfus argue that computers are unlike humans, for many more computing seems a perfectly obvious way to model human choice processes. Of course it seems difficult to imagine a process that can be explained which cannot, as a consequence, be rendered computable. But the emergence of connectionist machines has reminded us that we are just at the beginning of computing science, and that the relationship between computing and human choice may be far richer than we yet see.

In spite of the uncertainty surrounding the distinctions between the three threads of cognitive science, Simon and Kaplan's essay (1982) raises most of the issues which presently bedevil our field. First, we need explainable models of the human mind and the knowledge content that it processes. Second, we need to understand the relationship between the content and process modelled (knowledge and choice) and people's behaviour. Third, we need to understand the relationship between knowledge and choice and what people have to say about it. Meindl et al. (1994) certainly raise these points, but they also imply that the field will converge on some consistent answers. The contrary is far more likely as those working in the field on managerial and organizational cognition become familiar with the enormous amount of work that has already been done in cognitive psychology (for example, Posner, 1989) and social psychology. If we think about the assumptions underpinning most of the work in managerial and organizational cognition, we see they are relatively naïve. The model of mind and content is often based on von Neumann computing, action is typically tied closely to choice, and what people say is typically regarded as representative of their choice process. Yet few of today's cognitive scientists or social psychologists would be so sanguine. Network theory, which dates back to Hebb's work in the 1940s, seems far more viable now that neural network computing is a fact. Likewise there has been a widespread appreciation that much of human action is determined by non-conscious predispositions and modes of choice and everyone quotes Polanyi's pithy 'we know more than we can say'. In short, contrary to the predictions of Meindl et al., the editors feel that the field of managerial and organizational cognition is about to reach adolescence and become a vigorous and complex field. It is not likely to narrow down, nor escape the 'tired old problems related to level-of-analysis', nor soon to integrate content and process, nor to provide the links between knowledge, learning, choice, action and speech which resolve the problems noted above.

This volume reveals a variety of views and underlying assumptions. The editors, for example, focus on differing aspects of the nature of social cognition. One, following the behavioural psychologist F.H. Allport, argues that cognition belongs to the individual only, and that notions of group or organizational cognition do not address *thinking* but focus instead on the role and influence of symbols in organizational life. The other, following the lines of the old debate between Tarde and Durkheim (Doise, 1986) argues that an individual's consciousness and sense of self, which necessarily precedes and shapes all individual cognition, is grounded in interaction with the social, and that the social provides preconscious modes of cognizing.

Regrettably such richness and diversity in academic discourse is sometimes seen as the kind of disorder that should be shut down. There has been a fear that if the field encompasses individuals, groups and organizations then it will become too diffuse and general an interest group, and so a 'dumping ground' for research which cannot be accepted elsewhere. To some extent this fear has been realized. The Academy of Management MOC Interest Group meetings now include a vast range of material for which it would be difficult to find any unifying theme. But, as Kauffman observes in his study of self-organizing systems, life exists at the edge of chaos (1995: 26). There is considerable life in the field of managerial and organizational cognition, more than in some other better regulated and policed parts of the Academy.

Some comments on the chapters

J.-C. Spender, in Chapter 2, takes a hard look at the debate about the nature of organizational knowledge. He draws on a range of relevant literature from management, but more importantly from philosophy, cognitive science, social psychology and anthropology. It is an essay which attempts to bring the debate to a new level by drawing readers' attention to the fact that much of this material has already been covered in other disciplines. Drawing on these sources, Spender argues that the notion of organizational learning is complex. It cannot be captured by merely tracking shared cognition, rather there is a need to be concerned with 'tacit knowledge'. The chapter seeks to draw distinctions between explicit and tacit knowledge, conscious and automatic knowledge, and objectified and collective knowledge. Drawing further on developmental psychology, Spender argues that organizational consciousness is a necessary precursor to organizational learning.

In Chapter 3 Bo Hellgren and Jan Löwstedt introduce us to the role of social life as a context for understanding cognition. This chapter is concerned with drawing material from Greek philosophy and social theory into the field of organizational and managerial cognition but with a particular emphasis on organizational change. Within the context of organizational learning the authors are concerned to develop a synthesis of action and thought by addressing the assertions that 'organizations cannot think but they do act' and 'an organization can have a memory, but it cannot think'. Thus if we are to understand organizational learning then we must address some of the contradictions within our field. What is the relationship between thinking and acting? Are cognitive structures stable or continuously changing? Is cognition of importance on other levels than the individual?

Managerial and organizational cognition in strategic management

The next two chapters shift from discussion of the nature of managerial and organizational cognition to an exploration of its contribution within debates which are framed by the management literature. Chapters 4 and 5 are both concerned to understand the nature of strategy, strategic management and strategic decision-making from the perspective of managerial cognition. In each case the authors have sought to develop their thinking through an involvement within organizational settings and a focus on strategic organizational change. Research on managerial cognition as it relates to organizational change, strategic problem-solving, and strategy-making often involves 'action research' with real management teams (Eden and Huxham, 1996). There is little argument against the view that managerial cognition plays a significant role in the problem-solving processes and strategic decision-making of a management team. Research which depends upon intervention and change as the device for revelations in these fields can be more reliable than that which seeks to understand cognition through the analysis of speech acts, documents, or interview accounts. When the researcher can be close to the action by offering cognitive support then there is likely to be more trust between members of the management team and the researcher. Similarly the research data are rich because they relate to 'deeper' knowledge and can be collected over several organizational episodes. This type of research is dependent upon collaboration with 'elites' and so must attend to some of the difficult research method issues related to such groups. In both cases the authors take for granted the view that cognitive structures are not stable.

Van der Heijden and Eden are interested in managerial cognition to the extent that it can be changed. Their objective is to understand the ways in which organizational change can be attained by 'changing the minds' of managers. They use the equivocality of cognition, and designed group processes with computer support, to encourage both social (Fisher and Ury, 1982) and psychological negotiation. Lindell et al. have specifically sought to understand the nature of cognitive change in a senior manager. Each of these approaches are in contrast to the prevailing studies in the field where stability in cognition is presumed.

Van der Heijden and Eden reflect on years of working with a wide range of organizations, helping them to manage strategic change. They visit the debate about individual versus organizational cognition, but are particularly interested in the change as it relates to the management of meaning. Thus they consider the parallels between an evolutionary, processual, or rationalistic view of strategic management and the tensions between symbolic interactionism, semiotics and ethnomethodology as methods for understanding the management of meaning. It is within the context of these perspectives that they present approaches to the elicitation of cognition about strategy. They focus on exploring theories in use as the basis for eliciting cognition as it relates to decision-making and action.

Pia Lindell and colleagues, in Chapter 5, have been able to obtain continuing access to one top manager. They had to gain his trust within the context of the realities of organizational politics. They report on their understanding of his managerial cognition 'in action' and, as with Chapter 4, they raise issues of methodological import. The chapter explores, in depth, the cognitive development of the managing director of a large hospital. Based on interview data, the authors present some dimensions of the content of an individual top manager's way of thinking, and how it unfolds over three years. They discuss stability and change in managerial cognitions 'in action'. They also present their experiences in the use of a language-based interpretive technique for the analysis of their longitudinal data. As with the previous chapter, they use a theoretical framework derived from an integration of theories of strategic change and theories of managerial and organizational cognition. Thinking and acting are taken to go hand in hand, and mental structures are taken to be a mix of cognitions and emotions. Their data suggest that experienced managers change their cognition to develop relatively stable belief structures. These chapters act as a preface to the detailed discussions of methodology which appear later.

Research studies

Chapter 5 introduced an example of specific empirical research located within a strategic thinking arena. The next section features four different examples of empirical studies using a managerial and organizational cognition approach. The chapters deliberately present a variety of contexts and outcomes. There are examples of international joint venture practices, a large manufacturing company's experience in selecting and implementing a production innovation process, and a comparison of high- and low-performing organizations. In Chapter 9 Calori et al. not only document organizational outcomes and explicit national differences in joint venture management, but explore historical and educational sources for the differences in cognition and action.

Kjell Grønhaug and Joyce Falkenberg, in Chapter 6, take us back to some of the original research on managerial cognition – that of Dearborn and Simon (1958). Although the results of the Dearborn and Simon work are now being questioned and are proving difficult to replicate, they nevertheless provide a backdrop for the research reported in this chapter. The theoretical basis for the research reported here is that of attribution.

Jacky Swan and Sue Newell look at success in appropriating technological innovation in Chapter 7. The existing literature suggests that cognitive processes play a role in innovation. Here the authors address the role cognition plays in mediating the outcomes of decisions to adopt technological innovation. Cognitive mapping techniques were used to explore subjective beliefs in case studies involving the adoption of innovation. The authors report on the extent to which knowledge bases at the level of the organization and cognitions at the level of the individual are in a dynamic relation and change over time as innovations are introduced. Once again we see an orientation to considering cognition as something which changes, and so may be changed through social processes and changing contexts.

The primary aim of Chapter 8 by Phyllis Johnson, Kevin Daniels and Rachel Asch is to identify the level at which managerial cognitions of a competitive environment are held – the group or individual level. The question itself gives away one of the tensions in managerial and organizational cognition research. Researchers are, for practical reasons, attempting to focus on one aspect of cognition (individual, group, organizational, societal) rather than accepting that the interaction between context and the individual literally implies the social construction of reality (Berger and

Luckmann, 1966) – thus each aspect is inseparable. However, as we see from this mix of chapters each researcher chooses to focus on one rather than another aspect of the role of cognition. However, in addition, the chapter explores the impact of a number of organizational and environmental contingencies on the development of diversity in a group of managers' knowledge structures.

Roland Calori, Michael Lubatkin and Phillipe Very take us up a level of analysis by exploring the role of national context in determining cognition. The notion of 'collective knowledge' is now at centre stage in Chapter 9. This book is itself a reflection of some of the differences in approach to research in the field of managerial and organizational cognition. At some of the MOC research workshops we have seen a clear tension between the 'national cognitions' of different researchers. Some have argued that significantly different mental schemas exist between the Anglo-Saxon traditions (collective knowledge) of the USA, UK, the Netherlands and Scandinavia on the one hand and the 'Latin' traditions of Belgium, France, Italy, Spain and Portugal. This is only one of the propositions made. However, what it does demonstrate is the hunch that 'collective knowledge' of bundles of nations might be differentiated from those of others at the level of academics. Calori et al. explore, in particular, the national administrative heritages of the ways in which French and British firms manage their enterprises. Their approach is through a historical institutional analysis and its relationship to knowledge and managerial cognition.

Methodological issues in doing managerial and organizational cognition research

The final section of this book explores methodological issues in conducting managerial and organizational cognition research using mapping techniques. Contrary to *Mapping Strategic Thought* (Huff, 1990) which provided chapter-by-chapter comparisons of various methodologies, leaving readers to make their own comparisons, the chapters in this section provide stand-alone comparisons. In Chapter 10 Laukkanen outlines methodological ideas and options that researchers should be aware of when choosing methods like causal mapping. Eden and Ackermann (Chapter 11) discuss some of the issues in trying to make comparison between cognitive maps which have sought to represent the individuality of cognition. In Chapter 12 Bood examines various conceptions of organizational learning and matches mapping techniques with requirements imposed by the differing conceptions of organizational learning. Jenkins concludes with the issues raised by comparing maps of multiple organizations (Chapter 13).

The use of cognitive maps as cause maps to depict and explore the cognitive structures of members of organizations has become popular in recent years. The methods used for coding maps has varied between researcher and in relation to purpose. However, the theoretical basis for cause mapping, which allows an interpretation of analysis of those maps, is rarely made explicit, and so the link between a theory of cognition and the coding method is usually difficult to detect. Most methods follow the 'cause mapping' method developed by Axelrod in 1976 for use in political science, which was originally based on the practical demands of content analysis and the need for the analysis of documents. One clear exception is the approach to cognitive mapping developed so as to reflect the theory of personal constructs (Eden et al., 1979). However, there are few well-developed methods for the elicitation of cause maps.

An exception is the Self-Q method developed by Bougon (1983) which sets out a structured approach to interviewing research subjects. This approach contrasts with that used by Eden and colleagues who apply a deliberately open structure for interviewing which relies upon personal construct theory (Kelly, 1955) as the guide to elicitation as well as coding. The research processes involved in understanding cognition at the level of the individual are not trivial. Perhaps the most obvious point to be made is that the interview is the most common vehicle for elicitation and yet it is a social process. The nature of the social interaction changes the thinking of the interviewee. At the simplest level, poor interviewing skills, such as evaluative non-verbal signals and the interviewer taking too much air-time, vitally affect the size and shape of a map. As Eden (1992) argues, the differences between cognition and the models of cognition which researchers manage to collect and portray are likely to be large because the modelling of cognition by the researcher (whatever modelling method is used) is far removed from what a research subject may be thinking. In this section of the book we have four chapters which are designed to help researchers to make informed choices about how they do their research in the field.

One of the most notable differences that exists across different sorts of cause maps stems from the relative complexity of each of the maps. Most maps used in current organizational studies show a small number of nodes and links (6–20 nodes – see Huff, 1990), whereas others elicit large maps (30–120 nodes) from a single one-hour interview (see Laukkanen, 1990; Eden, 1991; Brown, 1992), and some strategy maps can be very large (800–2,000 nodes – see Eden, 1993).

As noted above, cause maps are directed graphs. They are therefore characterized by an hierarchical structure which is most often in the form of means/ends graph. However, the hierarchical form of a map is often destroyed by circularity in which a chain of means and ends loops back on itself; indeed circularity is often regarded as the fundamental structural characteristic of a map (Bougon and Komocar, 1990). When feedback of this nature occurs in maps everything which is a part of a circular structure is of the same hierarchical status unless collapsed to a single node describing the loop, when the general form of the remaining cause map can still be said to be hierarchical.

The tools and techniques for eliciting cognitive structures have rarely been set out in anything other than working paper documents. Such working papers have been in great demand. In this section we attempt to correct this problem by presenting some perspectives on the methods of cognitive mapping. In each case the authors have considerable experience of eliciting cognition through interview processes. The section examines the research task, processes of analysis and comparison, some aspects of the significance of the research setting and also compares a number of research approaches based on the idea of mapping as a model of cognition.

Laukkanen, in Chapter 10, provides readers with a basic overview of the issues in capturing cognition. He introduces some of the design issues in comparative cause mapping by considering the particularities of the research setting and context, the data type to elicited, the type of actor to be studied, and the domain of interest to the researcher. The chapter discusses the phases in planning research in the field of managerial and organizational cognition, including the procedures to be followed in data recording using computer software, and the subsequent data analysis methods for comparing cognitive maps.

Colin Eden and Fran Ackermann, in contrast with the previous chapter, consider the analysis of individual cognitive maps. Chapter 11 introduces a portfolio of analysis methods which seek to treat the cognition of an individual as systemic. They consider the reliability and status of a cause map for the purposes of making judgements about cognition and differences in cognition. The analyses introduced seek to uncover emergent properties of the map through analyses of the structure of the cognitive system.

Robert P. Bood, in Chapter 12, explores and compares four approaches to mapping an organizational learning process. The setting discussed is that of organizational learning during the course of a diversification project. Here it was of importance to understand changes in the conceptualization of the strategic portfolio of businesses and the developments of knowledge to run the business. The four approaches discussed are: content analysis; repertory grid combined with multi-dimensional scaling; cause mapping with CMAP2 (Laukkanen); and cognitive mapping with COPE (Eden et al.).

Finally, Mark Jenkins, in Chapter 13, addresses the issue of whether current approaches to eliciting comparative causal maps are appropriate to many research situations. In particular he considers circumstances that involve mapping across multiple organizations. The chapter suggests a resynthesis of approaches which places greater emphasis on the needs and requirements of the respondent in order to capture cognitions in a context where it is not practical to develop a high level of trust and commitment. The chapter addresses the issue of managing the balance between the capture of meaningful data and ensuring that there is a suitable basis for valid comparison across cause maps.

In summary, this book is an attempt to address some of the noted weaknesses of past publications. Specifically, its chapters make two contributions:

first, explicit links between managerial and organizational cognition's methods and findings and the concept and practice of organizational learning; second, new studies examining the linkage between cognition, behaviour and organizational outcomes.

References

Berger, P. and Luckmann, T. (1966) *The Social Construction of Reality*. New York: Doubleday.

Bougon, M.G. (1983) Uncovering cognitive maps: the 'self-Q' technique, in G. Morgan (ed.), *Beyond Method: A Study of Organizational Research Strategies*. Thousand Oaks, CA: Sage.

Bougon, M.G. and Komocar, J.M. (1990) Directing strategic change: a dynamic holistic approach, in A.S. Huff (ed.), *Mapping Strategic Thought*. New York: Wiley.

Brown, S. (1992) Cognitive mapping and repertory grids for qualitative survey research: some comparative observations, *Journal of Management Studies*, 29, 287–308.

Dearborn, D.C. and Simon, H.A. (1958) Selective perception: a note of departmental identification of executives, *Sociometry*, 21: 140–44.

Doise, W. (1986) *Levels of Explanation in Social Psychology*. Cambridge: Cambridge University Press.

Eden, C. (1991) Working on problems using cognitive mapping, in S.C. Littlechild and M. Shutler (eds), *Operations Research in Management*. London: Prentice Hall.

Eden, C. (1992) On the nature of cognitive maps, *Journal of Management Studies*, 29, 261–65.

Eden, C. (1993) Strategy development and implementation – cognitive mapping for group support, in J. Hendry and G. Johnson with J. Newton (eds), *Strategic Thinking: Leadership and the Management of Change*. Chichester: John Wiley.

Eden, C. and Huxham, C. (1996) Action research for the study of organizations, in S. Clegg, C. Hardy and W. Nord (eds), *Handbook of Organization Studies*. Beverly Hills, CA: Sage.

Eden, C., Jones, S. and Sims, D. (1979) *Thinking in Organizations*. London: Macmillan.

Fisher, R. and Ury, W. (1982) *Getting to Yes*. London: Hutchinson.

Huff, A.S. (ed.) (1990) *Mapping Strategic Thought*. New York: John Wiley.

Kahneman, D., Slovic, P. and Tversky, A. (1982) *Judgement Under Uncertainty*. New York: Cambridge University Press.

Kauffman, S. (1995) *At Home in the Universe: The Search for the Laws of Self-organization and Complexity*. New York: Oxford University Press.

Kelly, G.A. (1955) *The Psychology of Personal Constructs*. New York: W.W. Norton.

Laukkanen, M. (1990) Describing management cognition: the cause mapping approach, *Scandinavian Journal of Management*, 6, 197–216.

Laukkanen, M. (1991) 50 types of snow: exploring managers' core beliefs by cause mapping, Working Paper, Helsinki School of Economics.

Meindl, J.R., Stubbart, C. and Porac, J.F. (1994) Introduction, *Organization Science*, 5 (3), August, special issue.

Organization Science (1994), 5 (3), August, special issue.

Posner, M.I. (ed.) (1989) *The Foundations of Cognitive Science*. Cambridge, MA: MIT Press.

Simon, H.A. and Kaplan, C.A. (1989) Foundations of cognitive science, in M.I. Posner (ed.), *The Foundations of Cognitive Science*. Cambridge, MA: MIT Press. pp. 1–48.

Weick, K.E. and Bougon, MG. (1986) Organizations as cognitive maps, in H. Sims and D.A. Gioia (eds), *The Thinking Organization*. San Francisco, CA: Jossey-Bass.

2

THE DYNAMICS OF INDIVIDUAL AND ORGANIZATIONAL KNOWLEDGE

J.-C. Spender

Though cognitive theory has allowed organizational analysts to begin to operationalize Simon's (1958) concept of 'bounded rationality', it is in danger of becoming trivialized as the basis for a 'multiple lenses' model of management. Some of the deeper issues raised by information work, bounded knowledge, and organizational learning and memory need urgent attention before cognitive researchers' findings get dismissed as mere tautologies. In this chapter we argue that the current application of cognitive theory to organizational analysis is deficient in at least three major respects:

1   The models are applied freely at every level of analysis, even though most believe only individuals think.
2   The relationship between thought and action, and the dynamics of learning and forgetting remain unclear.
3   There is an assumption that there is but one type of knowledge. We draw on the work of Polanyi, Halbwachs, Weick and Roberts, Reber, and Vygotsky to sketch an alternative model of organizational knowledge and learning.

Modern cognitive science, which can be traced directly to Descartes' analysis of our 'impressions' of reality, reminds us that while we form mental representations of our situation, they remain profoundly problematic. We know that they are not the direct impress of reality on the blank substance of our consciousness. Instead they seem to be the result of complex selection, sorting, manipulation and conversion processes that are shaped by our existing knowledge, interests, and intentions. Our cognitive processes mediate significantly between what we take to be the facts and our behaviours. Since the facts alone do not determine our perceptions, the cognitive problematic is to find out what else influences their shape.

To some this seems a matter for biophysics, linguistic philosophy, psychology or the study of cognitive neuroscience. These fields want to know how the individual's mind–brain system works, how humans are able to construct and combine the processes of intention, representation, computation and behaviour. Organization theorists, on the other hand, have a different agenda. They want to know how organizations work and reflect management's intentions. It is not obvious how we are to connect these two types of inquiry. Managers make decisions, so we want to know about the cognitive frames in which these decision processes take place. Employees occupy roles and follow rules, so raising questions about how such constraints on workplace activity are determined and perceived. Strategists scan the competitive environment and try to comprehend the firm's resources and dynamics, so forming perceptions and making strategic decisions about the organization's 'workplace'. In addition to perceiving and deciding, managers, firms and employees are also experiencing, raising questions about the relationship between their perceptions and their experiences.

The easy way to deal with the resulting confusion is to assume that the manager's information is clear, complete and acted on without bias, that the employees understand the rules, that the competitive situation is certain, that the firm's resources are measured and controlled, and that the organization is a simple extension of the founder's or ruling group's mind and intentions. Curiously the bulk of economic and organizational analysis still depends on such heroic assumptions. Simon's (1958: xxv) well-known critique of economic rationality, albeit coming three hundred years after Descartes' speculations about the problematic nature of perception, warned organization theorists about the way these simplifications would shape their own analytic frameworks. In the years since the 'cognitive revolution' researchers have struggled to reveal intentions and representations, to work out their relationship to the situation perceived and to understand their effects on the behaviour of individuals, workgroups and organizations. For organization theorists rather than cognitive theorists, the state of the art is reasonably well summarized in Huff (1990), especially in the penetrating commentary by Stubbart and Ramaprasad (1990). This volume shows us a range of techniques for applying cognitive concepts to organizational analysis. For practitioners, whose agenda stresses practical application, progress towards understanding how to uncover and intervene in both the process and content of organizational decision-making is similarly summarized in Eden and Radford (1990).

This kind of analysis tends to suffer three defects. First, the idea of a cognitive map is applied freely to individuals, groups, organizations and institutions. This implicitly reifies each as cognizing entities. While this seems reasonable at the level of the solitary individual, it is clearly problematic at other levels of analysis. Second, the role of action and experience, the relationship between thinking and acting, and thus the dynamics of learning and forgetting, remain unclear. As Bougon and Komocar (1990: 136) have argued, a theory of change should also imply a theory of dynamic organization. Even so the typical organization theorists' underlying learning models tend to the simplistic, with experience leading directly to knowledge, an approach which effectively ignores the mediating effect of cognition and perception. Third, there is a presupposition that there is but a single kind of knowledge to be acquired and mapped. This is a reflection of the continued influence of the positivist empirical tradition which sees all knowledge as law-like, best modelled by the natural sciences.

To escape the third presupposition, a number of organizational researchers have recently turned to Polanyi's (1962) distinction between objective and tacit knowledge. Nelson and Winter (1982: 99), for instance, have argued that organizational routines, which embody the organization's memory, are learned by doing and therefore comprise knowledge that is both objective (explicit, symbolic and capturable in language) and tacit (implicit and embedded in action). Since cognitive mapping methods focus on cognition rather than on behaviour, they are likely to ignore by assumption those tacit components of knowledge which cannot be readily retrieved and explicated by respondents. It follows that cognition that focuses on symbols and ignores action may not be enough to deal with the problem Descartes identified, of knowing the status and truthfulness of one's perceptions. These deficiencies may be especially crucial to the study of organizations. Inasmuch as organizations are dynamic patterns of social activity, rather than scientifically designed tools for the achievement of well-understood objectives, the knowledge most evident in their day-to-day activity may well be more implicit rather than explicit. Organizations may be more systems of meaning and action than rule-bound production systems.

In this chapter we sketch a model of organizational knowledge that focuses on activity in the workplace. It is grounded in an expanding body of empirical research that goes beyond the rational decision-making paradigm. The central analytic concept is that of the 'activity system' (Asch, 1952). Rather than contrast only individual and collective entities, we argue that activity systems embrace individual and collective knowledge, both explicit and implicit knowledge. The key to the nature of activity system is the dynamic which leads to changes in the various types of knowledge, in its learning and unlearning processes. We consider the recent work of Weick and Roberts (1993) and the experimental work of a variety of those interested in 'practical' knowledge (Rogoff and Lave, 1984; Scribner, 1986), we borrow from social rationalism (Gergen, 1985, 1994) and from the socio-historical work of Vygotsky (1962) and others (Tharp and Gallimore, 1988; Moll, 1990).

Collective mind

So long as the cognitive problematic is ignored, organization theory is really about power, the division of labour in production and administration, and the quasi-scientific coordination techniques traditionally labelled POSDCORB (planning, organizing, staffing, delegating, controlling, ordering, resourcing and budgeting) (Gulick, 1977: 13). It is clear that the vast majority of organizational research is still focused at these modern rather than post-modern targets. A goal is established which remains logically prior to the analysis. The means to reach this goal is reflected in the knowledge evident in the chosen divisions of labour. The resulting set of roles is filled by people responding to an 'inducements–contribution' scheme which motivates them to take part in the organization. These role occupants are then coordinated, first by the system of explicit rules created for them and then by the authority system which attempts to align their behaviour with that required by the role. There may well be power in the situation which compels people to occupy roles, such as in a one-company town, but such complications are typically excluded from the analysis.

The power treated within the analysis is that which is applied to force behaviour to conform to the organization designer's expectations. As we know, power legitimated becomes authority, evidence of a structured system which employees accept as they 'buy into' the organization. The organizational power structure is explicit in its rules, and in its rewards and sanctions. There can be communication problems, in that the employee is not adequately informed about the role, but there are no fundamental knowledge problems. Indeed this kind of organization theory supposes that the body of knowledge necessary to design the organization pre-exists its formation, revealed, for instance, in the rational research and design homework we find in the entrepreneur's business plan.

When we speak of 'the organization' and use this kind of theory, we refer to the formally designed system which, we hope, coordinates the activities of all the role occupants. We assume these activities to be mutually supportive and convergent on the organization's goals. It is well known that 'real' organizations seldom meet such expectations. For instance, the interaction between the individuals and the power system often provokes dysfunctionality (March and Simon, 1958: 36). But this does not interfere with our preconception of the organizational 'mind' as a rational and mechanistic extension of the power-holder's views. It merely draws our attention to the fact that employees have minds of their own, and are as self-interested as the power holders. They are not tabulae rasae on which organization designers may draw or write as they please. The amelioration of the differences between the organizational and employee minds becomes the human relations problematic. But none of this specifically addresses the cognitive issues.

Simon (1958: xxiii), following Knight (1921) and others, reminded us that role occupants are at best only 'intendedly rational'. This introduced the problem of cognition into organizational analysis. Now even correct and complete information may be misperceived. Simon suggested that theorists, and managers, turn their attention to the employees' decision premises, which included their value systems and the way these might be influenced by their training. The concept of limited rationality introduced an indeterminacy or area of non-rationality into the tension between the rationality of the organization's 'mind', as evidenced in its coherent and purposive set of rules, and the rationality of the employee's mind, which is influenced by management's rule-making but is also under other influences which the managers do not control completely. The overlap between these 'minds' forms the finite 'zone of acceptance' (Simon, 1958: 12) within which the managers expect the employee to be aligned with the organizational goals. The science of administration is only necessary because of this tension and only possible because of the finiteness of this zone. Simon's administrative science is directed to the management of this zone. Simon (1958: 243) argued that collective or group mind is possible inasmuch as the members of the group share the objectives and values which influence their side of each participating individual's zone of acceptance. By determining, even only in part, both sides of the zone of acceptance, managers retain some control over both the organizational and the individual minds.

An organizational system of shared values, beliefs and norms is often labelled the organization's culture. Allaire and Firsirotu (1984) have demonstrated the complexity and ambiguity of the term 'organizational culture'. Suffice it to say that for many analysts the terms culture and collective mind are scarcely separable, though some distinguish the 'formal' rule system that deals with the rational elements from the 'informal' culture which deals with the non-rational value elements. This distinction demonstrates our field's debt to Simon's treatment of the ambiguous relations between the individual and the organization and the way the intersection between the formal and the informal establishes the zone of acceptance. But Simon's deft elision of the difference between the organization's mind and that of the power holder leaves us thinking that the idea of cognition can be applied to organizations just as readily as it is applied to individuals. Its merit is that it takes us beyond the limited mechanistic or 'scientific' notions of classical management theory and tells us that organizational knowledge comprises both facts and values and that the concept of mind must always deal with both.

Halbwachs and collective memory

Getting beyond the idea of the organization mind as a convenient way of speaking about either the power-based articulation of a single mind, or the presumption of uniformity shared between several minds, demands a substantive theory of cognitive collectivity. The notion of social collectivities which stand opposed to and shape individual cognition has been widely accepted since Durkheim's (1964, 1970) work on the *conscience collective*. Durkheim explained shared consciousness as the basis of 'mechanistic' solidarity, the condition of primitive society. The growth of knowledge leads to an increasing division of labour. Eventually differentiation and individual identity emerge. Society becomes the result of an active interdependence which Durkheim called 'organic' solidarity. Although

Durkheim was particularly concerned to refute Spencer's evolutionary theories, both offered dynamic concepts of society which contrasted vividly with the static and mechanistic theories of organization inherited from the classical theorists.

Halbwachs, who was befriended and directly influenced by Durkheim, theorized about the nature and process of organic solidarity and his theory of collective memory has been extremely influential. Its essence is that it is only through their membership of social groups (the organization is one type of social group), such as families, or religious or class-based groups, that individuals are able to acquire, localize and recall their memories (Connerton, 1989: 36). As Coser explained: 'It is, of course, individuals who remember, not groups or institutions, but these individuals, being located in a specific group context, draw on that context to remember or recreate the past' (in Halbwachs, 1992: 22). No one person is able to remember all the relevant facts about any social event. The Gospels, for instance, provide conflicting reports of the crucifixion. Collective memory requires the support of a social group delimited in space and time.

Halbwachs distinguished historical memory, which reaches the individual through records, artefacts, rituals and stories, from autobiographical memory, which the individual experienced personally. But even the latter is likely to fade and change unless it is supported by others. Halbwachs also argued that the past is a social construction inevitably and mainly shaped by the concerns of the present. Schwartz (1982) reinforced the dialectical nature of collective memory, in tension between continuity and change. Middleton and Edwards (1990: 1) following the same social constructionist line, emphasized the social practices that are integral with remembering and forgetting, as well as with the reconstruction of collective memory and with its change. Connerton (1989), suggesting further interesting parallels with Nelson and Winter's (1982) 'organizational routines', emphasized collective practice and argued that social memory is located in the society's myths and rituals rather than in its artefacts and records. Memory becomes embodied, to be revealed only through activity.

Weick's concept of collective mind

These themes have been recently reworked by Weick and Roberts (1993) in ways that are of considerable interest to organization theorists. Their initial interest was in 'high reliability organizations' (Weick, 1987; Roberts, 1989, 1990). Perrow (1984) had previously advanced the hypothesis that many modern organizations, such as nuclear power stations and genetic research laboratories, are liable to fail because in their design they attempt to combine tight coupling with interactive complexity. Tight coupling means that minor failures propagate rapidly through the system. Interactive complexity makes understanding these effects extremely difficult and theoretically unmanageable. Weick (1987) suggested that Perrow had over-looked the way in which organizational culture acted to contain these uncertainties (Bierly and Spender, 1995). Weick's work later shifted its focus from culture, as a loose metaphor for organizational cognition, to a specific model of collective mind which follows directly in the Halbwachs tradition. The attribution is primarily to Ryle (1949), Asch (1952) and Wegner (1987). According to Weick and Roberts (1993: 358) Wegner's insight was that group mind is not merely a result of shared understanding. Nor could collective knowledge be understood without paying attention to the communication processes going on among the group's members.

Following Sandelands and Stablein (1987: 137), Weick and Roberts (1993: 364) tried to avoid reifying the organization or imbuing it with any ability to cognize in ways detached from the cognizing of its members. Rather they argued that the collective mind emerged in the practices of social interrelating when these practices were conducted 'mindfully'. Mindfulness or 'heed' appeared as a quality of practice. Quoting Ryle (1949: 151), Weick and Roberts (1993: 361) suggested that people act heedfully when they act carefully, critically, consistently, purposefully, attentively, studiously, vigilantly, conscientiously, pertinaciously.

Three key aspects of such interrelating practice lead to the development of collective mind; contributing, representing, and subordinating. When these aspects occur together they create a collective situation or 'activity system'. The collective mind is evident when the individuals who form the group construct their activity (contribute) as they envisage the activity system (represent), and interrelate actively within the system envisaged (subordinate). The collective mind is located in the practice of the activity system since the particular manner of interrelating is not given, as in classical organization theory, but is continually constituted by and reconstitutes the individuals involved.

Weick and Roberts (1993: 366) turned next to the crucial question of the individual's entry into this kind of collective mind. They drew on symbolic interactionism (Blumer, 1969) and Mead's (1913, 1962) concept of the 'importation of the social process'. Their analysis came perilously close to suggesting merely the development of shared meanings and language. But it also displayed an appreciation of the special powers of narrative (Schön, 1983; Weick and Browning, 1986; Orr, 1990). In addition to Orr's useful example, both Hunter (1991) and Cassell (1991) have illustrated the power of narrative to capture the rich complexity and nuances of workplace life, and therefore of collective mind in organizations. Narrative actively involves both the hearer and the storyteller in a collective enterprise. Weick and Roberts (1993: 367) argued that as those entering into the collective mind hear the organization's stories and myths, and so begin to comprehend what heedful interrelating means in practice, the storytellers too renew their membership of the collective and discover that 'they had more thoughts than they thought they did'.

The concept of heed enabled Weick and Roberts (1993: 362) to distin-guish heedful from habitual performance. The latter is a replica of its predecessor whereas the former, though clearly conditioned by its prede-cessor, suggests each performance is novel and the actors are forever learning. But as the group matures, it tends to institutionalize, so the inter-relating tends to become routine and habitual. Performance becomes less mindful whenever individuals represent others in less detail, when con-tributions are shaped by less understanding of others' needs, and when the boundaries of the activity system are narrowed. Dysfunctions arise as attention is focused on local issues rather than on the system as a whole. Interrelating becomes careless and the collective mind dissipates.

Finally Weick and Roberts (1993: 374) attempted to disentangle the development of collective mind from the development of the group. They defined 'group' in terms of the movement of the individual from mere inclusion, through group control to affection, rather than by the develop-ment of a collective mind. Cognition is separated from affect. It follows that there can be well-developed groups without 'mind', such as messianic cults and those showing 'group think'. There can also be collective mind without a developed group identity. As examples Weick and Roberts offered film production teams, pickup jazz combos, airline cockpit crews and the ad hoc teams that respond to crises (Rochlin, 1989).

Weick and Roberts proposed collective mind to explain why Perrow's warnings are not borne out by our experience of 'high risk' organizations. In those workplaces and systems which seem most likely to fail, according to Perrow's thinking, failures are actually getting less frequent. While there have been nuclear accidents, they are remarkably few in number, espe-cially in the US Navy where the largest number of reactors has operated for the longest period under the most pressured circumstances (Bierly and Spender, 1995). Generalizing, Weick and Roberts (1993: 377) suggested that the key feature which distinguishes the different forms or types of organi-zation is the degree to which they facilitate or inhibit the development of collective mind. Rather than turn to the affect and motivation issues which were logically external to the organizational system, the concept of collec-tive added a crucial qualitative dimension to the analysis of organizational performance. It added a missing internal social dimension to the technical or mechanistic dimension which is the focus of classical theory. It reaf-firmed the Durkheim/Halbwachs argument that our understanding of not only the workplace but also of the human experience is socially con-structed and tightly contextualized.

Activity systems and the varieties of knowledge

The Weick and Roberts analysis paid considerable attention to the quality of the actor's knowing, but little attention to what was known, how it was learned or why its quality mattered. This was curious – given its intellectual roots. Both Durkheim and Halbwachs paid particular attention to the development processes that lead to collective mind. Both proposed a socio-evolutionary dynamic with the 'higher' individual mental function of the organic social system emerging after the period of mechanical solidarity. Weick and Roberts followed the same functionalist approach, and argued that collective mind leads to more robust and reliable organizations with a greater chance of survival. They also implied a specific sequence in that collective mind emerges after the individual mind, as the group evolves into the collective.

The relationship between the individual and collective mind remains ambiguous. Is what the collective mind knows simply the best of what each individual can contribute to the activity system? Is it, in this sense, a subset of the sum of what the individuals together know? Or is it, as Halbwachs suggested, the other way round, with each individual knowing only a subset of what the collective knows? While Weick and Roberts addressed the socialization of the individual into the collective, they did not consider the source of the knowledge received, nor the effect of entry on the collective, nor how the collective learns. How does the notion of quality become established? Through survival alone, after the fact, or through competition with other activity systems? Indeed, how can the notion of quality be detached from the content of what is known? In short, their analysis seemed a move towards rather than fully achieve the more comprehensive theory in which these matters would be taken into account. The result, which we can take as the specification of a theory of the dynamic organization, should be a theory covering both individual and collective cognition in the workplace. The individual and collective types of knowing would differ (Sandelands and Stablein, 1987: 149), thereby denying the kind of similarity at every analytic level suggested by most of the contributors to the Huff (1990) volume. This theory would also clarify its dynamic, the way the heedful activity system grows and declines. Thus it would also envelop a theory of learning (both knowledge acquisition and knowledge generation), of memory and of knowledge application.

One way to move towards this objective is to reconsider the place of activity in the analysis. For analysts such as Connerton, activity is central to the constitution and reconstitution of society and social knowledge. This suggests a contrast between social or collective knowledge and the kind of knowledge that can be stored in libraries or on hard disks. The distinction between abstract knowledge and that embedded in action might also be applied to the individual's knowledge, so distinguishing between the knowledge involved in mindful activity, and that merely stored, waiting to be remembered and applied in activity.

Narrative, whether we speak of the practice of diagnosis, as in the work of Orr or Hunter, or sacred myths (Pirsig, 1974; Schein, 1985), involves activity, not only from the storyteller, but also from the listener who must actively reconstruct its meaning. Narrative conveys nuance as well as value and moral content precisely because its active dimensions enable it to do more than communicate the facts. The quality dimension to which Weick and Roberts spoke is intimately associated with the way in which individuals move into the collective as an activity system rather than as a system of symbolic knowledge. There is not only learning through narrative, there is also learning through taking some part in activity, by watching and by doing under the tutelage of expert insiders (Arrow, 1962; Nelson and Winter, 1982). Thus an essential dimension of collective mind is that it is both contextualized in a particular field of activity, such as surgery or carrier-deck management, but it is also embedded in practice. The knowledge cannot be separated from the activity, its quality is only evident in that activity. It contrasts with knowledge which is abstract, decontextualized, and whose quality is measured by its conformance to the canons of positivist science.

Polanyi was one of a small group of 'philosophers of consciousness' (Webb, 1988) who explored the implications of the contextualization and coevolution of both knowledge and consciousness, rather than presuming that these can be separated. In the Platonic epistemology the highest form of knowledge is the Good, the abstractions of *noesis* and the mathematical purities of *diainoia*. These deal with the essential truth which lies behind any particular embodiment, much as time is the truth suggested by a watch. Plato regarded these truths as the ultimate kinds of knowledge. The lower forms of knowledge deal with the manifestations of these kinds of knowledge in an individual's appreciation of the concrete nature of the world, such as his/her perceptions and beliefs (*pistis*) and images of concrete objects (*eikasia*) (Ihde, 1993: 21). These distinctions cover the nature of the knowledge that might be contained in statements using language. They are the basis of epistemology, the study of the nature and origins of knowledge. But they focus on the abstractions, whether formal or linguistic. The Greeks also saw the possibility of types of knowledge other than *episteme* (abstract generalizations). The practical arts manifested *techne* (being able to get things done) (Ihde, 1993: 26). But there was also *phronesis* (practical wisdom about social practice) and *metis* (cunning) (Detienne and Vernant, 1978).

Today the primary distinctions are simpler, such as those suggested by James (1950: I221) between 'knowledge about' and 'knowledge of acquaintance'. The former is abstract while the latter is the direct result of experience. James suggested that knowledge of acquaintance is 'dumb' and cannot speak its value. Science is the process of abstracting from the subjective context of experience and generalizing beyond the specific so as to turn knowledge of acquaintance into knowledge about. This can be stored and communicated. Ryle (1949) similarly distinguished 'knowing what' from 'knowing how' (Smith, 1988: 1). Again the former is abstract, while the latter indicates knowing how to create mindful activity.

The implication is that the content of collective mind is likely to be oriented towards practice rather than to abstract knowledge. The abstract knowledge can be shared by individuals, much as a number of people can read the same book, but they thereby become a group without a developed collective mind or practice. Should they come together in a seminar and discuss the book, sharing in collective intellectual activity, they will develop other kinds of understanding such as the rhetorical knowledge (Yates, 1969) of how to present, defend and extend the book's argument. This kind of practice leads to collective mind and suggests parallels with deep or 'thick' knowledge (Geertz, 1983).

A further distinction, which is associated with but is not identical to that between abstraction and practice, is that between what one knows consciously and what one might know in some other way that can only demonstrate through practice. It may also be the case that actors may not be conscious of knowing this other type of knowledge. Polanyi (1962) distinguished between objective and tacit knowledge and remarked 'people know more than they can tell' (Polanyi, 1967: 4). The essence of Polanyi's distinction is less in activity than in the knowledge's communicability. It is also the essence of the similar distinction between the 'declarative' and 'procedural' types of knowledge (Anderson, 1983; Singley and Anderson, 1989).

This communicability oriented way of classifying knowledge creates some difficulty since we can neither know about nor really be much interested in that which cannot be communicated. Most commentators refer to the difficulty rather than the impossibility of communicating tacit knowledge (for example, Nelson and Winter, 1982: 77). It follows that 'tacitness' is defined as a quality of knowledge's communicability, a matter of degree, rather than as knowledge of a different type. In the end this kind of definition becomes more confusing than clarifying. On the other hand Nelson and Winter (1982: 78) also intimated a 'contingent' theory of knowledge transfer when they suggested that words may be better for communicating the skills required for algebra than those required for carpentry. Algebra is abstract (*diainoia*) while carpentry is *techne*, knowledge of a different type. Algebra is a type of language with its own discourse, limits, and syntax while carpentry is a practice. But how is carpentry to be communicated unless we consider it involves a different type of knowledge?

What is it about practice that leads us to think of it as evoking a different type of knowledge? Polanyi's (1962: 49) examples, swimming and bike riding, suggested that they involve a kind of knowledge that is implicit and inaccessible to its possessor, who is therefore not able to engage in the kind of deliberate symbolic communication which Nelson and Winter have in mind. It is this confusion between the inaccessibility of the relevant knowledge to its possessor and the ability of the possessor to convey that knowledge to another that renders this kind of explanation of tacit knowledge so unsatisfactory. We need to separate the internal communication or knowledge movement problem from the external interpersonal communication problem. To sort this out we need to consider directly the notion of the 'implicit' (Reber, 1993) or 'taken-for-granted' (Schutz, 1953, 1972) aspects of workplace life.

Implicit knowledge

The notion of implicit knowledge suggests that we rephrase Polanyi's quip as 'we know more than we know we know'. This avoids the communication dimension but plays instead on the different ways of knowing. The positivist approach, that analysis and prediction are the only ways of knowing, is exemplified by Simon's remarks that 'intuition is analysis frozen into habit' (Simon, 1987: 63) or that intuition, insight and inspiration are forms of analysis, and that there is no need to postulate any special mechanism of creativity or discovery (Simon et al., 1992: 117). Polanyi argued that scientific discovery grew from another kind of knowing which is grounded in the researcher's deep intimacy with the field of study. Here Polanyi suggested that the creative scientist knows more than he/she knows he/she knows.

Schutz similarly argued that participants in social life were only able to perform satisfactorily and so reconstitute society because they had acquired a substantial amount of knowledge which was then taken for granted. The question here is to distinguish between the sheer quantity of what one has to learn to take part in this kind of complex activity and the possibility that there might be some fundamental qualitative difference between the explicit knowledge of which actors are aware, and the implicit knowledge of which they remain unaware, even though both types are necessary for skilled performance. For instance, most people take the parameters and characteristics of their own culture for granted and would be hard put to explain how it differs from that of another person.

The boundary between these two types of knowledge may well be permeable, given that much of the sociologist's agenda is the discovery of both the taken-for-granted aspects of individuals' lives, and the exploration of the unintended and unforeseen consequences of their actions. Thus it need not follow from there being different ways of knowing that there could be no traffic between them. We saw that James took for granted a progression from knowledge of acquaintance to knowing about. Polanyi's beliefs about scientific work and its dependence on tacit foundations are similarly grounded.

Learning or developmental psychologists have explored these questions from the individual rather than the social perspective. Reber has recently provided a comprehensive overview and analysis of the empirical research into individual level implicit knowledge and learning. He defined implicit learning as the acquisition of knowledge that takes place largely independently of conscious attempts to learn and in the absence of explicit knowledge about what was learned (Reber, 1993: 5). More importantly, his focus, unlike Polanyi's, is not on physical activity. Reber clarified the distinction between conscious knowledge, kinetic knowledge and memory. He argued that careful observation of people working on solving problems showed that the elements which underpin the kinds of rational and logical model lauded by Simon, and which are absolutely central to management education, were often missing. It was not so much that the decisions were irrational, rather they were being made using processes that did not take the rational elements into account (Reber, 1993: 13). This suggests the existence of another kind of 'practical' knowledge. The same phenomena were also exhibited in studies by Scribner (1985, 1986), Lave (1988), and Langer and her colleagues (in Reber, 1993: 14). Apparently these behaviours were, contrary to the Weick and Roberts analysis, 'mindless'. People were making choices correctly but drawing on knowledge that they were not aware they possessed. Competent mindlessness has also been considered as the state of 'flow' (Csikszentmihalyi and Csikszentmihalyi, 1988).

While implicit knowledge may be different from objective knowledge, it also seems that there may be more than one method of processing knowledge. This runs counter to the common belief that the brain is simply a sophisticated computer with a single mode of processing (be that von Neumann, parallel, neural or some other yet-to-be discovered architecture). Indeed, it is the possibility, contrary to Simon's belief, that the human brain is capable of more than one kind of processing that underpins the literature criticizing artificial intelligence (Searle, 1987). In the same vein, Dreyfus (1987: 45) remarked that people recognize others without processing data in ways that can be captured by AI. Reber (1993: 15) noted that a century ago it was already known that many perceptual processes involved operations that lay outside consciousness. Far from being an isolated phenomenon, such extra-conscious operations are widespread, normal and underpin everyday life.

We can include the additional implication, that there are several different types of memory. It is commonplace to note the difference between short-term and long-term memory. But Reber (1993: 17) also dealt with the difference between the effects of explicit and implicit learning. He defined 'implicit' memory as evident when a subject displays memory of an earlier experience without being conscious that that experience took place, what is also known as the Korsakoff syndrome. Cognitive neuroscientists have also suggested that the different types of memory can be associated with different parts of the brain; the hippocampus being activated for episodic memories, the cerebellum during the process of recognition (Squire et al., 1991). This kind of local specialization becomes especially clear in cases where one of these memory sites has been damaged so causing proso- or visual-agnosia. These patients often have excellent memories about things that have happened to them and can perform data manipulations quite normally. But they cannot recognize members of their own family or where they are.

All this suggests that far from being a matter of degree, the conventional interpretation of Polanyi's work, the terms 'tacit' or 'procedural' may well allude to an alternative system of knowledge, complete with its own manner and means of representation, learning, storage, retrieval, and computation. While it is clear that the conscious system is involved in the processing of abstract symbols, the *episteme* types of 'knowledge about', it is less obvious what kind of tasks engage the implicit system. The *ah ha!* experience, in which understanding comes suddenly and unexpectedly, research by Lewicki (Lewicki, 1986; Lewicki et al., 1987, 1988) into the processes of recognition, as well as the difficulties involved in developing even the simplest recognition capabilities in AI and robotic systems, confirms one's intuition that recognition is one of the kinds of task that engages the implicit system.

From the cognitive scientist's point of view, it becomes necessary to theorize about the relationships between the two – or more – different cognitive systems. Applying an evolutionary perspective Reber (1993: 7) argued that the conscious system of cognition is built upon and emerges from the deeper 'implicit' system. We see that this is consistent with the older Durkheimian view. Phylogenetic theory also suggests that having evolved 'later' the conscious system will be a 'higher order' system and have characteristics that differentiate it from the 'lower level' implicit system. For instance, there should be less difference between individuals in their implicit cognitive capabilities, and greater difference between their higher order abilities. Second, the implicit system should be more robust and less prone to disruption than the higher order conscious system. Such disruption could be either neurological or clinical, and this prediction is borne out by the empirical literature (Reber, 1993: 7).

But the processes which arrest disorder can also be informational. Thus three hundred years ago Locke (in Spender, 1989: 45) wrote that 'the faculty which God has given man to supply the want of clear and certain knowledge in cases where it cannot be had is judgment'. The implication is that, from a cognitive point of view, every system of facts stands on a system of judgements. This is consistent with modern post-positivist epistemology (for example Popper, 1969; Gergen, 1994: 9). Rather than use the term judgement, which is used in so many other senses, we might employ the term 'automatic' to identify the individual's ability to recognize, to choose, and to perform when 'mindless' or in a state of 'flow'. This usage is consistent with clinical research into automatic processing (Bargh, 1989; Reber, 1993:15).

Here we have used Reber's analysis and the empirical work to drive a wedge between the explicit (conscious) and the implicit (automatic) types of knowledge for the individual. The distinction is far more substantial than that offered by Polanyi, who was arguing from philosophy rather than from cognitive psychology or cognitive neuroscience. But it remains to be shown that the same distinction can be applied usefully to collective knowledge or mind. There were suggestions in the work of Weick and Roberts (1993: 365) who noted that no single individual can fully represent the emergent properties of the activity system, and this recalled Halbwachs's sense of the distributed nature of collective memory.

The answer to the question about whether the same duality applies to the collective cognitive process is to compare, in ways that cannot be done properly in this chapter, the emergent implicit quality of culture and rational explicit quality of science, and so recall the old debate between *Kulturwissenschaft* and *Naturwissenschaft*. The comparison depends on the degree to which science can be successfully abstracted from the critique mounted by those who see science as socially constructed and therefore a mere subset of culture. We can recall those, such as C.P. Snow (1959, 1964), who saw science and art as two opposed cultures, or those who stress the gulf between scientific and social knowledge (Merton, 1973). Cultural and institutional studies of science and technology have shown that culture and science are intermingled. As Rouse (1993: 13) argued, the relationships between scientific and social knowledge clearly are extremely subtle and the boundary between them is permeable. Of course the same permeability applies to the division between the explicit and implicit dimensions of the individual's knowledge. But even though there is traffic across the boundaries, the typology is still analytically useful and empirically substantial.

Table 2.1   *The different types of cognition*

	Individual	Social
Explicit	Conscious	Objectified
Implicit	Automatic	Collective

Sources: Spender, 1994, 1995

To the extent that these distinctions are useful we can portray the various types of individual and collective cognition in a two-by-two matrix. This matrix summarizes the discussion above with the proposition that there are four distinct categories of cognition. We accept the arguments about collective or social knowledge, but argue that it has both explicit and implicit dimensions. This seems less controversial than the distinction between explicit and implicit cognition at the individual level, but it needs considerably more research to determine its validity or utility. For the remainder of this chapter we turn to the question of learning and the dynamic between the various types of knowledge.

Learning

As we noted earlier, there can be no theory of cognition which does not imply an associated theory of learning. One of the weaknesses of the mental mapping approach to cognition, whether at the individual level or at the organizational level, is that the learning mechanisms, the way the mental map came to be this way rather than some other way, are seldom explored. One exception, which illustrates well the need for a theory and a method of revealing the richness and complexity of the learning process, is the analysis of Law and Callon. They investigated the history of a single large British aerospace project, the TSR2 fighter aircraft. This project was eventually cancelled in 1965 as the British switched to the use of US-made F111. The Law and Callon (1992: 50) analysis showed the subtleties and dynamics of the project as various issues interacted over time. Their purpose was to rebut reductionist analyses which would give priority to one construct, such as politics or technology or individual inventiveness, even though each of these played a powerful part in the process, and illustrate instead the dialectical interplay of interests and perceptions among a set of actors. These actors learned and relearned the project's goals, possibilities and boundaries as their process unfolded.

As we learned from the Hawthorne Studies, cognition in the workplace is similarly a reflection of a historical process which has its own autonomous dynamic. The object of attention in Law and Callon's analysis is what they define as the 'actor-network'. This has its own logical 'space' and boundaries. Outside these boundaries are forces, and perceptions, which deny the network's autonomy – in this case the British government among others. Thus the autonomy is bounded, as are the cognitions of all concerned. We see that the actor-network is an activity system in the sense defined above. But we also see that it has a degree of autonomy which has not been previously brought out. Weick and Roberts, for instance, did not explain how the collective mind of the deck management system achieved the self-referencing quality that turned it into an autonomous actor. Embedded in the US Navy's strict hierarchical power system, it yet became proactive and able to resolve novel uncertainties without checking with the 'higher ups' who obviously determine its operational context. They only touched on this matter when discussing senior ranks' culpability for the serious on-board accident (1993: 364).

The more general question about cognition is thus not simply about learning as a metaphor for adaptation, but as a way of describing the development of the consciousness that cognizes, that is logically prior to the act of cognition. Reber (1993: 133) recognized that the question of consciousness cannot be separated from that of cognition. He offered an evolutionary model in which a self-referencing consciousness, able to view and model itself and so 'think' in the contemporary sense, emerges from a simpler or 'lower' type of observing awareness which merely responds 'automatically' to appropriate stimuli. The point is illustrated by reminding us that a frog's physical or 'operational' responses are little changed when its cortex, the centre of its 'higher' mental functions, is removed.

Many analysts construct this kind of two-level model into a systems theory framework and, referencing various derivations of the 'double loop' concept (Ashby, 1956; Argyris and Schön, 1978), propose a multi-level theory of organizational learning (for example, Ciborra and Schneider, 1992: 272). This kind of theorizing typically overlooks the debate about what it is that is learned, where it is stored, how it is applied and so forth. It attempts to treat learning as problematic, but without considering what is learned as equally puzzling. Such theorizing is an unreflexive prisoner of the notion that there is but one type of knowledge and that the only type of change envisaged is an increase in the quantity of knowledge. The method of learning is a given, a simple interpretation of experience. There is no reference to what is already known. The learning is then less adaptation to uncertainty than the process of equilibrating the knowledge imbalance between the cognizing system and the environment. In cognitive terms learning would be about getting the mental model to represent better the reality 'out there', as if this reality were available to us in some way that would allow us to monitor the congruence between it and the mental model. This is simply not what Polanyi's theory of scientific discovery is about. Indeed it would even be an uncharitable interpretation of Popper's post-positivist theory of scientific discovery (Popper, 1969).

In this chapter learning means the creation of knowledge, which is the resolution of uncertainty for the 'knower', and this cannot occur without a pre-existing level of consciousness and knowledge appropriate to the type of knowledge being newly acquired. The example of the decorticated frog suggests that a certain level of consciousness is 'native', a genetic endowment for all healthy members of the species. We can make the same assumption about human beings. But it is not at all clear that we can attribute a similar kind of native consciousness to organizations. We can reasonably ask where the organizational mind acquires its initial absorptive capacity.

This is a puzzle to which experienced team builders probably know at least part of the answer (for example, Larson and LaFasto, 1989). Broadly speaking it seems to be a matter of establishing an appropriate 'activity space', filling it with activity and guiding its attention towards challenges. The activity system begins from its native elements. This is fine for a healthy animal, but we must not forget that the organization is an artefact. It is artificial, created by people. It is neither emergent, nor natural in the sense of being the natural offspring of other organizations. Organizations do not beget organizations any more than they make decisions. On the other hand we see that the higher level functions of collective mind are not artificial, they cannot be created in the same way. They emerge in their own time and way, as successful team builders know. The problem of organizational cognition is not, therefore, to explain the development of a set of organizational roles and rules. These could easily be put in place by those that create the lower level explicit response system implied in classical organization theory. The puzzle is to explain the development of the higher level collective consciousness which lies behind the organization's self-referencing and autonomous cognition and behaviour.

We can make some progress toward understanding these phenomena by considering the work of Vygotsky and the many whom he influenced, such as Bruner, and who were interested in the intellectual development of children. We will suggest that we can map their ideas into organizational analysis to create a rather different model of the learning organization. Their work is both subtle and dynamic. Not only did Vygotsky's views change considerably during his own lifetime, but our understanding of them has also changed markedly since his death, in part because of the suppression of his work during the Stalinist period (Bakhurst, 1990).

Vygotsky shared much with Durkheim in giving priority to the social. Durkheim, who considered even our sense of time socially constructed, was more extreme, given Kant's position on the nature of space and time. We are now seeing a resurgence of Durkheimian thought in 'social construction' theory (for example, Gergen, 1994). Vygotsky searched for a subtler dialectic between the individual, defined as the newborn child, with only its native lower level learning capabilities, and the social context which provides its higher level activity system. He thought it clear that no amount of instruction would lead to the emergence of the child's higher level functions unless the child became actively engaged in the development process. Thus this kind of consciousness forming learning is activity based, giving rise to the name 'activity theory' and the quip that it proposes 'performance before competence' (Cazden in Moll, 1990: 3). The core of the theory concerns the 'space' in which this development activity occurs which, in activity theory, is known as the zone of proximal development (ZPD). The process of education which both socializes the child and leads to the emergence of the higher level functions revolves around the external (adult) management of the ZPD.

Tharp and Gallimore (1988: 33) argued that the management of the child's ZPD can be considered in four stages. The first is simple practice assisted by adults. Here the child begins the development of contextualized practice. Initially there is neither consciousness nor understanding, there is only performance. But with active native involvement with routinized performance comes the beginnings of representation and the awareness of the activity's immediate goals. As these emerge, there is the first of a series of 'handovers'. The child becomes a knowing participant rather than being simply passive. In the second stage the performance becomes actively assisted by the child. Vygotsky saw this as the stage at which performance became mediated by 'psychic tools', the beginnings of language and other symbolic representations of performance. Using these tools, the child develops self-directed speech, manipulating these symbols. With this comes deliberate and conscious self-referencing and control. In stage three this consciousness and control is internalized and routinized, becoming automatic. The child is now broadly, though boundedly, aware of both an internal psychic world and an external social world. He/she is a fully conscious, self-regulating activity system embedded within the larger system of meaningful social activity.

The fourth stage is where the activity context is changed in ways that de-automate performance and force the child, or the adult, back to stages one and two as performance is reconstructed after crisis with the help of others. This help, in its own turn, is discarded as new levels of consciousness develop and self-regulation takes over again. While self-control relates to the individual's response to goals established by others, self-regulation breaks the external link and establishes autonomy. Thus it is quite different from double-loop learning. The second loop still requires its own external referent. Even with infinite regression to higher and higher loops, there can never be the kind of autonomy which Vygotsky sought. Nor did Ashby ever intend his cybernetic automata to achieve such independence.

The essence of the second stage of activity theory is the development of the psychic tools which are part and parcel of higher mental functions. Thus consciousness is the ability to abstract oneself from the immediacy of experience, to achieve autonomy in a different universe of language. This is only possible with the use of tools or such other constructs as can be interposed between the native capabilities and the activity. The real objective of learning is the continuous development and refinement of these tools (Bereiter and Scardamalia, 1993). Since these psychic tools are the evolving synthesis of the increasing challenges presented by the ZPD and the previously developed capabilities, they will not evolve if the challenge is either too boring or too frightening. The ZPD then collapses. The teacher's task is to manage the ZPD so that this kind of disengagement does not occur (Hedegaard, 1990: 367). Vygotsky's notion of social priority, which makes the development of consciousness part of a broader system of cultural transmission through which the social system recreates and develops itself, contrasts with Piaget's much more natively constrained system (Butterworth, 1982: 8). Closer reading, of course, shows considerable overlap.

The purpose of considering Vygotsky's theory is to suggest a model of how the implicit components of social cognition are first communicated to individuals and then, second, communicated back again to the social level. Learning by doing under the tutelage of a master does precisely what we know it to do, communicate several types of knowledge, both explicit and implicit, both social and individual. The manner in which it works turns on the nature of native consciousness and on the psychic tools. Since these mediate social activity, they go well beyond the conscious and into the pre-conscious. Indeed Reber (1993: 9) argued that the surprise lies in there being any conscious function. The learning is holistic in that it embraces everything necessary to create controlled social activity. But inasmuch as it involves several types of knowledge, organizational learning deals with all.

A Vygotskian model illustrates how the dialectical tension between the individual and the social is not slavish copying, giving rise to a socially determined theory of consciousness, but one in which there is fundamental equifinality and indeterminism. Accidents and serendipity influence the process. Thus the socialized individual's consciousness is partly unique and partly 'path dependent', giving rise to an ongoing progressive dynamic as the social system is reconstituted while the child grows into adulthood. In a manner analogous to Giddens's structuration theory, the autonomous individual exerts a tension on the social and so, in the process of its reconstitution, reinterprets the past in terms of the concerns of the present. As we map this Vygotskian model into organizational analysis, we see how the individuality of the group's members creates a dynamic tension with the emerging collective mind or pattern of activities. Thus the organization is best envisaged as loosely coupled (Spender and Grinyer, 1995) and 'the way we do things around here' is a dynamic record of the individuals who took part in the development of the present consciousness of 'here'.

Workplace cognition

The model sketched above can be mapped directly into the organizational workplace. Lave researched the use of mathematics by adults in everyday settings such as supermarkets. The conventional supposition, standing on the Platonist ideas of *diainoia* which regards mathematics as an abstract truth, is that mathematics is acquired in school in ways that are context free and thus available for application in all subsequent contexts, impervious to change in the course of travel and use (in Lave, 1988: 9). However Lave found, on the contrary, that the way in which shoppers calculated quantities and prices was highly contextualized. She concluded that the cognition observed in such everyday practice is distributed, stretched over rather than divided among, mind, body, activity and culturally organized settings which included other actors (Lave, 1988: 1).

Scribner (1986) observed a similar contextualization of cognition and calculation among dairy product storage workers and packers. She found that the storage workers used mnemonics for calculating quantities and locations which were grounded in the social activity of storage and the specific dimensions of the storage facilities. The physical dimensions of the bays were understood in terms of the volumes of the products stored. The packers demonstrated their ability to find minimum effort solutions to their packing tasks contingent on the specific state and location of the unpacked materials. They saw packing as changing the state of the extant workplace rather than as a decontextualized task. They were able to change the base numbers of their calculations (like the computer programmer's switch from decimal to octal) depending on the quantities in the stored state. Suchman (1987) demonstrated similar 'situated learning'. Cassell (1991) demonstrated the similar social contextualization of the hospital surgeon's work and knowledge.

In the work of each of these 'socio-historical' or 'activity theory' researchers, and others such as Orr (1990), there is a clear tension between the social dimensions of cognition and that of the individual who takes action in that socially constructed context. As the individual enters into the collective mind there is a process of 'adult' or external assistance contingent on prior legitimate social structures, on the novice's experimentation and on the emergence of unassisted self-control and regulation. Finally the individual becomes an autonomous but socialized actor involved in the process of reconstituting both the universe of discourse and its corresponding community of practice (Brown and Duguid, 1991). The importance of the discourse and narrative is recognized as the stories and myths are exchanged between the experts and the novices, and among the experts themselves.

Conclusions

Our objective has been to consider the dimensions of individual and collective cognition in the workplace. Our point of departure was the current state of the art of mental mapping. We argued that this application of cognitive theory has suffered three major defects:

- these models are applied freely to all levels of analysis, even though the individual level still seems privileged as the only one at which thinking can occur;
- the lack of clarity about the relationship between thought and action, and thus about the dynamics of learning and forgetting;
- the underlying assumption that there is but one type of knowledge.

Driving beyond these constraints caused us to look again at the long tradition of inquiry into social cognition. We focused on the work of Durkheim and Halbwachs, though we could have usefully traced earlier roots in Greek epistemology. Weick and Roberts's analysis follows fairly directly in this tradition, as interpreted by Wegner. His insight was to see social cognition as a quality of the process of interrelating among the society's members. Where this is done mindfully, collective mind emerges. This insight provided a tentative answer to the first of our criticisms, and suggested the possibility of a dynamic between the individuals and the collective.

The next step was a consideration of Reber's analysis. This looks again at the long tradition of inquiry into implicit intelligence, forms of knowledge, processing and learning that lie outside the conscious rational model to which organizational researchers have paid so much attention. Reber summarized the empirical data as well as the theory. The evidence of an alternative mode of human cognizing is overwhelming. Reber proposed an evolutionary structure in which the conscious mode is seen as a higher order function that emerges from the preconscious implicit mode. He was not entirely clear about how this occurred. Nonetheless we applied the resulting explicit/implicit distinction to both the individual and collective mind to generate a two-by-two matrix of modes of cognizing. This provides a tentative answer to our third criticism, but similarly suggested a dynamic between the explicit and implicit modes.

The final step was to address the need for a multi-faceted learning model. We considered the socio-historical work of Vygotsky and his followers. They spelled out a specific theory of interaction between the social and the individual. Forgetting remains a puzzle. On the other hand Halbwachs implied that individual forgetting is partly autobiographical, a result of the passage of time. But it is also social in that the individual is no longer supported by the group in his/her remembering. Thus forgetting is the result of the disappearance of the set of practices which sustained the knowledge. Thus language disappears with the community of practice as the social context evolves. An even stronger argument comes from Vygotsky. Forgetting is the necessary consequence of every individual's process as they continually reconstruct both the present and the past.

It is interesting to note that all three answers revolve around two axiomatic concepts; (a) a space or zone; (b) the social and individual activity in that zone. Contextualized action is the principle on which we build notions of both cognition and recognition. Cognition implies more than response to external stimuli, whether these be electric shocks to the legs of the decorticated frog or the competitive impulses impacting the organization. Cognition emerges along with consciousness as the awareness of strategic choice (Child, 1972). This is just as true at the implicit level, where judgement is being exercised, as at the higher levels where deliberate and conscious choices are being made. The key to cognition therefore lies in the development of consciousness. Given the matrix above, we have to show the possibility of developing four types of consciousness, social and individual, explicit and implicit. A theory of cognition that offers neither a theory of learning nor a theory of consciousness does scant justice to the possibilities of the cognitive revolution.

APPENDIX

Critical research issues

This is a piece of theoretical work and, in that sense, intentionally speculative. It is grounded in the long tradition of *verstehen*, the idea that our task is less to 'explain' the nature of the social and economic world than to take part in the more general activity of making sense and searching out the meanings of our social and economic experiences. As theoreticians our primary objective is to help organizational analysts and, to a lesser extent, managers free themselves from the constraints of unproductive thinking and assumptions. Our main target is positivism, a legacy which so infuses our work that getting a sense of its boundaries and limitations is extraordinarily difficult. It is not uncommon to find writers, especially reviewers, who shout that positivism is dead but still ask for empirical evidence. These problems become especially severe when we are talking about disequilibrium, learning, change, evolution, chaos, creative destruction, innovation, or any of the other metaphors which are necessary to the kind of dynamic theory of organization that we all know we need. So the critical research issues are both epistemological and methodological. In this chapter we adopt an overtly post-modern epistemology which proposes multiple types of knowledge, learning and memory, and argues that management's crucial function is to intervene in their interplay.

Operationalizing a research programme

Although the discussion has been somewhat abstract and philosophical it is clear that there are many ways in which this epistemological framework might be operationalized. But the meaning of this term will be tied up with the nature of the process being observed. We are most comfortable with the 'objectified' type of knowledge. Our argument is that the most important dynamic emerges from the dialectic between the individual's explicit 'conscious' knowledge, and the implicit 'collective' knowledge that is embedded in the language and activities of the community of practice. Observing this requires some form of longitudinal study. However, other kinds of research opportunity do exist. We might contrast the sequence of knowledge types in the history of a particular organization, not only observing how one set of ideas is displaced by another after, for instance, the arrival of a new chief executive, but also how the types of ideas might change from a bureaucratic dependence on objectified knowledge to a more cultural dependence on collective knowledge.

Another more oblique kind of empirical programme might be focused on the different types of learning necessary to achieve effective action. Complex computer systems, which lead to major changes in the organization's practices, are remarkably difficult to implement. We would argue that, in part, this is because several different types of knowledge are necessary before skilled performance takes place. It has been characteristic to focus on classroom training which delivers objectified knowledge about how the system works. This is OK as far as it goes, but it overlooks completely the problems which the contextualized and situated practitioners (operatives and maintenance personnel as well as managers) face as they attempt to generate the appropriate collective knowledge. Among educators an increasing amount of research is being focused on understanding the knowledge necessary for skilled performance and thinking out new methods of delivery (DiBello and Spender, 1996). This literature offers us an entirely new dimension of empirical research among adult learners.

References

Allaire, Yvan and Firsirotu, Michaela E. (1984) Theories of organizational culture, *Organization Studies*, 5: 193–226.

Anderson, J.R. (1983) *The Architecture of Recognition*. Cambridge, MA: Harvard University Press.

Argyris, Chris and Schön, Donald A. (1978) *Organizational Learning: A Theory of Action Perspective*. Reading, MA: Addison-Wesley.

Arrow, Kenneth (1962) Economic welfare and the allocation of resources for invention, in Richard R. Nelson (ed.), *The Rate and Direction of Inventive Activity*. Princeton, NJ: Princeton University Press. pp. 609–30.

Asch, Solomon E. (1952) *Social Psychology*. Englewood Cliffs, NJ: Prentice-Hall.

Ashby, W. Ross (1956) *An Introduction to Cybernetics*. New York: John Wiley.

Bakhurst, David (1990) Social memory in Soviet thought, in David Middleton and Derek Edwards (eds), *Collective Remembering*. Newbury Park, CA: Sage. 203–26.

Bargh, John A. (1989) Conditional automaticity: varieties of automatic influence in social perception and cognition, in James S. Uleman and John A. Bargh, *Unintended Thought*. New York: Guilford Press. pp. 3–51.

Bereiter, Carl and Scardamalia, Marlene (1993) *Surpassing Ourselves: An Inquiry into the Nature and Implications of Expertise*. Chicago, IL: Open Court.

Bierly, Paul E. and Spender, J.-C. (1995) The culture of high reliability organizations: the case of the nuclear submarine, *Journal of Management*, 21: 639–56.

Blumer, Herbert (1969) *Symbolic Interactionism: Perspective and Method*. Englewood Cliffs, NJ: Prentice-Hall.

Bougon, Michel G. and Komocar, John M. (1990) Directing strategic change: a dynamic wholistic approach, in Anne S. Huff (ed.), *Mapping Strategic Thought*. Chichester: John Wiley. pp. 135–63.

Brown, John S. and Duguid, Paul (1991) Organizational learning and communities-of-practice: towards a unified view of working, learning, and innovation, *Organization Science*, 2: 40–57.

Butterworth, George (1982) A brief account of the conflict between the individual and the social in models of cognitive growth, in George Butterworth and Paul Light (eds), *Social Cognition: Studies of the Development of Understanding*. Chicago, IL: University of Chicago Press. pp. 3–16.

Cassell, Joan (1991) *Expected Miracles: Surgeons at Work*. Philadelphia, PA: Temple University Press.

Child, John (1972) Organisation structure, environment and performance, *Sociology*, 6: 1–21.

Ciborra, Claudio and Schneider, Leslie S. (1992) Transforming the routines and contexts of management, work, and technology, in Paul S. Adler (ed.), *Technology and the Future of Work*. New York: Oxford University Press. pp. 269–91.

Connerton, Paul (1989) *How Societies Remember*. Cambridge: Cambridge University Press.

Csikszentmihalyi, Mihaly and Csikszentmihalyi, Isabella S. (eds) (1988) *Optimal Experience: Psychological Studies of Flow in Consciousness*. New York: Cambridge University Press.

Detienne, Marcel and Vernant, Jean-Pierre (1978) *Cunning Intelligence in Greek Culture and Society*. Hassocks, Sussex: Harvester Press.

DiBello, Lia and Spender, J.-C. (1996) Constructive learning: a new approach to deploying technological systems into the workplace, *International Journal of Technology Management*, 11 (7): 747–58.

Dreyfus, Hubert L. (1987) Misrepresenting human intelligence, in Rainer Born (ed.), *Artificial Intelligence: The Case Against*. London: Croom Helm. pp. 41–54.

Durkheim, Emile (1964) *The Division of Labor in Society*. New York: Free Press.

Durkheim, Emile (1970) *Suicide – A Study in Sociology*. London: Routledge and Kegan Paul.

Eden, Colin and Radford, Jim (eds) (1990) *Tackling Strategic Problems: The Role of Group Decision Support*. London: Sage.

Geertz, Clifford (1983) *Local Knowledge: Further Essays in Interpretive Anthropology.* New York: Basic Books.

Gergen, Kenneth J. (1985) The social constructionist movement in modern psychology, *American Psychologist*, 40: 266–75.

Gergen, Kenneth J. (1994) *Toward Transformation in Social Knowledge*, 2nd edn. New York: Sage.

Gulick, Luther (1977) Notes on the theory of organizations: with special reference to the government of the United States, in L. Gulick and L. Urwick (eds), *Papers on the Science of Administration*. Fairfield, CT: Augustus M. Kelley. pp. 1–45.

Halbwachs, Maurice (1992) *On Collective Memory*. Chicago, IL: University of Chicago Press.

Hedegaard, Mariane (1990) The zone of proximal development as basis for instruction, in Luis C. Moll (ed.), *Vygotsky and Education: Instructional Implications and Applications of Sociohistorical Psychology*. New York: Cambridge University Press. pp. 349–71.

Huff, Anne S. (ed.) (1990) *Mapping Strategic Thought*. New York: John Wiley.

Hunter, Kathryn M. (1991) *Doctor's Stories: The Narrative Structure of Medical Knowledge*. Princeton, NJ: Princeton University Press.

Ihde, Don (1993) *Philosophy of Technology: An Introduction*. New York: Paragon House.

James, William (1950) *The Principles of Psychology*, vols I and II. New York: Dover Publications.

Knight, Frank H. (1921) *Risk, Uncertainty and Profit*. Boston, MA: Houghton Mifflin.

Larson, Carl E. and LaFasto, Frank M.J. (1989) *Teamwork: What Must Go Right/What Can Go Wrong.* Newbury Park, CA: Sage.

Lave, Jean (1988) *Cognition in Practice: Mind, Mathematics and Culture in Everyday Life*. Cambridge: Cambridge University Press.

Law, John and Callon, Michel (1992) The life and death of an aircraft: a network analysis of technical change, in Weibe E. Bijker and John Law (eds), *Shaping Technology/Building Society*. Cambridge, MA: MIT Press. pp. 21–52.

Lewicki, P. (1986) *Nonconscious Social Information Processing*. New York: Academic Press.

Lewicki, P., Czyzewska, M. and Hoffman, H. (1987) Unconscious acquisition of complex procedural knowledge, *Journal of Experimental Psychology: Learning, Memory and Cognition*, 13: 523–30.

Lewicki, P., Hill, T. and Bizot, E. (1988) Acquisition of procedural knowledge about a pattern of stimuli that cannot be articulated, *Cognitive Psychology*, 20: 24–37.

March, James G. and Simon, Herbert A. (1958) *Organizations*. New York: John Wiley.

Mead, George H. (1913) The social self, *Journal of Philosophy*, 10: 374–80.

Mead, George H. (1962) *Mind, Self and Society*. Chicago, IL: University of Chicago Press.

Merton, Robert K. (1973) *The Sociology of Science: Theoretical and Empirical Investigations*. Chicago, IL: University of Chicago Press.

Middleton, David and Edwards, Derek (eds) (1990) *Collective Remembering*. Newbury Park, CA: Sage.

Moll, Luis C. (ed.) (1990) *Vygotsky and Education: Instructional Implications and Applications of Sociohistorical Psychology*. New York: Cambridge University Press.

Nelson, Richard R. and Winter, Sidney G. (1982) *An Evolutionary Theory of Economic Change*. Cambridge, MA: Belknap Press.

Orr, Julian E. (1990) Sharing knowledge, celebrating identity: community memory in a service culture, in David S. Middleton and Derek Edwards (eds), *Collective Remembering*. Newbury Park, CA: Sage. pp. 169–89.

Perrow, Charles (1984) *Normal Accidents: Living with High-risk Technologies*. New York: Basic Books.

Pirsig, Robert M. (1974) *Zen and the Art of Motorcycle Maintenance*. London: Bodley Head.

Polanyi, Michael (1962) *Personal Knowledge: Towards a Post-critical Philosophy*, corrected edn. Chicago, IL: The University of Chicago Press.

Polanyi, Michael (1967) *The Tacit Dimension*. Garden City, NY: Anchor Books.

Popper, Karl (1969) *The Logic of Scientific Discovery*. London: Hutchinson.

Reber, Arthur S. (1993) *Implicit Learning and Tacit Knowledge: An Essay on the Cognitive Unconscious*. New York: Oxford University Press.

Roberts, Karlene H. (1989) New challenges in organizational research: high reliability organizations, *Industrial Crisis Quarterly*, 3: 111–25.

Roberts, Karlene H. (1990) Managing high reliability systems, *California Management Review*, 32 (4): 101–13.

Rochlin, Gene I. (1989) Informal organizational networking as a crisis-avoidance strategy: US naval flight operations as a case study, *Industrial Crisis Quarterly*, 3: 159–76.

Rogoff, Barbara and Lave, Jean (eds) (1984) *Everyday Cognition: Its Development in Social Context*. Cambridge, MA: Harvard University Press.

Rouse, Joseph (1993) What are cultural studies of scientific knowledge?, *Configurations*, 1: 1–22.

Ryle, Gilbert (1949) *The Concept of Mind*. London: Hutchinson.

Sandelands, Lloyd E. and Stablein, Ralph E. (1987) The concept of organization mind, in Samuel Bacharach and Nancy DiTomaso (eds), *Research in the Sociology of Organizations*, vol. 5. Greenwich, CT: JAI Press. pp. 135–61.

Schein, Edwin H. (1985) *Organizational Culture*. San Francisco, CA: Jossey-Bass.

Schön, Donald A. (1983) *The Reflective Practitioner: How Professionals Think in Action*. New York: Basic Books.

Schutz, Alfred (1953) Common-sense and scientific interpretation of human action, *Philosophical and Phenomenological Research*, 14: 1–38.

Schutz, Alfred (1972) *The Phenomenology of the Social World*. London: Heinemann.

Schwartz, Barry (1982) The social context of commemoration: a study in collective memory, *Social Forces*, 61: 374–97.

Scribner, Sylvia (1985) Knowledge at work, *Anthropology and Education Quarterly*, 16: 199–206.

Scribner, Sylvia (1986) Thinking in action: some characteristics of practical thought, in Robert Sternberg and Richard K. Wagner (eds), *Practical Intelligence: Nature and Origins of Competence in the Everyday World*. Cambridge: Cambridge University Press. pp. 13–30.

Searle, John R. (1987) Minds, brains and programs, in Rainer Born (ed.), *Artificial Intelligence: The Case Against*. London: Croom Helm. pp. 18–40.

Simon, Herbert A. (1958) *Administrative Behavior*. New York: Macmillan.

Simon, Herbert A. (1987) Making management decision: the role of intuition and emotion, *Academy of Management Executive*, 1: 57–64.

Simon, Herbert A., Egidi, Massimo, Marris, Robin and Viale, Riccardo (1992) *Economics, Bounded Rationality, and the Cognitive Revolution*. Aldershot, Hants: Edward Elgar.

Singley, Mark and Anderson, John R. (1989) *The Transfer of Cognitive Skill.* Cambridge, MA: Harvard University Press.

Smith, Barry (1988) Knowing how vs knowing that, in J.C. Nyiri and Barry Smith (eds), *Practical Knowledge: Outlines of a Theory of Traditions and Skills.* London: Croom Helm. pp. 1–16

Snow, C.P. (1959) *The Two Cultures and the Scientific Revolution.* Cambridge: Cambridge University Press.

Snow, C.P. (1964) *The Two Cultures and a Second Look.* New York: Mentor Books.

Spender, J.-C. (1989) *Industry Recipes: The Nature and Sources of Managerial Judgement.* Oxford: Basil Blackwell.

Spender, J.-C. (1994) Knowing, managing, and learning: a dynamic managerial epistemology. *Management Learning*, 25: 387–412.

Spender, J.-C. (1995) Organizational knowledge, collective practice and Penrose rents, *International Business Review*, 3: 353–67.

Spender, J.-C. and Grinyer, Peter H. (1995) Organizational renewal: top management's role in a loosely-coupled system, *Human Relations*, 48 (8): 909–26.

Squire, Larry R., Weinberger, N.M., Lynch, G. and McGaugh, J.L. (eds) (1991) *Memory: Organization and Locus of Change.* New York: Oxford University Press.

Stubbart, Charles I. and Ramaprasad, Arkalgud (1990) Comments on the empirical articles and recommendations for future research, in Anne S. Huff (ed.), *Mapping Strategic Thought.* Chichester: John Wiley. pp. 251–88.

Suchman, Lucy (1987) *Plans and Situated Actions: The Problems of Human–Machine Communication.* Cambridge: Cambridge University Press.

Tharp, Roland G. and Gallimore, Ronald (1988) *Rousing Minds to Life: Teaching, Learning, and Schooling in Social Context.* Cambridge: Cambridge University Press.

Vygotsky, Lev S. (1962) *Thought and Language.* Cambridge, MA: MIT Press.

Webb, Eugene (1988) *Philosophers of Consciousness.* Seattle, WA: University of Washington Press.

Wegner, Daniel M. (1987) Transactive memory: a contemporary analysis of the group mind, in Brian Mullen and George R. Goethals (eds), *Theories of Group Behavior.* New York: Springer-Verlag. pp. 185–208.

Weick, Karl E. (1987) Organizational culture as a source of high reliability, *California Management Review*, 29: 112–27.

Weick, K.E. and Browning, L. (1986) Argument and narration in organizational communication, *Journal of Management*, 12: 243–59.

Weick, Karl E. and Roberts, Karlene H. (1993) Collective mind in organization: heedful interrelating on flight decks, *Administrative Science Quarterly*, 38: 357–81.

Yates, Frances A. (1969) *The Art of Memory.* Harmondsworth: Penguin Books.

3

AGENCY AND ORGANIZATION: A SOCIAL THEORY APPROACH TO COGNITION

Bo Hellgren and Jan Löwstedt

Conflicting views on change – a recurrent theme

The year is 510 BC. It is springtime. A Greek philosopher is sitting in the shadow of an olive tree, fascinated by what he sees around him, the changing scenery of the spring. Even though he has seen it many times before, he still wonders how it can happen. How is change possible? The question of change and how it comes about has been with us for a long time. We know it was one of the issues which perplexed Greek philosophers. Today, with rapid change in Europe, Asia and elsewhere, it is understandable that the same questions of why, how and when change occurs remain of great interest to social scientists.

In ancient Greece a major concern of the debate among philosophers was nature itself and processes in nature. They took for granted that Mother Earth had always been there and asked themselves how it was that water, for example, could change into living fish, and soil into trees and flowers. Did such changes really occur, or were they simply perceived by human senses that had been misled? How could matter totally change its shape? Permenides (540–480 BC) offered a radical solution to the problem: nothing could change; elements were unchangeable![1] Another Greek philosopher, Heraclitus (494–434 BC) maintained the complete opposite: everything changes. He believed, from observing what happened around him, that change was an elementary characteristic of nature.[2]

In the social sciences (and management studies) the traditional emphasis on totalities or systems with specific structures and characteristic modes of operation is being challenged. The alternative view focuses on the impact of individuals and their actions on change in different societal and organizational settings. Social structures have lost their unchallenged position as the determinants of human (or organizational) conduct. Instead, they are seen as results – intended, unintended or even unrecognized – of individual or organization endeavour (Sztompka, 1993: 3) and as the means for the fulfilment of individual or organizational goals.

This chapter deals with managerial and organizational cognition. Our argument is that general theories of social change and social processes can act like a metatheory,[3] providing the basis for more synthesizing efforts and reducing the risk of dogmatism,[4] whether or not in terms of eclecticism.[5] Our hope is that the field of managerial and organizational cognition can learn from and apply some of the elementary assumptions in Greek philosophy and in modern social theory. The notion of (managerial) agency (Giddens, 1984; Sztompka, 1991; Whittington, 1992) offers a new view of the contradictory results in today's cognitive theory of management and organization and provides a route for further development of the field. Studies of management and organizations from a cognitive approach now constitute a field of their own in the social sciences in general and in business studies in particular. So far, the field is characterized by heterogeneity in theoretical assumptions and levels of analyses (Srivastra et al., 1983; Sims et al., 1986; Huff, 1992). Are cognitive structures stable or continuously changing? What is the relation between thinking and acting? Is cognition of importance in other contexts than the individual? Contradictions seem to dominate the field. In its early stages of development this is both natural and fruitful, but the time has come to emphasize more synthesizing efforts. This does not imply a belief in 'grand theory'. The great complexity of social life 'demands multiple sources of enlightenment and can be adequately explained only by a plurality of theories, or ultimately by a multidimensional theory' (Sztompka, 1991: 174). Instead of eclecticism or synthesizing efforts, the field needs a prosperous dialectic between the two. To obtain such a dialogue, there has to be an increased emphasis on the latter.

Empidocles and social theory

Empidocles (483–423 BC) offers a solution to the conflicting view of Permanides and Heraclitus. Briefly, Empidocles argued that things are neither unchangeable nor always changing. In other words, he believed that his two predecessors were both partially right. He denied that something could arise from nothing or that anything could be totally destroyed. His compromise suggested that all change derives from recombinations or separations of unchangeable elements.[6] His message is that change and stability are two sides of the same coin and that each is dependent on the presence of the other. With this assumption, Empidocles avoided the dualism between change and stability that had bewildered Heraclitus and Permenides. The essence of what we shall call the Empidoclian view is the avoidance of dualism, a dislike of extremes. A tendency towards extremism is present not only in Greek philosophy but also in today's social science and management studies. When thought structures about social phenomena undergo changes, the inherent force seems to be so powerful that the pendulum swings over to the opposite extreme. One way to limit this tendency is to reconceptualize dualism as duality: an opposite standpoint is complementary rather than polar. This reconceptualization can be a significant impetus towards a metatheory of managerial and organizational cognition.

Sociological theory tends to reconceptualize dualisms between contrasting and competing views as dualities. It stresses the dialectical interplay of the different forces behind societal changes. One of the most important and influential dualisms is that between objectivism and subjectivism. Objectivistic modes of thought (represented by structuralism and functionalism) focus on analysis of social institutions and their reproduction from a mechanical and deterministic view of behaviour. On the other hand, subjectivistic modes of thought emphasize the voluntaristic aspects of social life at the expense of structural or institutional analysis.

The 'structuration theory' of Giddens (1979, 1984) is an attempt to avoid the dualisms of subject and object, agency and structure, and structure and process (Bryant and Jary, 1991: 2). The theory of 'social becoming' (Sztompka, 1991) is another attempt in that direction. Here, the author tries to develop a theory 'where dialectic interrelations of individualities and totalities could be anchored, a level where actors and structures, actions and transformations merge into one multidimensional form' (ibid.: 40). These two examples – as representatives of social theory – have at least two things in common. The first is the dilemma of action and structure in processes of change and continuity. The second similarity is a focus on the impact and role of agency in social processes. According to Kilminster (1991), Giddens tries to reconceptualize our view of society to cover theoretical links between 'social integration' and 'system integration', that is 'between the face-to-face encounters of co-present actors and the wider social formation of which they form a part' (ibid.: 77). Sztompka (1991, 1993) makes the same claims. His 'two-sided world' (1991: 16) is a world in which men are both makers ('creators') and prisoners ('creatures'), a world which human actions construct and which is itself constrained by human action. This two-sided world (or social theory in general) is a synthesis between alternative models of society: structural, objectivistic, models which focus on social constraints and individual dependence, and action, subjectivistic models which focus on individual freedom in loose and flexible structures.

The theories of Giddens and Sztompka are not only an attempt to overcome the divergence between structure and action. They also deal with the divergence between the 'static model' and the 'dynamic model' – the opposition of continuity and transformation. It is possible to see these two oppositions – structure vis-à-vis action, and continuity vis-à-vis transformation – as defining the problematic field of sociological theory. Sztompka argues that before sociological theory was able to reconceptualize the two oppositions, it could offer only biased and imperfect models.

> Before sociological theory was able to raise itself above this maze and recognize both dualities as irreducible, as basic and indispensable traits of society, requiring a multidimensional, synthetic approach, it was vainly pursuing one-sided

solutions, splitting the ontological unity of opposites at the conceptual level and producing distorted, inadequate models. (Sztompka, 1991: 17)

We believe that a similar step from one-sided solutions to the 'two-sided world' is still to be taken in management studies, although the notion of (managerial) cognition might be an important move in that direction. If so, this emergent field of managerial cognition has to abandon the internal–external dualism of subjectivist and objectivist modes of theory. This dualism has to be replaced with duality 'wherein structure is implicated in action and action is implicated in structure' (Layder, 1987: 28). The field has to be concerned with the fundamental ontological question, the nature of human social existence. For this, a perspective of duality, incorporating the view that society is made by individuals within the context of material and non-material resources, and human meanings and rules, is essential.

The theory of agency

Social theory, as exemplified by Giddens and Sztompka, is an attempt to incorporate and transform the opposite views of structure vis-à-vis action and continuity vis-à-vis transformation into a metatheory. At the heart of this endeavour is the notion of agency. The theory of agency deals with the dichotomy between human action being thought driven or structurally constrained (Sztompka, 1991). The evolution of this theory since the 1960s is evident in such concepts as morphogenesis (Buckley, 1967), actors – systems interdependence (Crozier and Friedberg, 1982), duality of structure (Giddens, 1984), contextual analysis (Pettigrew, 1985) and social becoming (Sztompka, 1991).

The increasing use of the concept of agency by writers on organization is not generally accompanied by any careful analysis of the concept per se. Not even Giddens, who has achieved a position of considerable influence within management studies (Whittington, 1992) analyses the concept thoroughly. In his 'theory of structuration' (Giddens, 1984), he contributes to the development of agency in the structuration of human action. Yet he contributes to the fogginess surrounding the concept of agency by telling the reader that he is content to use the words 'actor' and 'agent' interchangeably (ibid.: xxii). This increases the risk of the concept being juxtaposed with what Meyer (1996) calls the 'acterhood', one of the more dominant constructions in the managerial discourse, and a solely voluntaristic, one-sided view of the actor.

Giddens presents the theory of agency as the 'studies of the active, constructive side of social life but with due to recognition of the structural framework within which human conduct takes place' (1984: 4) or, more frankly speaking, the capability of the individual 'to make a difference' to a pre-existing state of affairs or course of events' (ibid.: 14). In other words, the concept of agency is related to the possibility of altering patterns of actions commonly characterized as habits or routines. The student of management is not unfamiliar with such a capacity to make a difference. Over the last two decades, a prevailing view in management studies has been that management is able to exercise 'strategic choice' (Child, 1972). More recently, though, attempts have been made to synthesize organizational action, with thoughtful actors and structural constraints operating simultaneously (for example, Pettigrew, 1985).

Before any further discussion of managerial and organizational agency, a tentative definition of agency is needed which makes possible differentiation between such closely related concepts as actors and action. If actors are acting individuals, or collectives, and action is what actors do, such actions are always performed in a social context. Actions are, whether habitual or novel, interactions. This is interaction not only in the sense that is observed by, and affects other individuals, but also in the sense that it takes place within present structures of routines and institutions.

Action occurs, according to Silverman (1970: 30), not as a response to an observable stimulus, but as a product of what Parsons (1951) calls a 'system of expectations' arising out of the actor's past experience and defining his perception of the probable reaction of others to this act. Giddens (1984) discusses this as the inherent capacity of human actors to understand what they do while they are doing it. Such reflexive capacity operates only partly on the discursive level. Actors are not always explicitly aware of what they are doing. Yet their actions are not unintended; they are the result of their knowledgeability as agents which is largely carried in practical consciousness (ibid.: xxiii). Contributing to this practical consciousness are all the things that actors know about from daily experience. Many actions in life are repetitive and many of these day-to-day activities are dependent on experiences from earlier actions and interaction in the 'system of expectations' retained in cognitive schema. The concept of agency, then, represents neither the reflexive actor nor his or her constrained actions. Agency is characterized by being relational, the result of intentional or unintentional, active or passive, human action. Agency, therefore, can be defined as an analytical concept to be used for the analysis of how thought and action are co-present in the structuration of human conduct.

Types of agency

What types of agency are there? Are agencies always individual, or is it possible to consider organizational or other collective forms of agency? According to Sztompka (1991), it makes sense to consider three different types of individual as well as collective agencies. The first type of individual agency consists of common people in everyday life. Society at large consists of people working, eating, sleeping, travelling, and so on. Among those busy getting on with their day-to-day activities there are those who, by virtue of exceptional personal qualities, act as representatives of others. This is the second type of individual agency. The third type, according to Sztompka, comprises those who occupy exceptional positions, giving them authority irrespective of their personal qualities. Following this line of reasoning, the same author acknowledges collective agency as collective action taken to affect members in the group in some way or the other; for example, to help, support, mould or change them. Examples of such collectives are the family, fraternities, fitness clubs, and closed monasteries. Second, the collective agency engages in change, not only of itself, but also of society as a whole. In this type of agency are found lobby groups and political parties. The third type of collective agency is those bodies which institute rules, laws and regulations, such as governments, legislatures, boards and committees.

'Giddens does insist on our potential to choose actions deliberately, and to carry them through effectively, even in defiance of established rules and prevailing powers – in other words, the possibility of agency' (Whittington, 1992: 696). In the typology suggested by Sztompka, individuals as well as collectives can exercise such agency on (i) their own behaviour; (ii) their environment; and (iii) the formation of rules and regulations that constrain their behaviour. Such agency is not restricted only to the intended actions of individuals or collectives. Agency is also exercised in social situations unintended by the agent as a result of conditioned power (Galbraith, 1983), the acceptance of authority and when submission to the will of others becomes the preference of those submitting.

Examples of agency should not be confused with examples of types of agency. An influential family, for example, may be an agency of both the second and third collective type by trying to accomplish change in society or even to influence its rules and regulations. Therefore, a family, an organization, a church or a government can be both an agency and an entity, arenas located in time and space where agency is exercised. Our investigation needs some clarifications of the question of agency and organization – type or entity?

Agency and organization

If we first consider the organization as an arena for individual and collective agency, it is necessary to ascribe some importance to what Hägerstrand calls 'the life biographies of individuals', which are made up of 'internal mental experiences and events', related to the interplay between body and environmental phenomena (Giddens, 1991: 115). More important though than the unique history of individuals is that their actions in the organization (and elsewhere) are an ongoing interaction between past, present and possible futures. The development of modern western society has divided the life of the individual into several domains – work, family life, social and political activities. Managers and managed alike are also people who, as full members of society, operate in a diversity of systems and are therefore able to draw upon and respond to a multiplicity of rules and resources in the organizational arena. It is by active exploitation of the tensions between divergent structural principles that managers, and others in the organization, gain their agency (Whittington, 1992: 704–5). Of course, such a multiplicity of structural principles also influences the day-to-day actions of the organizational member.

Biz Ecosys

For managerial agency the organization is the arena. But what about the organization per se? Is it meaningful to talk about organizational agency? There are those who raise the possibility that organizations are mental entities capable of thought (Sandeland and Stablein, 1987: 136), but the concept of cognitive phenomena at the organizational level throws some doubt on the notion of organizational agency. Organizations do not literally think. Yet organizations do things; they operate in a market, together with other firms they constitute an industry, and so on. Take as an example a powerful and influential CEO in a major firm in an industry. Of course, as a person, he or she is an example of one individual exercising managerial agency, influencing both this particular firm and, indirectly, other actors in the industry. On the other hand, the influence of the CEO is to a certain extent mediated through the organization. We will later on give examples of organizations acting as agencies in the restructuring of industries and in reshaping 'industrial wisdom' (Hellgren and Melin, 1993).

How then can we say that organizations act or operate, but do not think? Some writers argue that information from the past can be stored in an organization (Walsh and Ungson, 1991). March and Simon (1958) wrote about the organizational memory being embodied in standard operating procedures. Writers on organizational learning have viewed organizational memory in terms of structural artefacts or roles (Walsh and Ungson, 1991) that over time lose their efficacy and become obstacles to change (Hedberg et al., 1976). In this sense, organizations, independently of individuals within them, 'remember' previous actions and are able to operate in accordance with the solutions to previous problems.

The discussion of organizational memory can be extended to interorganizational level. In most industrial sectors there seems to be a dominating recipe (Spender, 1989) or an industrial wisdom which expresses dominating opinions, shared by companies and actors, about the rules of the game and the freedom of action within the structural confines of a sector (Hellgren and Melin, 1993: 63). Therefore, we find it reasonable to consider the possibility of organizational agency since action at the industry level in many cases influences the operations and strategic orientation of significant organizations.

Implications for cognitive theory

In this part of the chapter we will put forward some implications of apply-ing an Empidoclian view and the idea of agency on managerial cognition. Both Empidocles and modern social theory recommend the avoidance of dualism because of the extremism it engenders. Cognitive theories of orga-nization and management characterized by extreme views can benefit from this approach. There is a number of concepts that capture different aspects of cognitive structures, 'conceptually related representation(s) of objects, situations, events, and of sequences of events and actions' (Markus and Zajonc, 1985: 143). Downey and Brief (1986) consider how cognitive struc-tures affect organizational design and the development of organizational structures. The importance of implicit theories for the development of dif-ferent organizational structures is exemplified by a comparison between those of Henry Ford in the Ford Motor Company and those of Alfred P. Sloan in General Motors. Examples of other conceptualizations of cognitive structures are beliefs (Donaldson and Lorsch, 1985), interpretative schemes (Ranson et al., 1980; Bartunek, 1984), maps (Weick and Bougon, 1986), and schema and scripts (Gioia, 1986). Each of these exemplifications can be said to represent extreme, one-sided views in the spectrum of structure vis-à-vis action and continuity vis-à-vis transformation.

These conceptualizations, although they are based on the assumption that mental structures facilitate and influence action, express different views about the relation between thought (mental structures) and action. Some of the authors referred to above (Donaldson and Lorch; Downey and Brief; Isenberg; Ranson et al.) assume that mental structures are thought driven in the sense that they are the result of thinking processes that precede and thereby rule the action; that is, actions undertaken are determined by these mental structures (Hellgren and Melin, 1993). An opposite view sees mental structures as predominately action driven, and so not a determining force on action. In fact, thinking and acting are simul-taneous and interrelated processes (Weick, 1983; Bartunek, 1984). Individuals learn while they act and not through rational stage models of decision-making.

The other exemplification of opposite (or one-sided) views in the field of managerial cognition is continuity or transformation. Are mental struc-tures stable assumptions that rarely change or structures that continually change to accommodate new experience? Donaldson and Lorsch (1985: 79) found that one function of beliefs is to provide continuity and stabil-ity when change threatens to undermine the lessons of experience. Furthermore, the authors found that managers in the twelve companies they studied had deep emotional commitment and were almost reli-giously devoted to their beliefs (ibid.: 111). When change occurred in the belief system, it was incremental and altered only one tenet of the system without altering the whole mental structure. Hellgren and Melin (1993: 61) drew a similar conclusion after studying two CEOs. Each CEO demonstrated a 'way of thinking', a mental structure, that was stable and distinctive and showed no strong tendency to vary with the situation.

In contrast to the findings of Donaldson and Lorsch and of Hellgren and Melin that beliefs and ways of thinking are stable, Weick and Bougon (1986: 132) argue that changes in cognitive maps often occur. People continually reorganize concepts to accommodate new experiences. Bartunek (1984) differentiates between the degree of change when discussing the stableness of mental structures. Second-order changes are less common than first-order changes (that is, incremental modifications in present ways of interpretations). Generally, behind the idea of managerial and organizational cognition is a basic and (one-sided) assumption of freedom of action. Individuals (and organizations) are able to make 'strategic choice' (Child, 1972) in accordance with their interpretations and are thereby able to 'create' supporting situations. Actors, exercising power, become the explanatory factor behind social and economic changes. To accord with the ideas advocated in this chapter, this assumption has to be redefined.

When actors exercise power, their influence is more or less constrained. This view on freedom of action was propounded (at the level of organization) by Stinchombe (1965), who pointed out that organizations are made by social actors but only when social structural conditions permit. Societies, organizations or other artefacts are made by individuals within the context of material and non-material resources and human meanings and rules; that is, the freedom of action is structurally constrained.

What particular bearing has this idea of structures as agencies on managerial cognition? There are some implications which need particular emphasis. First, the significance of cognitive framing is not restricted to the individual level. Second, the question of changing or stable mind sets becomes an important issue. Furthermore, it is clear that there are other than cognitive structures that act as agencies in the shaping of societies and organizations. Because the freedom of action of individuals and organizations is contextually constrained, there are not only individual mind sets but also ideational structures (Hellgren and Melin, 1993) reducing the power of an individual actor; that is the ability to implement a solution to an enacted situation. Ideational structures are patterns of shared beliefs in a community, or dominant ideas within the organization (Löwstedt, 1993) about such organizational issues as structure, strategy and management style. The notion of agency also implies that we cannot understand markets as socially constructed – that no single efficient economic logic or mode of organizing economic activities dominates in countries, industries and firms – solely from a cognitive perspective. This is so even if we take into account the impact of different cognitive spheres (Hellgren and Melin, 1993). Agency is also exercised by dominant institutional structures. The shape of a specific configuration, such as a 'business system' (Whitley, 1990, 1991) is the product of the institutional environment (a nation, a region or an industry) in which that configuration is embedded and of the history of this specific environment. Institutional factors, such as the financial system, the political system, and the legal system, act as agencies and balance the influence of cognition.

Some scholars argue that the mental structures of individuals are stable and rarely change, and then only incrementally. Other scholars argue that changes in cognitive structures often occur because of the tight connection between action and thinking. Of course, these two opposites can be extended to structures in other cognitive spheres. When applying the notion that action as well as structure can act as an agency in societal processes, each of these two general standpoints seems to be of less importance. A more plausible assumption, derived from what has been said about agency, might be that managerial cognition can be characterized by stable as well as changing mind sets. More interesting is to ask when, why and how structures in different cognitive spheres alter or not. This question leads to the connected, but more general issue of the role and relation of different cognitive spheres as agency in processes of continuity or radical change. For example, Hellgren and Melin (1993) describe the rather paradoxical result that three different and stable cognitive spheres (an individual way of thinking, organizational culture, and industrial wisdom) resulted in a radical change in a firm's business strategy. A change can be judged radical (or continuous) only when it is related to some other change. In this case, the change – introduced by the entrance of the new CEO – was radical in relation to the prevailing corporate culture and industrial wisdom. This was also the situation in one of our other cases. The CEOs in these two cases initiated a change that transformed the corporate culture, gave the firm a new market position, started a restructuring of the industry, and inaugurated a new industrial wisdom. In some of our cases (Löwstedt, 1988, 1993), individuals or groups of individuals were exponents of new ideas. These examples indicate that there has to be a tension between different cognitive spheres if there is to be radical change. Of course, tensions can also produce counter-productive struggles for power and control if there is no actor able to exercise powerful agency in social relationships (Barbalet, 1987).

Examples of agency

The theory of agency presuppose that insights into the cognition of significant actors making, for example, 'a strategic choice' are but one building block in the understanding of such a situation. The agency influential in such a situation also includes former and continuous behaviour and its contextual constraints. For researchers interested in managerial and organizational cognition this has, as already indicated, some important implications which we will now exemplify using our own empirical studies of change processes. Three business firms were chosen for a study of the introduction of a new technology which had the potential to alter the labour process dramatically. Despite considerable similarities between the three firms, the use of the technology and the gradual structuration of the work organization triggered by the new technology were significantly different in the three cases. These differences could be related to the content and differentiation in organizing frameworks held by a small group of significant actors in each firm. The influence of such a small number of people on the consequences of a change process, their possibility to 'make a difference', is only partially explained by their individual differences. Their agency is also the result of these actors having been chosen and legitimized to work on these issues by their organizations. Their personal qualifications and/or their formal position in the organizations explain why these persons were able to influence the change process at all. Their agency is also the result of their internal and external interaction during the organizing process triggered by the new technology (Löwstedt, 1993).

The role of individual actors in introducing new technology or new work organization in businesses has often been stressed. Such people are said to carry the new machinery 'on their bare shoulders' (Löwstedt, 1988), and to be 'souls of fire' (Stjernberg and Philips, 1993). Studies of the internal diffusion of technology and new forms of work organization show how the influence of such change agents is restricted in time and space. For example, individual actors were of major importance in the early phases of introduction of computer-aided design (CAD) in Swedish industry. When it came to large-scale internal diffusion of the technology in the company, the process changes from being solutions driven to being problem driven. The role of the entrepreneur was taken over by other actors and by traditional economical rationalities (Löwstedt and Norr, 1991). The 'souls-of-fire' study shows the importance of the legitimacy (especially top management acceptance) influencing the organizational change process. It was also shown how legitimacy was restricted in time and to only parts of the organization (Stjernberg and Philips, 1993). The examples show that actors can 'make a difference' but also the constraints within which such agency must work.

Organizational agency is also evident at the intermediate level. Swedish Telecom's consideration of a major administrative reform is such an example. Substantial change in the environment necessitated an improvement in the overall coordination of production. A new organization was tested in two out of 24 regional units. No changes were allowed in any of the other 22 regions before evaluation was completed. Yet, changes did occur in the other 22 regions. A case study of one of them showed these to be not the result of top managerial agency, but of an intermediate organizational agency. Top managers and some of the influential production people, together with union officials, had taken the opportunity presented by the centrally initiated reform to realize some of their own ideas about how production ought to be organized in their part of the organization (Löwstedt, 1991).

Finally, two examples from the perspective of organizations acting as agencies are appropriate. One is from the pulp and paper industry and the other from the welding industry. After 1984, the business idea and main strategies of the Swedish company Holmen AB changed significantly, though not because of changes in the company environment (further detail is given in Hellgren and Melin, 1992, 1993; Melin and Hellgren, 1994). The changes were brought about by the entrance of a new corporate leader. His strategy was in line with the firm's growth philosophy, but much more aggressively expressed: Holmen would become one of the leading Nordic companies in two of its business areas – wood-containing printing paper and wood-fibre based hygiene products. To reach such a market position, the company started to acquire Swedish competitors. Holmen also bought a minority share in a German producer of printing paper. While the company's strategy before the entrance of this new CEO was characterized by a rather defensive plan to grow with the market in one business area, this new strategy was much more offensive, including both related diversification and evident ambitions to take an active part in the restructuring of the industry. To undertake this more aggressive strategy, Holmen gave up its earlier ideas about internal growth. The new strategy implied a strong belief in both far-reaching alliances and acquisition.

Through the aggressive restructuring and growth of the Holmen group, the company was in part challenging the conventional wisdom of the pulp and paper industry. The new CEO and his company threatened the negotiated order of the industry where each company had a determined position. Before the entrance of the new CEO, Holmen had always been a medium-sized firm without ambition to take an active and leading role in restructuring the industry. At the same time, however, other players aspired to the role of leader in the Scandinavian part of the pulp and paper industry. In June 1988, after a power struggle, MoDo, one of Holmen's competitors, acquired 100 per cent of the company.

The second example also reveals a new CEO changing the strategy. When the strategy was implemented, the firm acted as an agency in the restructuring of the industry and in changes to its industrial wisdom. Unlike the first example, this is a success story. The firm is now one of the world's leading manufacturers of welding equipment. Esab AB changed its strategy from one of organic growth through product development to one of international acquisition in the early 1980s. Between 1980 and 1987 the company executed fifteen major acquisitions. In the restructure of the welding industry, Esab was the leading actor. Before the restructuring started, there were many domestic companies operating mostly in their local markets. Very few – Esab was one of them – were established in foreign markets. During the 1970s the industry had declined, mainly because of decreased demand for commercial steel. Esab – along with its competitors – had reacted with a focused strategy, removing business areas to consolidate the firm. Around 1980, when the acute economic difficulties were overcome and the new CEO had entered, the firm intensified its search for ways to survive in the mature welding industry. There was at this time a huge over-capacity and Esab wanted to avoid an intensified price cut. It became obvious that it was necessary to change the rules of the game. The company decided to acquire competitors and not to engage in collaborative strategies. The new CEO stated that there was only one way to cooperate with competitors and that was to own them.

In 1981 the board of directors made the final decision to follow an acquisition strategy. One crucial question remained: in what way could the strategy be implemented? How could the other actors in the industry be persuaded to accept Esab's efforts to dominate the industry? First, Esab organized a seminar with representatives from the industry and independent, highly esteemed experts. The next move was to announce that Esab under no circumstances would withdraw from the industry and that the intention was to take the lead in its restructuring. Esab declared that it intended to buy competitors at a price sufficiently attractive to allow owners of non-profitable businesses to leave the welding industry. By the late 1980s, Esab had been transformed into a modern, international, market-oriented company. The number of actors in the industry was significantly lower than it had been at the beginning of the decade.

These two examples show how the ideas of individuals are mediated through the organization. Furthermore, they show that organizations act as agencies when they provide the medium for individuals to carry out their beliefs. In both cases, the companies were vitally important in the restructuring of the industry and – especially Esab – in the reshaping of industrial wisdom.

Agency, managerial cognition and the contextual approach

The examples above illustrate different kinds of strategic changes. In general, the influences of modern social theory are rare in management studies and in studies of strategic change. An important and impressive exception is Pettigrew's 'contextual approach', an attempt to use modern social theory (especially Giddens) to understand strategic change processes. Some comments on his approach from the view of agency presented in this chapter are appropriate. Pettigrew's study of ICI (Pettigrew, 1985) is one of the first major empirical illustrations of structuration theory in management studies (Whittington, 1992). His approach is an effort to connect the inner and outer context, the content, and the processes of strategic change in companies as they operate within the competitive environment. Furthermore, it 'recognizes that processes both are constrained by structure and shape structures, either in the direction of preserving them or altering them' (Pettigrew, 1988: 27). Pettigrew wants to combine structural analyses stressing structural constraints with processual analyses stressing action and strategic conduct. This is done: 'by conceptualizing structure and context not just as a barrier to action but as essentially involved in its production (Giddens, 1979; Ranson, Hinings and Greenwood, 1980) and, secondly, by demonstrating how aspects of structure and context are mobilized or activated by actors and groups as they seek to obtain outcomes important to them' (Pettigrew, 1988: 27).

If one scrutinizes the contextual approach from the perspective of the mix of managerial cognition and agency theory considered in this chapter, at least one shortcoming is evident. The cognitive dimension becomes an aspect of the inner context in terms of 'frames of thought' and 'culture' and key actor 'assumptions' (content aspect). What does this imply? On the whole, according to Whittington (1992), the outer context is rendered alien 'with little sense of ICI as an organization actually constituted by the mobilization of the structural properties of the wider society' (ibid.: 701). Pettigrew's approach sees the failure of radical change in ICI as attributable to a few misguided idealists. Instead, Whittington proposes that the failure can be better understood in terms of different competing claims for managerial legitimacy, which he sees as capitalist, gentlemanly, scientific and social scientific. In terms of our own frame of reference, Pettigrew neglects the importance and impact of the shared cognitive structures of these agencies on the rise and fall of radical strategic change in ICI. But he does emphasize that behind the reorientation in ICI was not just the logic of economics and business. There were also processes of 'managerial perception, choice, and action influenced by and influencing perception of the operating environment of the firm and its structure, culture, and system of power and control' (Pettigrew, 1985: 665). Furthermore, he acknowledges that business strategies are likely to be rooted in the 'idea structure', cognitive structure or recipe institutionalized in an industry sector (ibid.: 666, Spender, 1989). But these cognitive structures, belonging to the outer context, are treated as more or less passive constraints and not as active agencies influencing the change process in ICI.

An outline of a research agenda

We have argued that an Empidoclian approach can handle some contradictions in the field of managerial and organizational cognition as it implies a reconceptualization of dualism to duality wherein structure is implicated in actions and action is implicated in structure. Furthermore, we argue that modern social theory, with its focus on agency, can act like a metatheory and provide a basis for further development of the field. We conclude the chapter by presenting an outline of a research agenda for studying societal and organizational change processes based on these arguments.

Studies of change from a cognitive perspective have, with a few exceptions (for example, Grinyer and Spender, 1979; Huff, 1992; Spender, 1989; Hellgren and Melin, 1993), been restricted to an 'internal perspective', focusing on the impact of individuals, groups or corporate culture. We believe that it is time to expand the research agenda. The notion of agency in modern social theory and the discussion of the contextual approach above indicate that it is not enough to incorporate the level of industry in the analysis. Indeed, as Whittington argues, other institutionalized groupings in society exert an influence on change processes. A first step in the development of the agenda would be to determine theoretically and empirically what are these institutionalized configurations, and to search for variations between, for example, nations and industries. The next step would be to capture shared beliefs and assumptions (the cognitive dimension) of members in these structures. By mixing institutional ruling and cognitive framing (Hellgren and Melin, 1992) in managerial and organizational cognition, the field can contribute both to the understanding and impact of the interplay between different cognitive spheres, and also to the structural and action role of agency in strategic change processes. Such a development of the agenda will certainly increase the field's contribution to the development of social theory. Finally, we must not forget that if anything can be guaranteed to change, it is, of course, change itself. To recognize that change changes might be a first step to avoid theoretical extremism whether or not in terms of dualism or duality.

Acknowledgements

We are grateful to Dennis Gioia, Stuart MacDonald and Andrew Pettigrew for comments and suggestions on earlier versions of this chapter.

Notes

1 An element may seem to undergo change, but Permenides argued that this is not due to an actual change. Our senses fool us into believing that the element changes. We therefore have to turn to reason instead of believing empirical observations.

2 This view is, of course, contrary to Permenides' idea about the sovereignty over empirical observations.

3 This view is, of course, contrary to Permenides' idea about the sovereignty over empirical observations.

4 Dogmatism can be associated with any particular standpoint. Sanderson (1987: 318) defines dogmatism as a form of thinking in which the actor clings to certain ideas and refuses to modify the ideas when confronted by contrary information.

5 Eclecticism refers to 'putting side by side disparate components of various theories in a purely additive fashion' (Sztompka, 1991: 174), or in other words, 'grabbing what you can from where you can, wrapping it all together and claiming it is distinctive' (definition offered by Prof. Michael B. Arthur, Suffolk University, Boston). Eclecticism is 'an a priori doctrine that multiple theoretical approaches must be used jointly in order to arrive at acceptable explanations' (Sanderson, 1987: 316). On the other hand, theoretical synthesis 'combines elements in such a way that the recombination produces a novel fusion, qualitatively distinct from any of the combined components' (Kilminster, 1991: 74). The recombination and fusion of elements from different research traditions produce a novel research tradition

similar to its parents, yet significantly distinct from them (Sanderson, 1987: 334). The new combination 'acquires assumptions, concepts and principles of its own, forming a new basis for research efforts' (Kilminster, 1991: 74). Thus, synthesis is basically different from eclecticism. The latter does not involve the recombining of elements into something new.

6 The four unchangeable elements are, according to Empidocles, earth, water, air and fire.

References

Barbalet, J.M. (1987) Power, structural resources, and agency, *Current Perspective in Social Theory*, 8: 1–24.

Bartunek, J.M. (1984) Changing interpretive schemes and organizational restructuring: the example of a religious order, *Administrative Science Quarterly*, 29: 355–72.

Bryant, C.G.A. and Jary, D. (1991) Introduction: coming to terms with Anthony Giddens, in C.G.A. Bryant and D. Jary (eds), *Giddens' Theory of Structuration. A Critical Appreciation*. London: Routledge. pp. 1–31.

Buckley, Walter (1967) *Sociology and Modern Systems Theory*. Englewood Cliffs, NJ: Prentice-Hall.

Bullock, A., Stallybrass, O. and Trombley, S. (eds) (1988) *The Fontana Dictionary of Modern Thought*, 2nd edn. London: Fontana Press.

Child, J. (1972) Organization structure, environment, and performance – the role of strategic choice, *Sociology*, 6 (1): 1–22.

Crozier, Michel and Friedberg, Erhard (1982) *Actors and Systems*. Chicago: University of Chicago Press.

Donaldson, G. and Lorsch, J.W. (1985) *Decision Making at the Top*. New York: Basic Books.

Downey, H.K. and Brief, A.P. (1986) How cognitive structures affect organizational design: implicit theories of organizing, in H.P. Sims, D.A. Gioia et al. (eds), *The Thinking Organization: Dynamics of Organizational Social Cognition*. San Francisco, CA: Jossey-Bass.

Galbraith, J.K. (1983) *The Anatomy of Power*. Boston: Houghton Mifflin.

Giddens, A. (1979) *Central Problems of Social Theory*. London: Macmillan.

Giddens, A. (1984) *The Constitution of Society*. Cambridge: Polity Press.

Gioia, D.A. (1986) Symbol, script and sensemaking, in H.P. Sims, D.A. Gioia et al. (eds), *The Thinking Organization: Dynamics of Organizational Social Cognition*. San Francisco, CA: Jossey-Bass.

Grinyer, P.H. and Spender, J.C. (1979) Recipes, crises and adoption in mature industries, *International Studies of Management and Organization*, 9: 113–33.

Hedberg, B. (1981) How organizations learn and unlearn, in W.H. Starbuck and P.A. Nystrom (eds), *Handbook of Organizational Design*, vol. 1. Oxford: Oxford University Press.

Hedberg, B.L., Nyström, P.C. and Starbuck, W.H. (1976) Camping on seasaws: Prescriptions for a self-designing organization, *Administrative Science Quarterly*, (1981), 21: 41–65.

Hellgren, B. and Melin, L. (1992) Business systems, industrial wisdom and corporate strategies, in R. Whitley (ed.), *European Business Systems. Firms and Markets in their National Contexts*. London: Sage. pp. 180–97.

Hellgren, B. and Melin, L. (1993) The role of strategists' ways of thinking in strategic change processes, in J. Hendry and G. Johnson with J. Newton, *Strategic Thinking: Leadership and the Management of Change*. Chichester: John Wiley. pp. 47–68.

Huff, A.S. (1992) Industry influences on strategy reformulation, *Strategic Management Journal*, 3: 119–31.

Kilminster, R. (1991) Structuration theory as a world-view, in C.G.A. Bryant and D. Jary (eds), *Giddens' Theory of Structuration. A Critical Appreciation*. London: Routledge. pp. 74–115.

Layder, D. (1987) Key issues in structuration theory: some critical remarks, *Current Perspectives in Social Theory*, 8: 25–46.

Löwstedt, J. (1988) Mot en förändrad arbetsorganisation, in P. Docherty and J. Löwstedt (eds), *Vägval inför CadCam*. Stockholm: Arbetsmiljöfonden.

Löwstedt, J. (1991) Structures and processes in administrative change, *Scandinavian Journal of Management*, 7: 143–50.

Löwstedt, J. (1993) Organizing frameworks in emerging organizations. A cognitive approach to the analysis of change, *Human Relations*, 46 (4): 501–26.

Löwstedt, J. and Norr, C. (1991) *Spridning av en innovation*. Stockholm: IMIT.

March, J.G. and Simon, H.A. (1958) *Organizations*. New York: John Wiley.

Markus, H. and Zajonc, R.B. (1985) The cognitive perspective in social psychology, in G. Lindzey and E. Aronson (eds), *Handbook of Social Psychology*. New York: Random House. pp. 137–230.

Melin, L. and Hellgren, B. (1994) Patterns of strategic processes: two change typologies, in H. Thomas, D. O'Neal, R. White and D. Hurst (eds), *Building the Strategically-Responsive Organization*. Chichester: John Wiley. pp. 251–71.

Meyer, J.W. (1996) Otherhood: the promulgation and transmission of ideas in the modern organizational environment, in B. Czarniawska and G. Sevon (eds), *Translating Organizational Change*. Berlin: de Gruyter.

Parsons, T. (1951) *The Social System*. New York: Free Press.

Pettigrew, A.M. (1985) *The Awakening Giant – Continuity and Change in ICI*. Oxford: Basil Blackwell.

Pettigrew, A.M. (1990) Longitudinal field research on change: theory and practice, *Organization Science*, 1 (3): 267–92.

Pettigrew, A.M. (1988) Context and action in the transformation of the firm, *Journal of Management Studies*, 24 (6): 649–70.

Ranson, S., Hinings, B. and Greenwood, R. (1980) The structuring of organizational structures, *Administrative Science Quarterly*, 25: 1–17.

Sandeland, L.E. and Stablein, R.E. (1987) The concept of organization mind, *Research in the Sociology of Organizations*, 5: 135–61.

Sanderson, S. (1987) Eclectisism and its alternatives, in J. Wilson (ed.), *Current Perspectives in Social Theories: A Research Annual*, 8. London: JAI Press.

Silverman, David (1970) *The Theory of Organisations*. London: Heinemann.

Sims, H.P., Gioia, D.A. Ass (eds) (1986) *The Thinking Organization: Dynamics of Organizational Social Cognition*. San Francisco, CA: Jossey-Bass.

Spender, J.-C. (1989) *Industry Recipes – The Nature and Sources of Managerial Judgement*. Oxford: Basil Blackwell.

Srivastva, Suresh et al. (1983) *The Executive Mind: New Insights on Managerial Thought and Cognition*. San Francisco, CA: Jossey-Bass.

Stinchombe, A.L. (1965) Social structure and organization, in J.G. March (ed.), *Handbook of Organizations*. Skokie, IL: Rand McNally. pp. 142–93.

Stjernberg, T. and Philips, Å. (1993) Organizational innovations in a long-term perspective: legitimacy and souls-of-fire as critical factors of change and viability, *Human Relations*, 46 (10): 1193–1219.

Sztompka, Piotr (1991) *Society in Action. The Theory of Social Becoming*. Cambridge: Polity Press.

Sztompka, Piotr (1993) *The Sociology of Social Change*. Oxford: Basil Blackwell.

Walsh, J.P. and Ungson, G.R. (1991) Organizational memory, *Academy of Management Review*, 16: 57–91.

Weick, K.E. (1983) Managerial thought in the context of action, in S. Srivastva et al. (eds), *The Executive Mind: New Insight on Managerial Thought and Action*. San Francisco, CA: Jossey-Bass.

Weick, K.E. and Bougon, M.G. (1986) Organizations as cognitive maps. Charting ways to success and failure, in H.P. Sims, D.A. Gioia et al. (eds), *The Thinking Organization: Dynamics of Organizational Social Cognition*. San Francisco, CA: Jossey-Bass. pp. 102–35.

Whitley, R. (1990) Eastern Asian enterprise structures and the comparative analysis of forms of business organizations, *Organization Studies*, 11 (1): 47–74.

Whitley, R. (1991) The social construction of business systems in East Asia, *Organizations Studies*, 12 (1): 1–28.

Whittington, R. (1992) Putting Giddens into action: social systems and managerial agency, *Journal of Management Studies*, 29 (6): 693–712.

4

THE THEORY AND PRAXIS OF REFLECTIVE LEARNING IN STRATEGY MAKING

Kees van der Heijden and Colin Eden

While the notion of a 'learning organization' is an important and relevant topic for managers and academics alike, it provides little help to those wishing to realize one, or to enhance organizational learning. De Geus (1988) contends that 'the ability to learn faster than your competitors may be the only sustainable competitive advantage'. This raises questions about whether, having postulated the concept of the 'learning organization', managers can do anything to improve learning qualities of organizations. The three dilemmas which make debate about practical learning difficult stem from three different schools of thought about organizational life. The first has been well rehearsed within the managerial and organizational cognition field – the organization as a reified unitary actor in tension with the individual acting on behalf of the organization. The second derives from the tension between the evolutionary, processual and rationalistic views of strategic management. The third reflects the tension between symbolic interactionism, semiotics and ethnomethodology as methods of understanding the management of meaning in organizations. These tensions frame discussion about the management and practice of organizational learning. We can only make progress by analysing organizational learning within a perspective that encompasses these three tensions. We suggest that a focus on the relationship between managers' cognition and their work on strategic issues is productive, even though there are problems with eliciting that cognition in the context of their everyday work on strategic issues. We offer a number of well-tried approaches to elicitation, which, while not perfect, deal with the inherent dilemmas and achieve an appropriate balance between theory and practice.

The learning organization or learning managers?

Garvin (1993) defines the learning organization as one that is 'skilled at creating, acquiring and transferring knowledge, and at modifying its behavior to reflect new knowledge and insights'. Similarly much of the organizational learning literature treats organizations as unitary actors whose knowledge and skills feed into action. This fails to distinguish between, on the one hand, organizations as unitary actors and, on the other, the individuals who act on the organization's behalf. The field polarizes, with some researchers attempting to map organizational cognition as if it were unproblematic (for example, Porac and Thomas, 1987; Spender, 1989) while others argue that cognition can only belong to individual managers (Bougon, 1992; Eden, 1992, 1993).

Models of individual learning are often projected onto organizations. For example, Piaget's (1971) model of the two levels of individual learning, by accommodation and by adaptation, is applied directly to organizations by Argyris and Schön (1978) in their concepts of single-loop and double-loop learning. Vickers (1965) makes a similar projection where he distinguishes an executive function (maintaining a course of current affairs in line with current governing relations) from a policy function (modifying the governing relations) leaving it open whether he is considering functions of managers or functions of organizations as a whole. Normann and Ramirez (1994) straddle both views, arguing that managers must be able to live in two thought worlds: first, the world of business, in which issues relate to the organization as a unitary actor in its environment trying to position itself skilfully to enhance its chances of survival; second, the world of management, in which issues relate to resolving the problems of multiple internal actors and their relationships, and the challenge of making things happen. They see thinking in the world of business and in the world of management as connected but consecutive tasks. We contend that an operational definition of organizational learning needs to take account of, and emphasize, the characteristics of groups of people developing corporate behaviour together, rather than individuals (or organizations as unitary actors) learning.

The three schools of strategy

The rationalistic, evolutionary and processual views of strategy may be used to illustrate different approaches to organizational learning (for example, Whittington, 1993). Mintzberg (1990) provides a larger taxonomy, which can be mapped into these three views. (See Figure 4.1.)

The rationalistic school codifies thought and action separately. The strategist thinks on behalf of the entire organization and works out optimal strategy as a process of searching for maximum utility among a number of strategic options. Once the best way forward has been chosen, the question of action (the 'implementation problem') can be addressed. Mintzberg (1990) lists the presuppositions of the rationalistic school as:

- predictability, with no interference from outside;
- clear objectives and intentions;

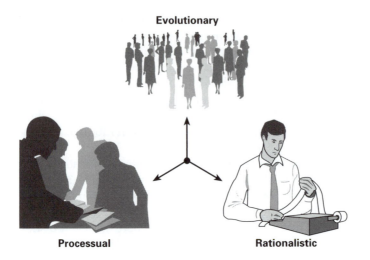

Figure 4.1 *Three schools of thought in strategy*

- implementation following formulation (thinking separated from action);
- full understanding throughout the organization;
- reasonable people will do reasonable things.

In spite of the fact that these assumptions are almost certainly false, the rationalistic school prospers and remains the largest dominant part of the field.

The evolutionary school emphasizes the complex nature of organizational behaviour, with aspects beyond the bounds of rational thinking (Lindblom, 1959; Mintzberg and Waters, 1985). Strategy is a perspective on emergent behaviour, and a winning strategy can only be articulated in retrospect. Evolutionary systems discriminate and generate emergent properties which comprise a transmissible memory of successful strategies. Discrimination may be self-applied or it may be exogenous, but it ensures that the strategies which survive are those which are best fitted to do so. For evolutionary systems, strategy is a process of random experimentation and filtering. The problem, in common with most other evolutionary theories, is that this theory has little predictive power. Most managers think about strategy in terms of their power to influence things, and therefore that strategic thinking is useful.

The processual school takes a middle position suggesting that, while it may not be possible to work out optimal strategies in a purely rational process, managers can create processes in organizations that make them more flexible and adaptable, and so better able to learn from their mistakes. The school looks at successful evolutionary behaviour as the ultimate strategic test. While academics have expended much energy on arguing the relative merits of these perspectives, strategy making in the real world manifests elements of all three. Rather than preferring one over another we suggest that it is more productive to see these as three aspects of a single complex phenomenon. Thus our approach to organizational learning attempts to integrate the three schools of thought.

Integration of theories of strategy (using Kolb's model)

Kolb and Rubin (1991) describe the nature of learning as a four-part loop or cycle, with concrete experiences feeding into a process of reflection, leading to the development of theories of how things work, on the basis of which new actions are planned and executed, leading to new experiences (see Figure 4.2). They describe the cycle as a process of individual learning, with individuals often having particular skills in one of the four activities indicated. They then apply the theory towards improved decision-making by increasing the blend of skills in a decision-making team, such that all skills are represented in the group. Their suggestion is that a blend of people with diverse aptitudes, so that all four boxes are represented, will improve the learning capability of a group. We use his model in a slightly different way.

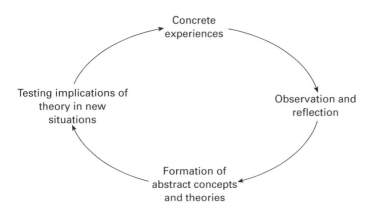

Figure 4.2   *The learning cycle (Kolb)*

The important point to pick out of Kolb and Rubin's model is the need for action to create experiences and learning (see Weick's 'how do I know what I think until . . . I see how I act', 1979). We extend his theory to institutional and organizational learning situations by introducing the notion of institutional action. We define the institution as 'a coherent set of individual actions which are supported as a set by a self-sustaining critical mass of opinion in the organization'. We suggest that one can speak of institutional action only if a minimum level of sense-making and response planning is shared. Without this we can speak only of unrelated individual actions, which lead to individual rather than organizational learning. Without any consensus or shared meaning, individual actions will not cohere and the organization will fragment and, if left in this stage, ultimately go under. However, if a minimum level of alignment of mental models has taken place within the organization, planning becomes a joint activity. Experiences will be common, leading to joint reflection in the group and reinforcement of a shared mental model. As we argue later, the minimum level of shared meaning required for coordinated and organized action is related to the demands for strategic opportunism. This is the ability to act fast with the confidence that the action will build appropriate strategic futures that can be set against the need for the creative tensions which come from differentiated meanings. We see that this institutional version of Kolb's theory introduces the additional factor of the degree of sharing of theories and meaning (Scheper, 1991). The learning cycle can feed on itself only when an initial critical mass is present. The inclusion of 'action' in the loop emphasizes the need for sharing of theories about the world if institutional learning is to take place (Bood; Lindell et al.; Spender, in this volume). For this reason learning requires an effective process of conversation, through which strategic cognitions can be compared, challenged and negotiated.

Effective conversation requires a language in which the concepts of strategy can be expressed. Some of this has been codified in a general way, as can be gleaned from strategic management textbooks. In addition most organizations over time build up an idiosyncratic strategic language based on the specific strategic breakdown situations experienced in the past. The existence and development of labels and jargon are manifestations of this language building, essential for organizational learning to take place. The language can only represent yesterday's strategic problems for specific strategic management concepts were generated in the past to categorize particular events, generally for use in coping with specific breakdown situations. This existing language will be the basis for categorizing new situations but will, almost by definition, stop short of completely describing new reality. We argue that the search for a response to a new situation is facilitated by the conversational process, using yesterday's concepts, but leading to a uniquely new response.

The conversational process needs to increase the alignment of the managers' ideas to make active the organizational learning cycle. This requires a process of rational comparison of the role of competing ideas by reference to a shared world view, from which the organization derives its purpose (van der Heijden, 1993). This shared world view (for example, Stern, 1906) provides the platform on which a line of logical argumentation will be built to compare views on the specific situation in the strategic conversation process, leading to the view preferred by the group. Rationality may not be the way in which strategy is created but it is essential in the strategic conversation process.

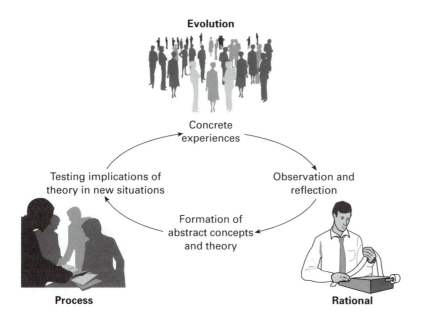

Figure 4.3   *The learning organization*

So far we see the contributions to the institutional learning process from rationality, through conversation based on rational argument, and through the process of creating alignment. However, the model cannot be complete without differentiation. Learning can take place only if experience deviates from plan in some unexpected way and this validates the contribution of the evolutionary school of thought. If we define evolution as a process that works through (i) a source of variation, (ii) a weeding out criterion, and (iii) a source of constancy, then every learning process is one of the evolution of ideas, their generation, testing and embedding. The deviation of the emergent strategy from intended strategy is the driving force of the institutional learning loop. Such deviation initially creates a divergence of views within the organization, with different people interpreting it in their own way. The alignment process then brings these views back together, establishing a new basis of rationality. In this way all three schools of thought in strategy have their role in the organizational learning process.

Symbolic interactionism, semiotics and ethnomethodology

The two tensions noted above hint at the importance of sense-making and the negotiation of meaning in the facilitation of organizational learning. The study of managerial cognition depends for its validity on the collection and representation of data that can depict the meaning which individuals attribute to events. It is for this reason that cognitive maps are used as a way of enabling personal constructs/concepts to be set within the context of other constructs. It is the context that gives meaning to what would otherwise be verbal tags. Modelling these meanings as cognitive maps enables them to be rearranged continually as they take on newly negotiated meaning (Eden, 1993). The negotiation of meaning is central to organizational learning, as old meanings are re-evaluated and new meanings are created through experimentation. Our earlier discussion of the learning cycle and the three schools of strategy paid particular attention to the role of negotiated shared meaning.

In a manner which almost parallels the three strategy schools, the schools of thought associated with symbolic interactionism, semiotics and ethnomethodology contribute to ways of working with meaning. Symbolic interactionism pays attention to everyday social interaction and is founded on the belief that events have no intrinsic meaning beyond that which managers give them in the course of everyday social interaction (Blumer, 1969). Here we are concerned with the management of social relationships – the manager is a part of an intimate social world (Vickers, 1965), requiring the maintenance of a negotiated social order (Strauss and Schatzman, 1963; Eden, 1992). This view of the making of meaning is related to individual learning. Within the context of organizational learning it is important to note the extent to which the 'conversation' may be dominated by individual managers attending to the negotiated social order rather than to the meaning of events to the organization.

At the other extreme, semiotics is concerned with uncovering broad and systemic patterns of meaning in society (Saussure, 1960). It parallels the debate between organizational and managerial cognition. Our view that organizational learning takes place in groups needs to attend to the role of symbolic interaction but to recognize that, in part, patterns of meanings develop within an organization. Patterns of meaning, and so the role of semiotics as a method for studying such patterns, are allied to the notion of an evolutionary or emergent strategy. In some senses these patterns of meaning express themselves through the culture of an organization, reflecting upon and so learning about the dominant patterns of meaning-making becomes a part of the process of facilitating organizational learning. However, the process of developing shared meaning within groups lies at the core of organizational learning. Pettigrew (1977) draws our attention to the extent to which the management of meaning (which we take to be shared meaning) is crucial to the politics of strategic action. Functional ethnography (Trice, 1985) and ethnomethodology, the 'science of sense making' (Heap, 1975), are concerned with the conversational and social processes through which members of an organization construct a sense of shared meanings (Garfinkel, 1967).

Each of these theoretical stances points to the need to recognize each of the three schools of strategy discussed earlier. Central to working with these three schools and to facilitating conversation about the meaning of strategic issues are:

• the recognition of intersubjectivity issues (Eden et al., 1981) and the world of shared culture and meanings (Schutz, 1973);
• the creation of meaning in organizational experience (Gioia, 1986);
• the dialectical power of different subjective meanings at the core of organizational learning.

Within the managerial cognition field Bougon and Komocar (1990) have explored shared meaning through the constructs that link individual cognitive maps. Others have been concerned with the formal identification of similarities and likenesses in cognition (Eden and Ackermann, this volume; Langfield-Smith and Wirth, 1992; Laukkanen, this volume; Markoczy and Goldberg, 1993). Shared meaning, 'can develop in all kinds of ways, as people interact, mutually adjust, learn from each other, conflict and develop consensus' (Mintzberg, 1987). But the resulting overlap between their 'mental models' is often based on the use of 'cryptic constructs' (Bougon, 1992). These cryptic constructs play an important role in maintaining the 'strategic conversation' as the organizational members explain meanings to each other. This is important when real action is considered for then discrepancies in the members' interpretation of concepts are surfaced and tested.

Organizational learning in practice

We have introduced a number of the perspectives which we believe should influence and guide the practice of facilitating organizational learning through the use of designed strategic conversations. In particular we have suggested that:

• the dichotomy between managerial and organizational cognition needs to be resolved by attending to cognition and shared meaning in groups;
• organizational learning depends on attention to reflecting on each of rationalistic, processual and evolutionary aspects of strategic management seen as elements of a learning cycle (Figure 4.3);
• the focus of symbolic interactionism, semiotics and ethnomethodology are all relevant to developing an understanding of sense-making and shared meaning as it relates to organizational learning.

Each of these three rather different frameworks will influence the process and the methods used to facilitate organizational learning. Guided by the frameworks we have discussed, and by our considerable experience of working with management teams, we find that the task of facilitating organizational learning encompasses some or all of the following processes.

1   Creating overall awareness of emergent processes of organizational decision-making, their strengths and weaknesses, and the attention and time they require.

2   Surfacing the decision-makers' definition of strategic breakdown situ-
    ations which are seen to require immediate attention, and their mental
    models of the world around it.
3   Helping decision-makers toward conceptualizing and categorizing
    aspects of their situation as they use their own strategic management
    language.
4   Helping managers to surface and dislodge obsolete mental models and
    recipes by facilitating discussions of multiple futures (Ingvar, 1985)
    each grounded in the emergent strategic situation.

The most crucial part of developing learning as one of the successful outputs of strategy making is that of eliciting the managers' 'taken-for-
granted' mental models of their world. As Lindblom (1959) has suggested,
these are often kept tacit in order to avoid confrontation and to maintain
flexibility in the negotiation that strategy development entails. However,
tacit models may slow down the conversation and negotiation process
and may sometimes disable it. If the breakdown situation requires a fast
response and a degree of deliberate action, it is important to acknowledge
the existence of the embedded patterns that guide strategic problem solving. This may reveal that a more efficient process be required, based on
quicker surfacing of the managers' embedded knowledge, views and
positions. It follows that the ability to elicit the participants' views is a
necessary skill underlying effective organizational learning. It helps participants to articulate their theories and provide effective input to the
strategic conversation. The facilitator can also judge the degree of overlap
in the managers' mental models, and the possible need for greater diversity and fresh outside inputs. The rest of this chapter reviews the
requirements for strategic elicitation.

Elicitation

The task of strategic elicitation within the context of organizational learning is to get at deep knowledge and embedded wisdom – the theories in
use, rather than the espoused theories or the mere rhetoric of strategy.
The embedded norms and values, role definitions and the 'organizational recipe' all need to surface. As this has been shaped by historical
events the task of surfacing requires a clear recognition of the role that
history plays in forming deep knowledge (Bryson et al., 1995) and developing theories in use (Argyris and Schön, 1978). The retrospective
designation of intentions is an efficient way of describing both organizational and personal action. This view is close to that of Weick when he
developed his thesis for the relationship between thinking and acting:
'how do I know what I think until . . . I see how I act' (Weick, 1979).
Similarly Mintzberg (1990) argued that 'emergent strategy means unintended order'.

In this section we consider four approaches to this process of discovery (see Bood, in this volume, who discusses the methodological aspects of these approaches within an organizational learning context):

Approach 1: Look at the concrete record of strategic intentions, through, for example, a study of the documentation which is designed to direct behaviour.

Approach 2: Look at decision-making in action, get involved in the orga-nization (an anthropological or participant observer approach). Watch decision-making, listen to stories.

Approach 3: Work with managers on strategic breakdown situations. Become immersed in the thinking and the social process of 'strategic fire fighting'.

Approach 4: Use well-designed trigger questions in interview situations to replicate immediacy and relevance so that 'theories in use' can be detected. Follow interviews with feedback to individuals and to the team.

The first approach can be very revealing of the way in which the orga-nization manages its bureaucracy, but conclusions based on analysing recorded statements alone can be a poor representation of institutional strategy, and ignore almost every aspect of the framework discussed in the early part of the chapter. Nevertheless this procedure has become com-monplace among many researchers studying organizational cognition. The analysis of formal procedures through written documentation reveals one slice through the strategic life of the organization but misses the social processes of negotiation and bargaining about the future, and the aspects of thinking and acting which documentation often attempts to rationalize away.

Eden and Cropper (1992) spent four years working with the Director-General of the England and Wales Prison Service, seeking to understand the patterns and coherence of strategic statements. The project was designed to understand the strategic significance of the framework of statements made by senior staff to Ministers and to different but interre-lated parts of the Service, and the emergent 'system' of reporting by the staff responsible for managing prisons. In many respects the project was extremely successful in enabling the Director-General to understand and reflect upon the strategy of the Service as it was delivered through the reporting about strategic direction and problem solving. As the work pro-gressed, the analysis of strategic learning sat in tension with the deliberate and rational strategy making. The dialectic between two understandings provided the drive towards more effective strategy development. In such circumstances, the extent to which the particular slice of strategic learning detected was complete or 'true' was less important than its role as a dialec-tical learning device.

The second approach gets away from trusting documentation and seeks to understand the social processes of decision-making, of relating, of strat-egy in action. However this approach is extremely time consuming and lengthy, and other methods are probably more practical. It is more time consuming than the first approach and has the added disadvantage of displaying little added value to the management team until all the data have been collected and understood. Yet it does enable particular attention to be paid to the more subtle aspects of shared meaning and uncovering systemic patterns of meaning within the organization.

The third approach is more promising because it wraps the process of detecting strategic learning within another activity which demands immediate attention from the top management team. Looking into real strategic problem solving is likely to provide the best assurance of detecting 'theories in use'. However it does depend upon such opportunities presenting themselves at the time when strategy making is regarded as important and relevant. Therefore we arrive at the fourth approach of using well-designed trigger questions in interview situations to replicate immediacy and relevance so that 'theories in use' can be detected and fed back to individuals and to the team. The rest of the chapter will discuss these latter two approaches within the context of example cases.

Working with 'breakdown situations' (Approach 3)

This example follows the use of an interactive modelling technique for strategic problem solving, triggered by study of particular issues, but subsequently taken wider into strategy development. It depends on the researcher working with the managers who 'feel pain' about a situation which they believe has strategic consequences. Normally strategic transformation is only triggered by crisis, and crises about strategic issues ('fire fights') happen frequently. One powerful method of detecting strategic learning is to uncover the embedded theories in action that are used during the analysis of these strategic 'breakdown situations'. By introducing a self-monitoring conversational interactive modelling tool as the problem-solving support mechanism, beliefs and values gradually become explicit and recorded as an aggregated system of 'theories for action'. One successful approach uses a 'Group Decision Support System' (Bostrom and Kinney, 1992) such as the 'Strategic Options Development and Analysis (SODA)' (Eden, 1989) and more recently 'Journey Making' (Eden and Ackermann, 1998) which use 'cognitive mapping' as the method of recording beliefs and values. This enables the strategic learning embedded in the managers' problem solving to be recorded and reflected upon. Whatever approach is chosen must be capable of modelling the 'theories in action' and allow a focus on shared meaning and on the processes of negotiating new meanings. As managers work jointly on their model (cognitive map) of the strategic breakdown situation they face, existing recipes and a degree of interpretation of the data emerge in 'real time'. The model is then used as a device for negotiating a way forward, for building consensus about behaviour (Lindblom, 1959), and for developing commitments. As such the model becomes a form of organizational memory and serves as a 'transitional object' (de Geus, 1988). Because a cognitive map is amenable to analysis through its structure and content (Eden et al., 1992) it provides the researcher with opportunities to extract beliefs and values that are part of the 'organizational recipe' for strategic transformation. These data, embedded in the problem-solving episode, model the managers' strategic learning.

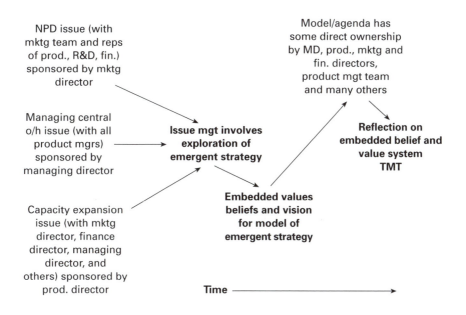

Figure 4.4   *Detecting emergent strategy from issue management*

Figure 4.4 shows an example of the process. Individual members of the top management team commissioned the group decision support approach as a way to deal with the strategic problems which they presumed to be discrete and separable. The same approach to group problem solving was used in each case, and so slices of strategic learning in practice (the 'coal-face' theories in action and embedded wisdom) could be merged to form a single model. This method of extracting fundamental theories in use which had strategic importance and exploring their relationship to one another in a merged model is a part of the process of encouraging a shift from single- to double-loop learning (Argyris, 1977; Argyris and Schön, 1978). The resulting model was introduced to the top management team as something about which they might be curious. Feeding back collective 'theories in action', especially as applied to specific problems, typically has a profound effect on the participants' understanding of the implicit content of their management process. As Figure 4.4 indicates, this model became the basis for their decision to proceed with strategy development. It recognized and respected their past (as expressed by the initial model) and their wishes for the future (as expressed in contrast to the initial model). Although time consuming, this process can be very powerful with top management teams who are unused to the idea of a joint strategy and group learning but have become committed to the principle (as had been the case in the example above). Because it facilitates their problem solving the time consumed to surface the organizational learning is productive and is not considered a cost.

Interview and feedback (Approach 4)

When there is no strategic crisis, interviews with key actors can be a substitute. The extent to which the interview procedures can be designed as a substitute for working on a strategic breakdown situation will determine whether they succeed in uncovering their 'taken-for-granted' world. The objective is to present the interviewees with unexpected and non-confirming perspectives on their world view, triggering articulation of their own mental map in order to rectify the imagined breakdown created by the interviewer. The model for this approach to detecting strategic learning is shown in Figure 4.5. The procedure is cyclical and depends upon using different techniques at each stage of the process.

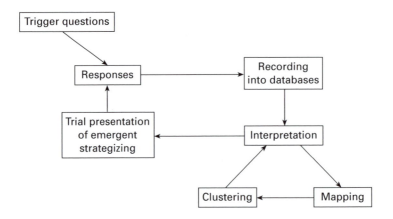

Figure 4.5   *Elicitation cycle*

The elicitation cycle is built on responses to designed triggers. The process uses dialectic and non-confirming statements and involves the cycle of triggering responses, recording responses, interpreting and relating responses (creating theory of action), feeding back the resulting strategic framework, and back to triggering responses. The iterative process should converge after a few cycles provided the interviewer is skilful in using several techniques.

1   The interview must be as open-ended as possible. The interviewer does not know what needs to be uncovered, and should therefore attempt to let the interviewee set the conversation's agenda.

2   It is important to move away from the 'espoused theories' as soon as possible. This can be achieved by creating a 'playful' atmosphere in which it is easier to deviate from the formal phraseology and the 'official script'. Instead of asking what the interviewees see as the main uncertainties, it is often more effective to enquire what they would ask a clairvoyant, had they half an hour to discuss the future (the 'oracle question'). Putting the interviewees in the position of asking this question often leads them to a new perspective for people who are used to being expected to provide the answers (Bougon, 1983).

3   It can be useful to set the interviewees up against themselves. After asking the 'oracle question' it may be helpful to suggest that the interviewee takes the oracle's position and answers the questions asked, first in a 'good' scenario and then in a 'bad' one (Amara and Lipinsky, 1983). The introduction of multiple futures helps by exposing the contrasts between representations of the future (Ingvar, 1985).

4   The objective is to create dialectical tension by asking the interviewees to adopt unusual roles, for example, by asking which competitor they would prefer to join were they not part of their present organization (Sparrow, 1992).

5   Finally the interviewer needs to listen carefully for internal inconsistencies in what is being said. When seeming inconsistencies are noted, the interviewees can be triggered into offering further explanations and so exposing more of the underlying structure of their belief systems. Such inconsistencies can often be uncovered by discussing 'purpose' in the context of the organization and its actions (Checkland, 1981). However, inconsistencies should not be treated as 'wrong' and interviewees 'punished'. Inconsistencies represent a common part of organizational life.

Following the interviews the researchers analyse and interpret the record. After more team feedback, apparently underlying divergence becomes a powerful trigger for further articulation of views on the 'taken-for-granted' world. These should not be brushed under the carpet with the idea of minimizing disagreement. It is essential, in order to ensure the maximum diversity of opinion, that the initial interviews achieve a personal tone. Managers almost invariably underestimate the range of views existing within the team so the elicitation process creates a 'natural dialectic' (Eden, 1992). Provided the different views are tenable, the result is a vigorous debate which surfaces, to a considerable degree, the group's tacit assumptions. A good example of a management team discovering their emergent learning through exploiting this dialectic was an intervention in an upstream oil exploration and production company (van der Heijden, 1993). After the initial interviews, the first feedback meeting showed significant differences in perspective on the business, mostly based on three starting points:

- an operational definition as oil producers and traders;
- a more strategic definition, based on a traditional generic (for example, Porter, 1980);
- a business definition based on the managers' own intuitive recipes for success in the industry (Spender, 1989).

Reframing the situation, the team looked at the 'recipes for success' in the industry for pointers towards different interpretations. One ingredient was the importance given in the industry to government relations. Whatever was being done in this industry in terms of engineering, commerce and competition there was always a sense of the overriding importance of the relationship with government in the background. In one interview a senior manager had said that although the business might look like engineering and commerce, he thought that it was really a relationship business. Should the industry be reframed as a service industry, with government as the prime customer, rather than as the oil industry? This question made the team think about the competitive 'moment of truth'. They asked themselves questions about how companies created their competitive positions. Given that the crude oil market is one of the most efficient, there is little a company can do to reposition itself to strategic advantage. Therefore competitive success must come from advantageous costing capabilities which, in an extractive business, means 'mining rents' (Schoemaker, 1990). Thus success or failure is conditional upon having access to the most favourable reserves where significant 'mining rents' could be earned.

The rents associated with owning good oil reserves can be very high when compared to the cost of developing them. Typically, only a small fraction of this rent ends up with the company developing the resource, the larger part returning to the local government in the form of taxes and levies. It follows that whether companies do well or not depends on the division of profits between the government and the concession holders. Since it is government that grants the concessions, the real determination of profit takes place when the concession deal is struck. From this perspective the oil companies provide an extraction and rent-raising service to governments, realizing the governments' natural resource-based rent streams. As the customer, government will try to negotiate the best deal considering the reliability and performance of the service provider. A 'fly-by-night' company may be prepared to develop the resource for a low price, but this will not lead to a good long-term outcome if they perform below standard in reservoir maintenance, or are unable to move oil when the market is glutted. The companies differ in their ability to provide good overall service and so determine their competitive success.

The conversation between the three deviating perspectives led to a new business definition, a new shared world view driven by the need to ensure organizational survival. The new definition put a different emphasis on the business. Even though it was always already embedded within the tacit knowledge of those in the field, the result made a remarkable impact on the strategy team. What had long been known intuitively fell into place and could be articulated. The reasons for organizing in particular ways became more widely understood. Cultural and managerial dilemmas became subject to debate and more manageable, having a strong strategic enabling effect within the company.

Conclusions

As the examples show, effective elicitation which models the organization's strategic thinking leads to strategy making with an action orientation. The process highlights the significance of learning through a synthesis of experience, sense-making and action into a holistic sense of the organization. The synthesis allows for an interplay between individual and group cognition. The process of a designed conversation (van der Heijden, 1996; Eden and Ackermann, 1998) leads to a shared or aligned system of meanings which allows the organization to behave in a strategically organized fashion. This level of alignment should not lead to 'group think' but rather a system of views which permits contingent and coordinated action. With a shared vision, managers will be able to capture strategic opportunities immediately they arise, knowing that the meaning of such actions has an appropriate strategic fit.

Differentiation in meaning across the management team is still important. It will persist through the appropriate processes of continual reflection, as organizational learning, acting in tandem with individual learning, enables change in response to new ambiguities and uncertainties. For organizational learning to be effective there must be:

- sufficient alignment to trigger organized action, based on joint experiences and perceptions;
- sufficient variety in ideas to allow selection of a suitable response.

Increasing differentiation reduces alignment and vice versa, so organizations and their strategic facilitators must try to find an appropriate balance for each situation. Which side needs to be emphasized depends on the state of the organization. In good times differentiation may need to be encouraged, in bad times alignment may be more important. The facilitator/researcher needs to respect both differentiation and alignment, sometimes at the same time. The apparent contradiction in this conclusion is a manifestation of the fact that learning, like anything else in the managerial world, is a matter of balance.

References

Amara, R. and Lipinsky, A. (1983) *Business Planning for an Uncertain Future, Scenarios and Strategies*. New York: Pergamon Press.

Argyris, C. (1977) Double loop learning in organizations, *Harvard Business Review*, Sept–Oct.

Argyris, C. and Schön, D. (1978) *Organizational Learning: A Theory of Action Perspective*. Reading, MA: Addison Wesley.

Blumer, H. (1969) *Symbolic Interactionism: Perspective and Method*. Englewood Cliffs, NJ: Prentice-Hall.

Bostrom, B. and Kinney, S. (eds) (1992) *Computer Augmented Teamwork*. New York: Van Nostrand and Reinhold.

Bougon, M.G. (1983) Uncovering cognitive maps: the self-Q technique, in G. Morgan (ed.), *Beyond Method: Strategies for Social Research*. Beverly Hills, CA: Sage.

Bougon, M.G. (1992) Congregate cognitive maps: a unified dynamic theory of organization and strategy, *Journal of Management Studies*, 29: 369–89.

Bougon, M.G. and Komocar, J.M. (1990) Directing strategic change, a dynamic holistic approach, in A. Huff (ed.), *Mapping Strategic Thought*, Chichester: John Wiley.

Bryson, J.M., Ackermann, F., Eden, C. and Finn, C.B. (1995) Critical incidents and emergent issues in the management of large-scale change efforts, in D. Kettl and H. Brinton Milward (eds), *The State of Public Management*. Baltimore, MD: Johns Hopkins University Press.

Checkland, P. (1981) *Systems Thinking, Systems Practice*. Chichester: John Wiley.

Eden, C. (1989) Strategic Option Development and Analysis, in J. Rosenhead (ed.), *Rational Analysis for a Problematic World*. Chichester: John Wiley.

Eden, C. (1992) Strategic management as a social process, *Journal of Management Studies*, 29: 799–811.

Eden, C. (1993) Strategic development and implementation, cognitive mapping for group support, in J. Hendry and G. Johnson with J. Newton (eds), *Strategic Thinking: Leadership and the Management of Change*. Chichester: John Wiley.

Eden, C. and Ackermann, F. (1998) *The Journey of Strategy Making*. London: Sage.

Eden, C., Ackermann, F. and Cropper, S. (1992) The analysis of cause maps, *Journal of Management Studies*, 29: 309–24.

Eden, C. and Cropper, S. (1992) Coherence and balance in strategies for the management of public services, *Public Money and Management*, 12: 43–52.

Eden, C., Jones, S., Sims, D. and Smithin, J. (1981) The intersubjectivity of issues and issues of intersubjectivity, *Journal of Management Studies*, 18: 37–47.

Garfinkel, H. (1967) *Studies in Ethnomethodology*. Englewood Cliffs, NJ: Prentice-Hall.

Garvin, D.A. (1993) Building a learning organization, *Harvard Business Review*, Jul–Aug.

de Geus, A.P. (1988) Planning as learning, *Harvard Business Review*, March–April.

Gioia, D.A. (1986) Symbols, scripts and sensemaking: creating meaning in the organizational experience, in H. Sims and D. Gioia, *The Thinking Organization*. San Francisco, CA: Jossey-Bass.

Heap, J. (1975) What are sensemaking practices?, *Sociological Inquiry*, 46: 107–15.

Ingvar, D. (1985) Memories of the future, an essay on the temporal organization of conscious awareness, *Human Neuro-biology*, 4 (3): 127–36.

Kolb, D. and Rubin, I.M. (1991) *Organizational Behavior: An Experiential Approach.* Englewood Cliffs, NJ: Prentice-Hall.

Langfield-Smith, K. and Wirth, A. (1992) Measuring differences between cognitive maps, *Journal of the Operational Research Society*, 43: 1135–50.

Laukkanen, M. (1998) Conducting causal mapping research: opportunities and challenges, this volume.

Lindblom, C.E. (1959) The science of muddling through, *Public Administration Review*, 19: 79–88.

Markoczy, L. and Goldberg, S. (1993) A method for eliciting and comparing causal maps. Paper presented to the First International Workshop on Managerial and Organizational Cognition, Brussels, 11–15 May.

Mintzberg, H. (1987) Crafting strategy, *Harvard Business Review*, July–Aug.

Mintzberg, H. (1990) The design school, reconsidering the basic premises of strategic management, *Strategic Management Journal*, 11: 171–95.

Mintzberg, H. and Waters, J. (1985) Of strategies, deliberate and emergent, *Strategic Management Journal*, 6: 257–72.

Normann, R. and Ramirez, R. (1994) *From Value Chain to Value Constellation, Designing Interactive Strategy.* Chichester: John Wiley.

Pettigrew, A. (1977) Strategy formulation as a political process, *International Studies in Management*, 7: 28–87.

Piaget, J. (1971) *Structuralism*, London: Routledge.

Porac, J.F. and Thomas, H. (1987) Knowing the competition: the mental models of retailing strategists, in G. Johnson (ed.), *Business Strategy and Retailing.* Chichester: John Wiley.

Porter, M. (1980) *Competitive Strategy.* New York: Free Press.

Saussure, F. (1960) *Course in General Linguistics.* London: Owen.

Scheper, W. (1991) Group decision support systems: an inquiry into theoretical and philosophical issues. PhD thesis, Tilburg: Katholieke Universiteit Brabant.

Schoemaker, P. (1990) Strategy, complexity and economic rent, *Management Science*, 36: 1178–93.

Schutz, A. (1973) *Collected Papers I: The Problem of Social Reality.* The Hague: Martinus Nijhoff.

Sparrow, O. (1992) *Management Options.* London: Shell UK.

Spender, J.-C. (1989) *Industry recipes, An Enquiry into the Nature and Sources of Managerial Judgement.* Oxford: Basil Blackwell.

Stern, W. (1906) *Person und Sache.* Leipzig: Verlag von Johann Ambrosius Barth.

Strauss, A. and Schatzman, L. (1963) The hospital and its negotiated order, in E. Friedson, *The Hospital in Modern Society.* New York: Macmillan.

Trice, H.M. (1985) Rites and ceremonials in organizational culture, in S.B. Bacharach (ed.), *Research in the Sociology of Organizations.* Greenwich, CT: JAI Press.

van der Heijden, K. (1993) Strategic vision at work: discussing strategic vision in management teams, in J. Hendry and G. Johnson with J. Newton (eds), *Strategic Thinking: Leadership and the Management of Change.* Chichester: John Wiley.

van der Heijden, K. (1996) *Scenarios: The Art of Strategic Conversation.* Chichester: John Wiley.

Vickers, G. (1965) *The Art of Judgement.* London: Harper and Row.

Weick, K.E. (1979) *The Social Psychology of Organizing.* Reading, MA: Addison Wesley.

Whittington, R. (1993) *What is Strategy and Does it Matter?* London: Routledge.

5

STABILITY AND CHANGE IN A STRATEGIST'S THINKING

Pia Lindell, Leif Melin, Henrik J. Gahmberg, Anders Hellqvist and Anders Melander

The cognitive perspective has proved to be a powerful instrument for researching the management of change. But to develop our understanding of the strategic impact of managerial cognition we need to do a better job with capturing and interpreting empirical data on managers' thought structures and thinking processes. Furthermore, we need longitudinal data in order to understand the role of cognition as a dynamic process, with a special focus on the degree of stability in the mental structures of managers. In this chapter we present the results of our examination of the cognitive activity of one top manager over a five-year period. We make a text-based analysis of his thinking-in-use as it related to his attempts to create strategic change in the organization he was managing. This analysis is mainly based on the language used as he communicated to the firm, especially with concepts that came to play a crucial role in his ambition to transform a public professional-driven organization to a more customer-oriented one.

Our purpose in this chapter is to describe and analyse the way-of-thinking of an individual top manager leading a strategic change process in a large organization. A number of more specific questions will be in focus: the unfolding of this way-of-thinking over time – that is, the question of stability and change of managerial cognition 'in action'; the use of specific concepts in the communication of strategic intentions – that is, the sense-making and sensegiving dimension of the strategic issues introduced by the top manager in order to influence the change process. Another aim of this chapter is to present some experiences regarding the methodological dimension of studying managerial cognition. We will discuss both the possibility of capturing the content of a manager's thought processes in in-depth interviews, and the advantages and disadvantages of the use of a language-based interpretive technique in the analysis of interview-based texts.

The chapter builds on strategic change theories (for example, Pettigrew, 1985; Johnson, 1987; Gahmberg, 1992; Hellgren and Melin, 1993) and on theories of managerial and organizational cognition (for example, Weick, 1983; Bartunek, 1984; Gioia and Chittipeddi, 1991; Lyles and Schwenk, 1992). From earlier studies on managerial cognition we have developed a tentative understanding of the field that includes the following basic assumptions:

- thinking and acting are mutual and intertwined processes;
- experienced top managers develop rather stable belief structures or strategic ways-of-thinking regarding how to develop, manage and lead an organization;
- mental structures function in an holistic mode and are a mix of cognition, values and emotions, an assumption which means that our perspective might be labelled 'socio-cognitive'.

The empirical basis is a series of in-depth interviews with the managing director of a Swedish hospital. We taperecorded nine interviews between 1990 and 1994 that express his thoughts, ideas, opinions, values, beliefs and emotions about the ongoing strategic change process which he initiated in 1989, half a year after he moved into this position. The interviews are part of a broader case study of the change process in this hospital.

Theoretical perspective: chains of thinking and acting shape strategic change

In order to develop further our knowledge of organizations we need a better understanding of action and change, which implies a process view on organizations. We question the assumption that change processes are uniform and readily labelled evolutionary or revolutionary; proactive or reactive; rational or political. Strategic change as a whole can instead be described as a prism of different processes (Hellgren et al., 1993), some more action oriented than others. It is the result of the interplay of external forces and internal cognitive, cultural and political processes. Action and change take place in an organizational reality that is socially constructed and where individuals with different mindsets and subjective world views interact. Therefore research on strategic change should focus not only on actions but also on the interplay of managerial cognition and actions, for these chains of thinking and acting shape the strategic processes. In this chapter we stress four interrelated and conceptual themes; which relate to the strategic change process as a whole:

- managerial cognition as the strategist's way-of-thinking;
- managerial cognition and strategic action;
- the identification of strategic issues and processes of sensemaking and sensegiving;
- stability and change in the strategist's way of thinking.

By managerial cognition we mean the cognition of the top managers.

Usually cognition refers to emotion-free mental structures, moulded by past experience. Mental structures help us to organize and interpret information, thereby creating meaning and making the world understandable. They also reduce uncertainty. When there is too much information the mental structure helps us to simplify and when there is an information gap the structure fills in the missing parts. Due to their function these structures play an important role in the process of thinking. The literature on managerial cognition offers a number of concepts about mental structures as maps which 'assimilate uncertain events to existing structures. Because maps relate an uncertain event to existing concepts, they generate meaning for the event' (Weick and Bougon, 1986: 131); or schemes which are 'used to impose structure upon, and impart meaning to otherwise ambiguous social and situational information to facilitate understanding' (Gioia, 1986: 56); or beliefs which 'translate a world that can be overwhelmingly complex and ambiguous into comprehensible and familiar terms' (Donaldson and Lorsch, 1984: 79); or 'the fundamental basis of implicit theories is that their holders seek to create an environment in which they all will have some elements of control' (Downey and Brief, 1986: 173). Other concepts with similar meaning are frames of reference (Shrivastava and Mitroff, 1983), paradigms (Johnson, 1987) and perceptual filters (Starbuck and Milliken, 1988).

Cognitive structures are usually considered to be pure knowledge structures. There is no indication that these structures are constructed by human beings with emotions, hopes and values. The need to take these aspects into consideration is stressed by Sims and Lorenzi (1992), who argue that affect and emotion influence cognition and behaviour in a social situation. This view of cognition, including both knowledge and emotional aspects, is the basis for our own concept 'way-of-thinking' (Hellgren and Melin, 1993) and has been developed from empirical studies of strategic change. A strategic way-of-thinking held by a top leader consists of a number of thematic sets of values, assumptions, beliefs, ideas and thoughts about leadership and strategic development in organizations. The way of thinking is shaped by the leader's personality, history and earlier managerial experience, and his/her interpretation of the environment.

As noted, managerial cognition is closely interrelated with action. Mental structures 'guide action' (Isenberg, 1986: 252) and 'have an important impact on management's strategic choices' (Donaldson and Lorsch, 1984: 111). In these quotations thinking is viewed as preceding acting. Hence thinking and acting are regarded as more or less separated, step-by-step processes. Another view is held by Weick (1983), who argues that thinking and acting are simultaneous processes and that managers act 'thinkingly'. They learn as they act rather than through the rational stages of decision-making. Thought precedes action as general expectations ('maps') about the orderliness of what will occur rather than in the form of rational analysis. A similar processual view of thinking and acting is held by Bartunek (1984), who suggests that second-order change (radical discontinuous shift) in interpretative schemes is mediated by the actions organization members take in response to a changed understanding of the situation which the organization is facing. In an earlier study (Hellgren and Melin, 1993), we found that the top managers' way-of-thinking plays a significant role in the strategic change process and that two top leaders may act differently in the same strategic situation. These findings were supported in a later study of the strategic change process in a Swedish department store chain (Lindell, 1993). Here we argue that thinking and acting go hand in hand as mutual processes.

In the growing field of managerial cognition studies there has been a lot of interest in the link between individuals' cognitive representations (of the environment) and organizational action (Daft and Weick, 1984; Dutton and Jackson, 1987). According to Dutton and Jackson strategic issues are identified to help decision-makers impose some order on the environment. However, the meaning of a strategic issue is not inherent in external events. Instead internal organizational characteristics determine the meaning that evolves for a specific issue. Dutton and Jackson argue that linguistic labels are used further to specify the meaning attached to strategic issues. These classify the issues and suggest how the organization should respond. Action regarding one strategic issue follows from the meaning attached to it, which means that organizations may respond quite differently to similar environmental events (Dutton and Jackson, 1987: 77). A related view on cognition and strategic change is taken by Gioia and Chittipeddi (1991), when identifying two processes, sensemaking and sensegiving, that are crucial for the top management's success in initiating strategic change. They define sensemaking as the construction and reconstruction of meaning 'by the involved parties as they attempt to develop a meaningful framework for understanding the nature of the intended strategic change' (ibid.: 442). Sensegiving is the process through which managers attempt to influence 'the sensemaking and meaning construction of others toward a preferred redefinition of organizational reality' (ibid.: 442).

Another aspect of managerial cognitions concerns stability and change. Different opinions can be found in the literature. Some scholars regard the mental structures as unlikely to change and, should they do so, would change only incrementally and in ways that affect only parts of the system (for example, Donaldson and Lorsch, 1984). Others see these structures as more changeable (Weick and Bougon, 1986). The same argument is used by both sides. Donaldson and Lorsch (1984) argue that one function of beliefs is to provide continuity and stability when change threatens to undermine the lesson of experience. Weick and Bougon (1986), on the other hand, view maps as continuously changing when adding new experience. These differences may be real or mere questions of definition. Bartunek (1984) differentiates between incremental modifications in present ways of interpretation (first-order changes) and more radical changes in the mental structure (second-order changes), which are much more rare compared to the first type. Second-order changes are the only type likely to have significant impact on the organization's way of acting. Lyles and Schwenk (1992) adopt similar reasoning when they divide the knowledge held by the management into a relatively stable core and a peripheral set which is more open to changes. However, in contrast to Bartunek, they argue that it is change in the peripheral set which leads to radical change. Strategic change is facilitated through a loose coupling between the core and the peripheral set. It should be noted that the knowledge structure, as defined by Lyles and Schwenk, has no affective or emotional elements and hence 'is more subject to change' (ibid.: 157). Donaldson and Lorsch (1984), view stability in mental structures partly as a result of emotional forces that enhance commitment to beliefs. One conclusion from our earlier studies is that the way of thinking of top managers, which includes emotional elements, is not easily changed, even when confronting new situations (Hellgren and Melin, 1993; Lindell, 1993). Thus the scope of change in managerial cognitions, and whether or not emotional elements are considered, seem to be important aspects when discussing stability and change in managerial cognition. To conclude, while a cognitive perspective is not sufficient for understanding strategic change, it can supply important pieces to the whole. It is not the thinking process alone that is interesting, but rather the interplay over time between thinking and acting – between cognitive processes and what actually happens in the strategic development of organizations.

Methodological considerations

The empirical focus of this study is a managing director's thinking, acting and sensemaking in a strategic change process over a five-year period. It employs new tools of analysis and interpretation to a set of interviews with this strategist and is part of a more extensive case study, based on a traditional qualitative and interpretive approach, of the overall change process in the organization led by the managing director. Within the broader case study, there were over 50 interviews with other actors.

The data are drawn from eight interviews conducted with the strategist between November 1990 and October 1993. The data, over 200 pages of typed text, were transcribed and available on a microcomputer. These interviews do not totally capture the interviewee's real discourse, since they were partly structured. The interviewers asked open questions in an effort to create a dialogue with the managing director about the ongoing change process. The questions mostly stated general themes about the change process, or specific additional questions within each theme. In each interview the managing director commented upon what had happened since the previous interview, what issues and problems were on the agenda at the time of the interview, and what plans, thoughts and ideas he had for the future. This means that the interview data were not optimal for a grounded theory type of analysis, but were still gathered within the hermeneutic spirit.

To identify and interpret the central issues, concepts and meanings that came out of the eight interviews, we analysed the text with the help of the NUD.IST 3.0 program. This program has been developed for grounded theory research at La Trobe University, Australia, and is one of about twelve text analysis programs currently available. Only one of the authors had prior experience of the program in general, and none with this new version. Eventually we mastered it, but our analysis procedures so far have not been entirely orthodox. There is a fairly agreed upon set of principles and procedures for doing textual analysis (Tesch, 1990; Huber, 1992). The description, classification and connection of the microcomputer-assisted qualitative analysis follow the paths of the original work of Glaser and Strauss (1967). When working with texts in the social sciences, we are not primarily interested in words, but rather sentences or any other sequence that carries a meaning. Ambiguity of meaning is a pervasive characteristic of human communication and we need to pay attention to the context and the intentions versus actions of subjects under study. Based on our earlier analyses of data from the change process in this organization, we already had knowledge of some strategic issues in this specific case. We had also developed a conceptual scheme, where major concepts of implementing change were connected, in a tentative interpretation of the overall process. This prior knowledge was an important piece of pre-understanding, so we decided not to start from the beginning by reading through interview by interview and coding, sentence by sentence, various sequences into categories. Instead we used another option in the NUD·IST program: coding by computerized string searches of certain terms or wordings that we considered central to the interviews. We also made use of a word-crunching program through which we identified the most frequent words in each interview and compared them with our pre-understanding of the labels attached to the strategic issues at different periods.

This search yielded the core concepts that became our main categories. In the process we became aware of the danger of 'slicing' interview data in a certain way. In some cases we picked up conflicting or irrelevant data for a specific category because our search words had been used by the interviewee in different ways, resulting in quite opposing meanings. Such contradictions were further input for the study. But mechanical slicing of a long text by one or more words is not recommended. The categorization and slicing should be based on meanings which are normally embedded in longer sequences of words. Thus our method has some shortcomings. However, the NUD·IST program gave us the opportunity to manage and operate on a considerable amount of text data. With its help we could identify the timing of the appearance and disappearance of specific issues, such as the concept 'centre', through the eight texts. Additionally, we could see the emergence of related concepts and their replacement by others over time. The NUD·IST software program was useful in many ways and, with experience, we shall learn more sophisticated ways to apply it. But even though it provides for effective handling and classification techniques of large amounts of text, it should be kept in mind that the creative inter-pretation stage of the analysis is done by the researchers and is their responsibility.

The strategist's way-of-thinking

The strategist in this study is the managing director (MD) of a large Swedish university hospital (with 6,200 employees and 1,700 beds). When appointed in 1988, the MD directly controlled 36 different specialized clin-ics. This made him look for a new structure with a reduced span of control. He also wanted to develop a new strategy so the hospital could meet the impending threats in the public sector, to increase the effectiveness of the hospital, in spite of reduced resources, together with an expected intro-duction of market competition. The MD's strategy revealed an incremental and processual view of strategic management. In this turbulent environ-ment – a public sector threatened by budget cuts, controlled by politicians who try to introduce internal markets through a buyer/seller model – the MD did not see formal strategic planning as the right mode of strategy making. Furthermore, the MD did not see bold strategic decisions made at the top as the right way to achieve legitimacy and get commitment for strategic change in an organization with a strong professional culture which the physicians dominated.

To capture the MD's thinking in use during the strategic change process, we chose, in this first step of the analysis, to focus on the 'centre' concept. This implies a new structure for the hospital. The MD used several other concepts, such as 'care chain', 'quality', 'the patients' and 'leadership', which are also useful for the analysis. The care chain concept is directly related to the centre concept in that the latter throws the focus on the first. At the start of 1990 the care chain and its flow of patients was considered a means for attaining quality and improving effectiveness but it turned out to be difficult to identify the care chain in the organization. A new way of thinking was necessary but the established belief structures in the hospital were very stable. In order to force the change process, the MD turned to the quality concept as a means for driving change. Even though quality was seen as an ambiguous concept, the MD thought that it would be easier to understand and so prove more easily accepted by the members of the organization. This indicates that the way-of-thinking is rather stable, at least in the form of a shell within which the concepts used can shift their roles over time. In the following sections we will concentrate on the centre concept, its introduction, use and meaning over a period of almost five years.

The centre concept

In order to cope with the turbulent environment and internal control problems, the newly appointed MD wanted to develop a new strategy for the hospital. At an internal conference in February 1989 with 15 persons (the principal physicians and administrative managers), two new ideas were agreed upon for the strategic change process that was now initiated:

- a focus on the patient through an organ-based clinic structure;
- the development of a more efficient health care chain.

The idea was to reorganize the hospital by merging a number of clinics into organ-based groups, that is, to adopt a divisionalized structure. During 1990 the MD introduced the term 'centre' as a label for these divisions:

Centre = an organ-based group of clinics (a division).

In November 1990 the MD regarded the centre concept as an instrument for changing the thinking in the organization. The centre concept focused on the patient around whom the organization should be built as a method of improving its efficiency and effectiveness. His purpose was to create an organization that would be able to cope with the market-oriented way of managing healthcare which was becoming widespread at that time. The centre concept matched the idea of the hospital as a divisionalized organization with centres corresponding to product divisions. One objective was to reduce the number of levels in the hierarchy. The centre concept should broaden the understanding of the clinics and make them cooperate. Even at the beginning of the strategic change process, the centre concept had several different meanings. But so far its role was mostly instrumental.

Centre = an instrument for focusing the organization on the patient.
Centre = an instrument for improving efficiency and effectiveness.
Centre = an instrument for improving control.
Centre = a metaphor for changing the thinking in the organization.
Centre = an instrument for creating cooperation.

Around the end of 1990 discussions began about the need for more holistic management of the centres' administrative and medical aspects. The need for medical competence was questioned, but because of the strong professional culture, it was considered necessary for creating legitimacy in the organization. The management of the centres was also crucial to the strategic change process. Parallel with the introduction of the centre concept, a decision was made concerning the structure: managers were appointed to be responsible for the medical as well as financial results of the clinics. Without intending it, this introduced another level of leadership, so making the change process even more difficult. To handle the difficulties resulting from having new leadership at the clinic level, the MD concluded that formalization of the structure was necessary. By May 1991 the meaning of 'centre' had been broadened and now explicitly implied a formal structure in which centres were profit centres, each controlled by an internal board. It also became a way to overcome the negative associations with earlier attempts to reorganize the hospital.

> Centre = a formal governance structure (divisionalized).
> Centre = a profit centre with a board and a centre manager.

At the general meeting in September 1991 a new proposal regarding the centre structure was presented. During the autumn representatives from the proposed centres met and discussed two questions: how the new structure could meet the new demands of the hospital; and how the clinical units could be made up into centres. The last question was not tackled with pleasure, but rather with a feeling of necessity. At the same time, the MD's thinking was focused on the management of the centres and the conflicts between the old power structure and the new. One problem was the new role of the hospital's administrative team. The MD even considered that it might be redundant, though he saw himself as the indispensable promoter of the change process, but at the same time felt exhausted and thought that he was 'tearing himself apart'. Despite the problems, he expected that the centre structure would be implemented by January 1992. In November 1991 the new structure was presented at a conference. It comprised 10 real centres, each with a board, 4 existing clinics, with boards, and 4 clinics which should be further investigated. Even though there was some hesitation and negative feeling about the new structure, the centre managers began to develop a pioneering attitude.

In January 1992 the leading actors in the change process met for a half-day conference. Two issues emerged as crucial: the role of the centre managers, and the engagement of lower levels in the change process. Naturally no answers were given and the debate continued during the spring. In May 1992 the group of centre managers was able to present the centre concept as 'a vehicle to meet tomorrow's problems':

- the centre organization was a tool to keep the hospital as a coherent unit, and a framework for future organization models;
- the current organization structure would be adjusted and developed in line with the changes in internal priorities and with the changes in the organization's environment.

Parallel with these discussions, a number of centre managers were appointed. They were recruited from the medical staff. In spite of their lack of management experiences, the MD was pleased with their interest in and attitude towards their new positions. However, they had to be trained to handle their new roles. The centre concept now gathered new meaning as a strategic business unit, with a consequent shift of focus onto the leadership of these units.

Centre = a strategic business unit under strategic leadership.

Even though the appointment of centre managers had proved unproblematic, the MD still felt that it was hard work to change the structure of the university hospital. He characterizes the process as full of 'Catch 22' situations. The integration of the medical faculty with the centre structure became a new problem. He also experienced difficulties in making professional managers out of the centre managers. They had some insight but, for instance, did not fully understand the quality concept which would have enabled them to manage the care chain. They also had to learn how to act as leaders and not just as 'one of the best among equals'.

So long as the focus had been on the management of the centres, the rest of the organization had been more or less excluded from the change process. The MD now felt that it was important to get everyone involved in the process. One problem was the low awareness of the crisis, generally unanticipated by the healthcare sector, and this inhibited change. Thus in the fall of 1992 the MD began to question the role of the centre as an instrument for change in the thinking of the organization. What remained was a new hierarchical level without the means of control that he had initially wanted. But he felt it important to continue the process.

Centre = a hierarchical level.
Centre = not a useful concept for driving change.

When the MD no longer considered the centre concept as a tool for driving change he introduced three new ideas or, to use his own expression, 'catchwords'. They were to serve as instruments for changing attitudes and values toward a market-oriented organization, new tools to overcome the previous resistance to change and make the realization of the centre idea possible. They absorbed the original meanings of the centre concept. The MD felt these catchwords would also create positive attitudes among the patients and, in a way, describe the patients' needs, expectations and roles. The new concepts were competence, security and participation. Before September 1992 these concepts rarely appeared in the interviews. Participation, meaning getting organizational members at all levels involved in the change process, was not used at all. Now it became a metaphor for how the process should be continued to realize the centre idea. It also became the means to overcome resistance to the change in the organization. Security had been used three times with two different meanings. First it was regarded as a symbol which could be used in marketing the hospital. Then the MD used security to characterize his own situation, and that of the vice managing director. However, when security was introduced as a catchword, its meaning was extended to 'good care', 'professional information' and 'education'. The MD expected the organization's members to feel secure and not fearful or negative towards change. Security would be operationalized through education.

The third concept, competence, was frequently used by the MD before being introduced as a catchword. In 1990 it meant the professionalism of the administrative and medical personnel. But it also meant the new quality which had to be developed to make decentralization possible. Another meaning referred to the lack of management knowledge of the clinics. In 1991 the meaning of competence was related to specific issues concerning the distribution of medical competence and, in 1992, it became a regional issue concerning the distribution of work between the university hospital and the other hospitals in the region. This change illustrated the MD's conceptual internalization of processes going on in his environment. He focused on what he considered to be important at the time of the interviews. As a catchword, the meaning of competence developed an internal focus on the professional competence held by the university hospital as a research organization, but also as an organization taking care of its patients. The introduction of competence as a catchword could be interpreted as both stick and carrot. It stressed what was important for the organization to maintain and improve, but also focused on something about which the organization could be proud.

During the eighteen months following the introduction of the catchwords, they were gradually operationalized in different actions. However, progress towards the MD's objective was slow. By 1993 the centre organization had begun to work. The economic conditions for healthcare got worse and the focus was shifted again to cost efficiency. According to the MD several centre managers were unable to meet the new conditions with rationalizations. A different meaning of the centre concept, which reflected the MD's way of coping with the new situation, was then introduced – 'the super centre'. The super centre would be composed of centres but might include units from the local hospitals, and the new structure would be imposed on the organization as a rationalization which would force the centres to cooperate. At the time some of the centres consisted of just one clinic and the MD thought that these could be forced together into a super centre.

Centre = super centre, composed of several centres and units from the local hospitals.
Centre = an instrument for rationalization.

In January 1994 the idea of changing the centre structure was abandoned because the MD concluded that change had to come from within the organization and could not be forced upon it. Problems with the management of the centres continued. The centre managers had neither the instruments for controlling their centres, nor full acceptance of their management role in the organization. Some centres were more successful than others, but changing values and beliefs was slow, even though there was an increased focus on the patient as customer.

The role of the centre concept

As shown in the previous section, the centre concept had several different meanings during the period studied. When introduced, it was a label for a new way of organizing the hospital, but soon afterwards the number of meanings expressed by the MD increased. In most cases, they were related to structural and control problems and so described important character-istics of the new structure. There was also a symbolic meaning since the MD considered the label to be a powerful metaphor that could change the thinking in the organization. Behind the different meanings lay his vision of the hospital as an M-form organization, a multidivisional organization with several strategic business units. All the meanings were related and interdependent. The different meanings generated and supported each other and, in some cases, one meaning served as a prerequisite of another. This could be exemplified by the meaning of a centre as both an instrument for improving control and an instrument for improving efficiency and effectiveness. The meanings reflected the role which the label played in the change process. When introduced, the concept was a 'magic formula' which would solve the internally and externally generated problems faced by the MD. It was a means to create change in the organization and, more precisely, realize the idea of improved efficiency and effectiveness. But as the centre label also expressed the desired characteristics of the future state of the hospital, it was also a goal. The label's roles as a means and a goal complemented each other.

As the change process continued, new meanings were developed. Interacting with and adapting to the change process, the centre label shifted the focus onto new issues which in turn generated new meanings. But this does not necessarily imply that the 'old' meanings were 'worn out'. The new meanings created by the MD were, at least at the beginning, elaborations and respecifications of the original meaning in response to new situations. However, as the new meanings were developed and imple-mented, the role of the centre concept as a metaphor was reduced, at least as a driving force for change. The magic formula lost its power and 'centre' became a simple label. When the MD realized that the centre concept was no longer a useful tool for change, he introduced three new concepts – security, participation and competence – as catchwords with both sub-stantive and symbolic meaning. Thus, the use of labels loaded with meanings was important to the MD's management of the change process.

The label can also be related to the processes of sensegiving and sense-making. When introduced, the centre concept was an important part of the MD's sensegiving process, obliging the organization members to redefine their sense of organizational reality. As the process continued, and the symbolic meaning of the term was reduced, its role as a sensegiving instrument declined. Thus, the new meanings created by the MD could be seen as evidence of his own process of making sense of internal and external events. This could be illustrated by the meaning of the centre concept, when relaunched by the MD, as a label with a new utopian meaning – a 'super centre' – which defined a response to new budget cuts and turbulence in the environment.

To conclude, the centre label appeared in different shapes and with several roles: as a means to create necessary changes; as a goal, indicating a desired outcome; as a description of the situation, both existing and desired; and as a metaphor for changing thinking and acting in the organization. These roles are intertwined, related, and exist simultaneously. The principal role of the label is determined by the situation and it seems that its role as a means and especially as a metaphor dominates the early stages of the change process. As soon as the substantive meaning of the centre label is implemented, it loses its instrumental power from the point of view of its user. However, for other organizational members it still functions as a metaphor, but now with a negative meaning. This adds a value dimension. It is also possible to identify a time dimension here covering both present and future. The notion of future is inherent in the label's role as a means and as a goal. It is related to the use of the label in the MD's process of sensegiving to other members of the organization as well as in his own sensemaking process. When expressing the present state, it is related to the role as a 'description of facts', illustrated by the meaning of centre as a 'hierarchical level'. The analysis in this section shows that a label is loaded with meanings which, when employed by dominant actors, can play an important role in the change process. Labels are full of nuances and appear in different shapes during a change process. Thus we can broaden our understanding of the thinking and acting in strategic situations by investigating the use of conceptual labels.

The strategist as sensemaker and sensegiver

The strategist in this case, the managing director of a large hospital, proved very efficient in the sensemaking process, for he constructed new meanings regarding the nature and direction of the strategic change process. The sensemaking process is evident in his introduction of new concepts, and redefinition of the meaning of some of the concepts already in use. His way of thinking was future oriented, and this may have facilitated his construction of new meaning. However, his ability to manage the sensegiving process – the deliberate attempt to influence the sensemaking of other organization members toward a redefinition of their shared organizational reality – was not as well developed. As partly shown in this case study, he was not especially successful with influencing the construction of new meaning by the middle managers. One reason was that he seldom communicated clearly the new concepts he developed through his own process, not even when he gave his presentation at the strategy seminar held once a year for the top and middle management of the hospital. However, he was more successful in the sensegiving process in informal meetings, especially with other members of the top management group. So future research in the field of managerial cognition might focus on managers' sensegiving, especially on the role of the language used and on the role of formal and informal communications.

Stability in the strategist's way-of-thinking

Our case illustrates not only the use of specific concepts in the change process but, more generally, management's strategic way-of-thinking. Behind the language communicated, with its changing concepts, labels and meanings, we can find a stable way-of-thinking about strategic issues. Such an individual way-of-thinking may contain several sets of beliefs and values about managerial and organizational themes. Our interpretation, based on a broader empirical picture than shown in this chapter, is that the MD's way of thinking was stable between 1990 and 1994. His belief structure within each basic theme, such as degree of decentralization, role of formal planning, role of leadership, and patient orientation, can be characterized as highly stable. For example, in his view of the hospital as a coherent organization he saw the hospital as an enterprise and wanted it to act as a business, meaning that it should identify its customers and markets and stress increased efficiency and effectiveness. However, within this set of basic beliefs about how a hospital should function, using the private firm as his model, the MD also showed strong respect for the specific circumstances of the hospital, its strong professional culture with medicine's caring and curing values in focus and its institutional embeddedness in the (Swedish) public sector with its political orientation toward the short-term. He also had stable views on change processes in organizations. He showed a strong belief in the incremental mode of organizational change which included both a step-by-step view of change and a focus on efforts to legitimate change through actions which generated commitment from influential actors in the hospital before the new steps were taken.

The way-of-thinking includes several stable beliefs which, once established, occupied the mind of this manager over long periods of time. The MD had formed these beliefs early in his managerial career through experiences in management positions in big private firms and in the healthcare sector. They also reflected his education and personality. The dynamic stability of the way-of-thinking means that it may change gradually over time through unlearning and learning, but most changes seem to be more situational within the stable set of core beliefs. Our analysis shows that such cognitions are more sensitive to situational issues than to fundamental managerial issues. The way-of-thinking shapes a 'shell' of strong beliefs, world assumptions and values within which beliefs and opinions on situational issues related to the specific business context in question change more easily than the core beliefs comprising the shell. The situational cognitions that change show the continuous mental adaptation of the top manager to the ongoing external and internal forces. One example is when severe budget cuts are imposed from above by the politicians. The MD reacts by introducing the 'super centre' idea, which he saw mainly as a strong means for the necessary rationalization. But his basic thoughts about how the centre idea could alter the way of organizing healthcare within the hospital did not change. We stress that the focus on an individual manager's way-of-thinking does not, on its own, tell us whether his thinking influences the organization's strategic change processes. But the perspective gives us an important supplementary tool for understanding how and why the strategic thinking of top managers comes to play a significant role in the dynamics of the strategic change process.

Reflections on the methodology in use

The analysis of the role of managers' cognitions in an ongoing change process requires a specific type of data. Our approach, a series of in-depth interviews over a period of several years with the manager, results in rich empirical material consisting of an extensive text with all original interview dialogues. Through the longitudinal approach, the interviewee is expressing, in his own language, reflections about the past, comments on the ongoing daily activities, and thoughts about the future. This means that in each interview, after the first one, the 'future' from the previous interview becomes part of the past, resulting in reflections about what really happened and new thoughts about the future. This approach lets the researcher capture chains of thinking and acting and so more valid empirical data for an interpretive analysis of the managerial cognitions in action.

   Our conclusion is that a series of rather unstructured interviews, done in an interpretive mode with one actor, gives the researcher a good possibility to catch managerial cognitions and to understand their meanings. The understanding of the specific context, in our case the whole strategic change process in which the interviewed top manager is a key actor, facilitates the interpretation of meanings. Rather than analysing single words, the focus must be on full sentences in context, so identifying constructed meaning and changes in meaning. If the analysis only includes single words or groups of rather few words, the researcher will not be able to understand the meaning of these words. The NUD·IST program gives the researcher the possibility of interpreting sentences and combinations of words in context. However, even if the computer-based analysis helps us to categorize a text, the deeper understanding of the meanings of the spoken language cannot be reached without the interpretative and creative contribution of the researcher.

References

Bartunek, J.M. (1984) Changing interpretive schemes and organizational restructuring: the example of a religious order, *Administrative Science Quarterly*, 29: 355–72.

Daft, R.L. and Weick, K.E. (1984) Toward a model of organizations as interpretation systems, *Academy of Management Review*, 9: 284–96.

Donaldson, G. and Lorsch, J.W. (1984) *Decision Making at the Top*. New York: Basic Books.

Downey, H.K. and Brief, A.P. (1986) How cognitive structures affect organizational design: implicit theories of organizing, in H.P. Sims, Jr., D.A. Gioia and associates, *The Thinking Organization: Dynamics of Organizational Social Cognition*. San Francisco, CA: Jossey-Bass. pp. 165–90.

Dutton, J.E. and Jackson, S.E. (1987) Categorizing strategic issues: links to organizational action, *Academy of Management Review*, 12: 76–90.

Gahmberg, H. (1992) Strategy as signification of meaning: building on the interpretive view, in J. Näsi (ed.), *Arenas of Strategic Thinking*. Helsinki: Foundation for Economic Education. pp. 163–77.

Gioia, D.A. (1986) Symbols, scripts and sensemaking, in H.P. Sims, Jr., D.A. Gioia and associates, *The Thinking Organization: Dynamics of Organizational Social Cognition*. San Francisco, CA: Jossey-Bass. pp. 49–74.

Gioia, D.A. and Chittipeddi, K. (1991) Sensemaking and sensegiving in strategic initiation, *Strategic Management Journal*, 12: 433–48.

Glaser, B.G. and Strauss, A.L. (1967) *The Discovery of Grounded Theory: Strategies for Qualitative Research*. Chicago, IL: Aldine.

Hellgren, B., Lindell, P. and Melin, L. (1993) Strategic change as a prism of different perspectives: integrating multiple theoretical perspectives. Paper presented at the 13th Annual Strategic Management Society Conference, Chicago.

Hellgren, B. and Melin, L. (1993) The role of strategists' way-of-thinking in strategic change processes, in J. Hendry and G. Johnson with J. Newton (eds), *Strategic Thinking: Leadership and the Management of Change*. Chichester: John Wiley. pp. 47–68.

Huber, G.L. (ed.) (1992) *Qualitative Analyse*. München: Oldenbourg.

Isenberg, D.J. (1986) The structure and process of understanding: implications for managerial action, in H.P. Sims, Jr., D.A. Gioia and associates, *The Thinking Organization: Dynamics of Organizational Social Cognition*. San Francisco, CA: Jossey-Bass. pp. 49–74.

Johnson, G. (1987) *Strategic Change and the Management Process*. Oxford: Basil Blackwell.

Lindell, P. (1993) Thinking, acting, and transformation: the case of Åhléns, a Swedish department store chain. Paper presented at the British Academy of Management Annual Conference, Milton Keynes.

Lyles, M.A. and Schwenk, C.R. (1992) Top management, strategy and organizational knowledge structures, *Journal of Management Studies*, 29 (2): 155–74.

Pettigrew, A.M. (1985) *The Awakening Giant. Continuity and Change in Imperial Chemical Industries*. Oxford: Basil Blackwell.

Shrivastava, P. and Mitroff, I. (1983) Frames of reference managers use, *Advances in Strategic Management*, 1: 161–82.

Sims, H.P. and Lorenzi, P. (1992) *The New Leadership Paradigm: Social Learning and Cognition in Organizations*. Newbury Park, CA: Sage.

Starbuck, W.H. and Milliken, F.J. (1988) Executives' perceptual filters: what they notice and how they make sense, in D.C. Hambrick (ed.), *The Executive Effect: Concepts and Methods for Studying Top Managers*. Greenwich, CT: JAI Press. pp. 35–65.

Tesch, R. (1990) *Qualitative Research: Analysis Types and Software Tools*. London: Falmer Press.

Weick, K.E. (1983) Managerial thought in the context of action, in S. Srivastva and associates (eds), *The Executive Mind: New Insights on Managerial Thought and Action*. San Francisco, CA: Jossey-Bass. pp. 221–42.

Weick, K.E. and Bougon, M.G. (1986) Organizations as cognitive maps. Charting ways to success and failure, in H.P. Sims, Jr., D.A. Gioia and associates, *The Thinking Organization: Dynamics of Organizational Social Cognition*. San Francisco, CA: Jossey-Bass. pp. 102–35.

6

SUCCESS ATTRIBUTIONS WITHIN AND ACROSS ORGANIZATIONS

Kjell Grønhaug and Joyce S. Falkenberg

In *Administrative Behavior* (1957) Simon suggested that executives would perceive those aspects of the situation that related specifically to the activities and goals of their own departments. Empirical support was provided by a group of business executives responding to a business case during an executive programme (Dearborn and Simon, 1958). The results showed that sales personnel focused on problems related to sales and production people were more aware than others of production problems. Dearborn and Simon explained their findings in terms of selective perception and heuristics. Due to limited perceptual capacity, actors focus their attention in a specific direction. Thus what is perceived represents only limited aspects of the complex problem with which they had been confronted. Since selective perception follows directly from the assumption of limited cognitive capacity, it is an important element of what we mean by cognition. The findings give rise to intriguing questions, such as: 'Why did the actors perceive what they did?' One answer is that the actors know more than others about their own department and the activities in which they are involved. The question may be followed up by a second: 'Why do people use heuristics?' This is a broad question, much of which is beyond the scope of this chapter. But we can emphasize one element of the answer, that of the actors' need to understand of their surrounding contex. Actors' sensemaking is dealt with extensively in the fast-growing literature on individual and social cognition. For an excellent introduction, see Sanford (1987).

Our chapter focuses on how organizations and their members come to understand their internal and external environments, and so act purposefully. The theoretical basis is attribution and attributional theories. The chapter is organized as follows. First, aspects of attribution and attributional theories are emphasized. The findings reported by Dearborn and Simon (1958) are reinterpreted in this attributional perspective. Also included in this section is a set of indicative hypotheses on attribution of success for members of managerial teams and organizations. Next, the research methodology of and findings from a small-scale study are reported. Finally, the findings are discussed and theoretical and managerial implications are highlighted.

Attribution

One class of theories that aims at explaining human understanding is that of theories of attribution. Attribution research is concerned with all aspects of causal inference: how people arrive at causal inferences, what sort of inferences they make, and what the consequences of these inferences are. The basic point of departure in attribution theory (which actually consists of several theories) is that the individual tries to make sense of the social context in which they are embedded (for overviews of attribution theories and research, see Harvey and Weary, 1984; Folkes, 1988). In order to operate, human beings are inclined to seek causal understanding, as this is needed to operate purposefully. Central to the concept of attribution is the inferred relationship between cause and consequence. Similarly Kelly (1967; 1973) focuses attention on the process of making sense of the world through a construct system which can be seen attributing sense by the way in which constructs imply one another (Eden et al., 1979; Eden, 1988). By making such inferences people are assumed 'to achieve greater understanding of, and hence greater control over, their environment' (Kelly, 1967; Harvey and Weary, 1984: 428). Sanford (1987: 99) also claims that 'everyday explanations (that is, attributions) revolve around chains of connected events, either real or imaginary, and occur either in response to a demand for an explanation or because something is not understood'. Of particular importance for understanding (which is the prime focus here), Sanford continues: 'an event is only understood to the extent it can be mapped into an existing knowledge structure' (1987: 100).

The general scheme (perspective) underlying most attribution research can be depicted as shown in Figure 6.1 (based on Kelley and Michela, 1980). The linkage between antecedents and attributions (arrow a) is related to attribution theories, that is, theories on how individuals make causal inferences, and factors influencing the inferences made, which can be depicted as cognitive maps (see Eden and Ackermann; Laukkanen; Jenkins, this volume). Prior research has identified motivation, information and prior beliefs as important antecedents for causal inferences. (For overview, see Kelley and Michela, 1980.) The linkage between attributions and consequences (arrow b) refers to attributional theories, that is, theories on how actors make use of their causal inferences. The use made of the causal inferences is of utmost importance, as such inferences influence future behaviour. Buss (1978) even claims that such inferences represent necessary and sufficient conditions for behaviours of individuals.

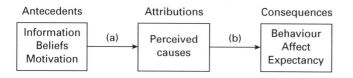

Figure 6.1   *The field of attribution*

The findings of Dearborn and Simon revisited

Can the findings reported by Dearborn and Simon (1958) that actors focus more on problems (and solutions) in their own department than on other aspects of the organization be explained by attribution theory?

When newcomers enter an organization and are assigned to a specific position, they enter the job as a stranger (Simmel, 1971). Many details of the job and its social context must be learned. Applying for and accepting a job also implies that the person is willing to comply or, as claimed by March and Simon (1958: 90), 'in joining the organization he accepts an authority relation . . . [and] will accept as the premises of his behavior orders and instructions supplied to him by the organization'. It is also reasonable to assume that new employees want to perform, as performance is expected to impact their future career. On-the-job activities expose the newcomers to information, enabling them to understand requirements and to make sense of activities in which they are involved. Focus on and information of tasks and motivation to perform also influence the actor's beliefs (for example, 'the job is important' and 'the others are dependent on me/us'). On-the-job activities thus influence and shape the antecedents to attributions (Figure 6.1). The employee also observes/gets information on organizational performance, such as changes in profit, market share and new contracts, and may make inferences that what they (the department) are doing 'causes' the resulting outcome. From the above description, it follows that all three types of antecedents, motivations, information and prior beliefs may explain the focus on one's own department and activities as reported by Dearborn and Simon (1958).

Use of attributed causes

People not only make inferences about causes (Figure 6.1, arrow a), but they also learn cause–effect (consequence) paths. Such paths represent schemata, that is, knowledge structures facilitating future attributions. Thus the learning that the newcomers to the organization undergo (including the attributions they make), will be manifested in their knowledge structure (Sanford, 1987), which they will use when appropriate (Figure 6.1, arrow b). As acquired schemata will be applied as long as they are conceived relevant by the actor, attributions tend to be stable, which is concordance with the idea of the actor as a 'cognitive economizer'. This also explains why organizational actors, well-acquainted with their roles and activities to which they have assigned meaning, tend to focus their attention and make causal attributions within a limited domain. Inferred attributions are based on retrospective rationality. When attributions are used in future activities they represent prospective rationality (Staw, 1980), that is, the typical view of rationality which implies that the actors attempt to process information in such a way as to maximize future benefits relative to costs. The relationships between making causal inferences (attribution) and applying the acquired attributions, and their inherent rationalities, can be illustrated as shown in Figure 6.2.

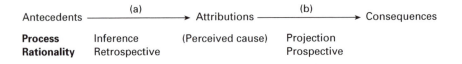

Figure 6.2   *Processes and rationality*

Figure 6.2 shows that different types of inferences are present in forming versus making use of attributions. Attributions are inferred based on retrospective rationality between observed consequence(s), for example, a specific event and some potential cause(s) (part a). When the individual makes use of the inferred attribution(s), the prior cause–effect relationship is projected, that is, the underlying rationality is projective.

Change in causal attributions

Acquired attributions may be changed. This follows from the way in which actors make causal inferences. By changing the antecedents, for example, if certain beliefs are created, motivation changed, or new information supplied (Figure 6.1, arrow a), attributions may be modified. For example, if the actor changes job and thus is exposed to new information, his or her attributions may change. Intuitively it can be expected that people exposed to job rotation will be less rigid in their organizational related attributions compared to employees (executives) exposed to only one position. In a similar way, both reorganization which alters present positions in the organizational structure and also efforts to change the organizational culture (Wilkins and Dyer, 1988) may change antecedents and modify rigid attributions.

Attribution of success and failure

Research has demonstrated that attributions based on motivations may be 'self-serving' or 'hedonic', typically expressed as attributing favourable outcomes to causes internal to oneself and unfavourable outcomes to external forces (Miller and Ross, 1975; Zuckerman 1979). By noticing the firm's success, the actors may infer the success to their departments' or own activities, that is, they may use retrospective rationality to explain the observed outcome (Staw, 1980). In addition to noticing their own activities, the actors also observe indicators of organizational performance, for example, changes in profit or sales. According to the covariation principle, they may infer their own activities as causing the resultant outcome (Kelley, 1967). To what extent this (causal inferences based on covariation) will be the case, will be influenced by consensus, distinctiveness and consistency of the information and criteria on which the attributions are based. To tell whether attributions are motivational or cognitive (based on information) requires, however, detailed information of the circumstances under which the causal inferences are made (Tetlock and Levi, 1982).

Another explanation from attribution theory which may explain the focus on self-centred activities is the discounting principle (Kelley, 1973), that is, an attributor gives less weight to a particular cause in producing an effect if alternative causes also are present. The executive/employee may be aware of other causes of organizational performance, but their own activities are overemphasized while other potential causes are de-emphasized. A similar finding from attribution research is that the salience of stimuli influences the attribution of causality, where salience is used synonymously with availability or vividness. This may also explain the findings reported by Dearborn and Simon (1958) as causal factors available in the actors' immediate surroundings often are the most salient.

Hypotheses

People and organizations seek success. The concept of 'success' and its derivatives, for example, 'successful' and 'to succeed' are positively laden words as demonstrated in examples such as: 'the firm increased its sales by 40 per cent and became the most successful in the industry'; 'the manager succeeded in saving the company from bankruptcy'. According to the *Random House Dictionary*, success is 'a favourable result that one has tried or hoped for', and to succeed is 'to accomplish what is attempted or intended'. Inspection of these definitions shows that success is related to goal-directed behaviour, implying that actors hold goals, whatever they are – and if goal(s) is (are) reached, the outcome(s) may be considered successful (for more complete discussion, see Grønhaug and Falkenberg, 1990).

Attribution of success (and failure) has received substantial attention in attribution research. Based on the observation that attribution can be 'self-serving', research findings have shown that individuals tend to attribute positive outcomes (success) more to internal causes, that is, factors over which they have control, while negative outcomes (failures) are attributed more to external causes outside the control of the actor (Miller and Ross, 1975, Zuckerman, 1979). Most studies have focused on individual attribution of success and failure. A noteworthy exception is the study reported by Bettman and Weitz (1985) examining the attributions of boards of directors as reflected in companies' annual reports. They found that the typical self-serving pattern of attributions observed for individuals was also present in their corporate level analysis. From these biases in perceptions the following tentative hypotheses can be proposed:

H1a: Successful, more than unsuccessful, organizations will attribute the performance outcome to internal, controllable causes.

H1b: Individuals in successful, more than individuals in unsuccessful organizations, will attribute the performance outcome to internal causes over which they can exert control.

The first hypothesis (H1a) builds on the assumption that individuals belonging to the same organization are exposed to some common information, and that collectively they will exhibit attributions as observed for the individual.

The second hypothesis (H1b) rests on research findings from individual attribution of success and failure. Managers (as other employees) possess positions related to specific activities and want to perform. This hypothesis (H1b) implies that the pattern hypothesized in (H1a) is also expected to be present at the individual manager's level. If in the case of unsuccessful performance outcomes attributions are made to external causes, this may be explained by ego-defensive motives.

From our above discussion of the importance of organizational positions, and how the actors' positions may influence antecedents to attributions, we will posit that:

H2a: Definition of factors causing success within an organization will vary among organizational members (managers) depending on their organizational positions.

In many industries similar organizational structures with the same positions across organizations are present. This leads us to the following hypothesis.

H2b: Members (managers) across organizations holding the same (or very similar) positions will be more similar in their perceptions of success factors, than will be members holding different positions.

It is often assumed that organizational success presupposes the concerted efforts of the organizational members (Drucker, 1973). For example, the literature on organizational successes (Peters and Waterman, 1982), organizational culture (Schein, 1985), and Ouchi's (1980) clan-mode of governance (when rules and procedures are insufficient) all emphasize the importance of shared values and understanding. Consensus among managerial teams is also considered important for successful strategy implementation, often assumed as prerequisite for subsequent successful performance outcome (Burgois and Brodwin, 1984).

Previous research regarding consensus and organizational performance has, however, not resulted in conclusive evidence. Dess (1987) has suggested that a reason for the inconclusive findings may be due to the disregard of the heterogeneity of organizational environments. In a study based on a sample from a homogeneous population of organizations, he found that consensus on either objectives or methods was positively related to organizational performance.

Consensus very much relates to attribution as both phenomena are related to cognition and understanding. Here it is believed that the degree of consensus in organizational attribution of success will be positively related to performance outcome. Moreover, as managers in particular are supposed to exert impact on the organizational performance consensus among managerial teams is assumed crucial. Thus it is hypothesized:

> H3: Degree of consensus on success criteria among managerial team members will correlate positively with organizational performance outcome.

Research methodology

Below is reported a small-scale study conducted to explore the proposed indicative hypotheses.

Design

In order to explore the hypotheses, the following requirements must be met:

- organizations both high and low in performance should be included;
- information from more than one manager in each organization should be gathered, that is, managerial teams should be included;
- the positions in the managerial teams should be the same (similar) in each of the organizations included in the study.

The present study is restricted to one industry only in order to eliminate inter-industry variation (Dess, 1987). By meeting the above criteria and by obtaining variability along the crucial dimensions covered by the hypotheses (Campbell, 1975), comparisons can be made:

- between high and low performing organizations (H1a, H1b);
- between positions within the organization (H2a);
- between positions across organizations (H2b, H3).

Research context and sample

The newspaper industry in Norway represents the present research context. Norway – though a small country with approximately 4 million inhabitants – has a multitude of newspapers. Most of its 165 newspapers have a limited, local circulation. Only a few truly nationally distributed newspapers exist. The organizational structure for most medium-sized newspaper firms is very similar. In most such organizations the following positions are present:

- the president (who is responsible for the newspaper as a business firm);
- the editor (who is responsible for the content of the newspaper. Traditionally the editor holds a very dominant position);
- the advertising/marketing manager (who is responsible for marketing of advertisement space).

The newspaper industry is intriguing in several ways. First, the product – the newspaper – has to be renewed every day. Yesterday's issue has almost no market value. Second, most newspapers represent a 'double' product, that is, both the news and the advertisements. The news(paper) is primarily intended for consumer markets representing ultimate demand, while advertising space is intended for firms (and other advertisers) representing a derived demand good. For most newspaper firms the monies derived from sales of advertising space constitute an important part of their income. Studies have shown that advertising income correlates with circulation, but also that the dominant newspaper in the market area tends to receive an overproportional share of advertising space and income.

Four medium-sized newspapers, each being dominant in its local market area, were included in the study. (The reason for restricting the sample to newspapers dominant in their local market areas was to reduce possible influences due to intra-industry variations in competitive positions.) Measured by profitability two of the firms are high performers (profitability > 4 per cent) and two are low performers (profitability < –2 per cent). In each of the four firms information was collected from the managers holding each of three roles mentioned above (president, editor and advertising/marketing manager). Thus at the firm and manager (position) levels the sample sizes are 4 and 12 respectively.

Data and measurements

The data used are from a larger research effort conducted at the Foundation for Research in Economics and Business Administration,

Norwegian School of Economics and Business Administration, on the behalf of the Norwegian Newspaper Association.

A variety of methods, each possessing advantages and disadvantages, has been used in prior attribution research (see Elig and Frieze, 1979, for an overview and discussion of the various methods). Here open-ended questions were used to capture attributions due to modest a priori information of the actors involved. An interview guide based on prior discussions with representatives from the newspaper industry was developed and pretested before the interviews took place. A series of open-ended questions, for example, 'What factor(s) is (are) important to succeed for the newspaper?' and 'How can your newspaper achieve success?' were used to capture attributed success factors. In addition unobtrusive information about economic performance, circulation and distribution of the newspaper was included, obtained from the National Newspaper Association.

Interviews were conducted with the president, the editor and the advertising/marketing manager in each of the four newspapers. Prior to the interviews a letter was mailed to each of them explaining the purpose of the study and asking for access. Appointments for the interviews were made by phonecalls. Each interview lasted approximately 1 hour and 30 minutes. The interviews were taperecorded and transcribed. A coding scheme was developed and used to classify the performance-related reasoning of the actors, that is, perceived success factors and improvements needed. Factors perceived as important and focused on by the respondents, that is, factors believed to influence the organizational performance, were considered as 'perceived success factors'. Inspection of the deduced success factors showed that they could be grouped according to focus, that is, whether they were directed towards readers of the newspaper, advertisers and economical/technical factors respectively. Suggestions offered by the respondents to improve the organizational performance were coded as 'improvements needed', for example, 'we need to change the format of the newspaper', or 'we need to develop a better consulting service for the advertisers'. Suggestions pointing at specific improvements, for example, 'we need to improve the coverage in the south part of the region', were classified as 'specific', while more imprecise suggestions, for example, 'we should improve the quality', without specifying what aspect of the quality should be improved, were classified as 'general'. The interview data were coded independently by the two authors. The coding of the perceived success factors and needed improvements were then compared. In the few cases of disagreement we went back to the transcribed interviews and discussed the coding until agreement was obtained. Unfortunately it was impossible to consult the managers interviewed.

Findings

Table 6.1 summarizes the findings regarding performance attribution:

Table 6.1   *Performance, success and success factors*

Performance/ position		Newspaper			
		A	B	C	D
1 Performance		High	High	Low	Low
2 President	(a)	Economic resources/ profit	Economic resources/ profit	Economy	Economy/ journalism circulation/ more readers
	(b)	Technical/ advertising service (S)	Technical changes (S)	—	
3 Editor	(a)	Readership/ journalistic quality	Readership	Readership	Increase in circulation
	(b)	Tech./emphasis on market (S)	—	Better techn. quality (G)	—
4 Adv. mngr	(a)	Advertisers/ business	Advertisers/ business	Readers/ advertisers	Advertisers
	(b)	Techn. improve (S)	Change format (S)	—	Improve print quality (G)

(a) Success factors.
(b) Suggestions for improvements.

Line 1 reports actual organizational performance (profitability) based on unobtrusive, standardized accounting data. Lines 2, 3 and 4 refer to the various organizational positions. For each of the organizational roles line (a) reports perceived success factors while line (b) reports perceptions of needed actions to improve.

Our two first tentative hypotheses suggest that at the organizational level (H1a) and at the individual level (H1b) attributions of performance are expected to be directed more towards internal, controllable factors in high-performing organizations than will be the case in low-performing organizations. Inspection of the perceived success factors (lines a) reveals mixed results. The support for the stated hypotheses (H1a and H1b) is modest. The findings regarding the suggested improvements (lines b) are, however, surprising. It is seen that five of six actors among the high-performance firms have specific (S) suggestions for improvements related to internal causes. In the low-performing firms, only two actors focus on internal related factors and then only in a general way (G). The various suggestions can be interpreted as 'biconditionals', that is, 'by doing X (cause), the outcome Y will be'. In other words, the suggestions reflect projection of previously inferred causes, that is, attributions based on ret-rospective rationality are used to project future outcomes (prospective rationality) as emphasized in Figure 6.2. This also supports the observation made by Buss (1978), that the inferred causes represent necessary and suf-ficient condition for action.

We also hypothesized that perceived success factors depend on the actors' organizational positions (H2a), and that actors from different orga-nizations holding the same (similar) positions are more similar in their perceptions of success factors than managers holding different positions (H2b).

Table 6.2   *Perceived success factors and organizational positions*

	President	Editor	Advertising/Marketing
Readers	2/4	4/4	1/4
Business/advertiser	2/4	2/4	4/4
Economic factors	4/4	–/4	–/4

Table 6.2 (based on Table 6.1) reports perceived success factors for each of the managerial positions. The upper left number in each cell shows the number of position holders emphasizing the various success factors; the lower right number is the number of managers holding that position. Inspection of Table 6.2 shows that more editors emphasize readers than do the other managers. It is also observed that advertising managers focus more on the business/market for advertisements, and presidents more on economic factors than do the other position holders. These findings sug-gest that the actors' definitions of success are related to their organizational positions (H2a). It is also seen that organization members holding the same (similar) position are more similar in their subjective success definitions than are members holding different positions (H2b). These observations are also in concordance with the findings reported by Dearborn and Simon (1958) discussed at the beginning of this chapter.

Our last hypothesis (H3) suggests that consensus on success criteria will be positively related to organizational success (see Table 6.3).

Table 6.3   *Degree of consensus*

	Newspaper			
	High performance		Low performance	
	A	B	C	D
1 Emphasis on technical improvement	3/3	2/3	1/3	1/3
2 Specific suggestion (solution)	3/3	2/3	—	—

The upper left number in each cell in line 1 shows the number of managers in each newspaper emphasizing technical improvements. Line 2 shows suggestions for improvements. The lower right number in each cell is the size of the management team in each newspaper. From Table 6.3 (derived from Table 6.1) it is evident that the degree of consensus, as reflected in more emphasis on technical (internal) improvements and specific solutions, is greater in the high-performance organizations than is the case for their lower performing counterparts, that is, an observation in concordance with the stated hypothesis (H3).

Discussion

The reported findings deserve some further comments. In going back to our hypotheses and findings, an important question remains: Why is it that consensus on success criteria is seemingly related to organizational success (H3 and Table 6.3)? By recasting Table 6.1 (from which Tables 6.2 and 6.3 have been developed), the following can be extracted.

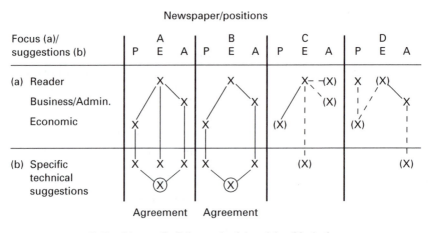

P = President;   E = Editor;   A = Advertising/Marketing

Figure 6.3   *Focus and specific suggestions*

Inspection of Figure 6.3, part (a) shows – as discussed above – that the actors' focus is influenced by their organizational positions, indicated by X. It is seen, however, that the focus for several actors in the low-performing organizations is more ambiguous (indicated by parentheses), that is, what to look for is less clear compared to the case in the high-performing organizations. How can this be explained? For the actors, their focus represents the point of departure for actions. The more specific the focus, the more precise is the point of departure for choosing and positioning the departmental activities.

Moving down to part (b) of Figure 3, it is seen that five of six managers in the high-performance organizations (A and B) came up with specific suggestions, while none of the managers in the low-performing organizations did so (Table 6.3). When looking more closely at the suggestions, it is also found that the suggestions are very much the same for the managers within the firm. In other words, the managers seemingly agree regarding what has to be done. Moreover, the fact that they have specific suggestions also implies that they know what to do. But how do we explain the discrepancy in focus and agreement in suggestion? In our opinion the explanation can be subsumed under the discounting principle, that is, by doing X (improvement) this will cause Z, say attract more readers (editor) or sell more advertisements (adv./marketing), which in turn will result in Y better organizational performance. The actors are probably aware that a specific improvement X may be beneficial for several activities and tasks in the organization, but their focus is on own activities and tasks.

The reported findings show that actors focus on tasks involved in and aspects perceived as important, and thus the 'selectivity in perception' as suggested by Dearborn and Simon. This as such makes sense: based on their knowledge related to the tasks involved and on observations and attributions, they have learnt what is important. This knowledge is used in new situations. It should be noted, however, that Walsh (1988) did not find support for the selectivity hypotheses as suggested by Dearborn and Simon. This might be due to differences in methods used. The study reported by Dearborn and Simon (1958) is based on solved cases, and thus what is focused in the subjects' (participants') solutions and perceived problems. In contrast, the Walsh (1988) study first solved a sorting task to measure belief structure. Walsh also took into account the whole work history of the participants, while Dearborn and Simon (1958) considered 'departmental' belongingness. The time difference, 30 years between the two studies, may also explain differences in findings. Job changes were much less frequent 30 years ago, with consequent greater identification with and focus on the individual department.

Findings from this small-scale study should be interpreted with care. Some preliminary conclusions may, however, be drawn. The fact that the theory-based, tentative hypotheses were supported by the observations from our study, suggests that this theory base possesses both descriptive and predictive power. An important point, which has only received scant attention in previous attribution and attributional research, is that these findings indicate that this body of theory is also valid for individuals in organizations and organizations themselves.

The observations have managerial implications as well. What organizations do largely determines whether they succeed or not (Porter, 1985). However, doing presupposes some sort of prospective rationality. If not, the actors easily end up being inactive, as partly reflected in the findings for the team members in the low-performing organizations. It should also be noted that this study only includes managers, that is, organization members assumed to be able to exert influence on organizational actions and outcomes. For lower level employees this will often not be the case. An interesting question is whether lack of understanding of the relationship of own effort on organizational outcomes may impact work performance and commitment. This question relates implicitly to the basic assumptions underlying the believed relationship between organizational culture and performance (Schein, 1985). Actors, neither individually nor collectively, are omniscient. Their construed, prospective rationality – often based on retrospective causal inferences (Figure 6.2) – may be erroneous. In order to improve organizational performance, assumptions underlying managerial and organizational actions should be examined. Individual and group reflective processes (such as those discussed elsewhere in this volume) that allow for organizational learning need to be emphasized.

APPENDIX

This is a 'theory-driven' exploratory study. Key emphasis is on raising an interesting question (see Davis, 1971). Here we have reinterpreted Dearborn and Simon's seminal article on the selective perception of executives. In other words, we have tried to construct a 'novelty' to get attention (see Blakeslee, 1994). The introductory discussion guides our empirical investigation as we have tried to get variation along the theoretic derived dimensions assumed important to explain the phenomenon under scrutiny in our study.

References

Bettman, J.R. and Weitz, B.A. (1985) Attribution in the board room: causal reasoning in corporate annual reports, *Administrative Science Quarterly*, 28 (2): 165–83.

Blakeslee, A.M. (1994) The rhetorical construction of novelty: presenting claims in a letter forum, *Science, Technology & Human Values*, 19 (1): 88–100.

Burgois, I.J. and Brodwin, D.R. (1984) Strategic implementation: five approaches to an elusive phenomenon, *Strategic Management Journal*, 5: 241–64.

Buss, A.R. (1978) Causes and reasons in attribution theory: a conceptual critique, *Journal of Personal Sociology Psychology*, 36: 1311–81.

Campbell (1975) Degrees of freedom and the case study, *Comparative Political Studies*, 8 (2): 1978–93.

Davis, M. (1971) That's interesting, *Phil. Soc. Science*, 1: 309–44.

Dearborn, D.C. and Simon, H.A. (1958) Selective perception: a note of departmental identification of executives, *Sociometry*, 21: 140–44.

Dess, G.G. (1987) Consensus on strategy formulation and organizational performance: competitors in a fragmented industry, *Strategic Management Journal*, 8: 259–77.

Drucker, P.F. (1973) *Management, Tasks, Responsibilities, Practices*. New York: Harper and Row.

Eden, C., Jones, S. and Sims, D. (1979) *Thinking in Organizations*. London: Macmillan.

Eden, C. (1988) Cognitive mapping, *European Journal of Operational Research*, 36: 1–13.

Elig, T.W. and Frieze, I.H. (1979) Measuring causal attributions for success and failure, *Journal of Personal Social Psychology*, 37: 621–34.

Folkes, V. (1988) Recent attribution research in consumer behavior: a review and new directions, *Journal of Consumer Behavior*, 14 (March): 548–65.

Grønhaug, K. and Falkenberg, J.S. (1990) Organizational success and success criteria, conceptual issues and an empirical illustration, *Scandinavian Journal of Management*, 6 (4): 267–84.

Harvey, J.H. and Weary, G. (1984) Current issues in attribution theory and research, *Annual Review of Psychology*, 35: 427–59.

Kelley, H. (1967) Attribution theory in social psychology, in D. Levine (ed.), *Nebraska Symposium on Motivation*. Lincon, NE: University of Nebraska Press. pp. 192–238.

Kelley, H.H. (1973) The process of causal attribution, *American Psychologist*, 28 (February): 107–28.

Kelley, H.H. and Michela, J.L. (1980) Attribution theory and research, *Annual Review of Psychology*, 31: 457–501.

March, J.G. and Simon, H.A. (1958) *Organizations*. New York: John Wiley.

Miller, D.T. and Ross, M. (1975) Self-serving biases in attribution of causality: fact or fiction, *Psychological Bulletin*, 82: 213–25.

Ouchi, W.G. (1980) Markets, bureaucracies, and claus, *Administrative Science Quarterly*, 25: 129–41.

Peters, T.J. and Waterman, R.H. (1982) *In Search of Excellence*. New York: Harper and Row.

Porter, M. (1985) *Competitive Advantage: Creating and Sustaining Superior Performance*. New York: Free Press.

Sanford, A.J. (1987) *The Mind of Man: Models of Human Understanding*. Brighton: Harvester Press.

Schein, E.H. (1985) *Organizational Culture and Leadership*. San Francisco: Jossey-Bass.

Simmel, G. (1971) The stranger, in G. Simmel, *On Individuality and Social Forms*. Chicago, IL: University of Chicago Press. pp. 143–9.

Simon, H.A. (1957) *Administrative Behavior*, 2nd edn. New York: Free Press.

Staw, B.M. (1980) Rationality and justification in organizational life, in B.M. Staw and L.L. Cummings (eds), *Research in Organizational Behavior*. Greenwich, CT: JAI Press.

Stein, J. (1980) *The Random House Dictionary*. New York: Ballantine Books.

Tetlock, P.E. and Levi, A. (1982) Attribution bias: on the inconclusiveness of the cognition–motivation debate, *Journal of Experimental Social Psychology*, 18 (January): 68–88.

Walsh, J.P. (1988) Selectivity and selective perception: an investigation of managers' belief structures and information processing, *Academy of Management Journal*, 31: 873–96.

Wilkins, A.L. and Dyer, W.G. (1988) Toward culturally sensitive theories of cultural change, *Academy of Management Review*, 13 (4): 522–33.

Zuckerman, M. (1979) Attribution of success and failure revisited, or the motivational bias is alive and well in attribution theory, *Journal of Personality*, 47: 245–87.

7

MAKING SENSE OF TECHNOLOGICAL INNOVATION: THE POLITICAL AND SOCIAL DYNAMICS OF COGNITION

Jacky Swan and Sue Newell

Since the successful appropriation of the results of technological innovation is key to maintaining the organization's competitive advantage (Hayes and Wheelwright, 1984), understanding the innovation process is crucial. There is a substantial literature on technological innovation and, while it recognizes that cognitive processes play a role, it does so implicitly and has yet to address this issue explicitly. Recent research suggests that cognitive processes are important in mediating the outcomes of decisions to adopt technological innovation (Löwstedt, 1985; Weick, 1990). In particular, the technology's success or failure may depend on the cognitions of the decision-makers who shape the organization's choices about the adoption of innovations. This chapter summarizes the findings of a study of the adoption of computer-aided technologies for production management (CAPM). We draw from two projects: first, a series of cases studies examining the cognitions mediating the outcomes of firms' attempts to adopt CAPM technologies (Swan and Clark, 1992; Swan, 1994); second, the use of a cognitive mapping technique to investigate managers' understandings about factors which lead to successful adoption of CAPM (Swan and Newell, 1995). The chapter draws these studies together and reviews the relative advantages of these two methodologies for understanding the innovation process.

A variety of definitions of, and approaches to, innovation exist (Tushman and Moore, 1988). In conducting our research we have found Van de Ven's (1986) definition of innovation to be useful: 'the development and implementation of new ideas by people who over time engage in transactions with others in an institutional context'. This definition highlights the importance of the social and cognitive processes through which people acquire new ideas and translate them into practice, the point at which they are seen as innovations. It also suggests the need to consider innovation in the context of the adopting organization. Other innovation theorists recognize the importance of cognitive processes. For example, Rogers (1983) describes the first stage of the innovation process as 'awareness' on the part of user organizations that an innovation exists.

Gerwin (1988) notes the importance of 'uncertainty' in understandings of particular innovations. Clark and Staunton (1989) suggest that innovation is embedded in organizational recipes and languages. All these writers imply that cognitive processes underlie innovation in that adopting organizations need to perceive, interpret, reconstruct and communicate information. But they tend to deal with these issues at the level of the organization, even though theoretical approaches to technological innovation suggest that it could be important to focus on the cognitions of the individual making decisions in the innovation process.

Acknowledgement of the relevance of the cognitions mediating the outcomes of the innovation process is implicit in early theoretical approaches to technological innovation. For example, socio-technical approaches suggested that the social and technical systems have properties that are independent. The problem for users is to develop innovations that harmonize the fit between these systems (Trist and Bamforth, 1951). These approaches implied that the knowledge, beliefs and assumptions of managers were important when making choices about the socio-technical system (Swan and Newell, 1994). More recently, writers on innovation have explicated the notion that managerial cognition is important in the process of technological innovation. For example, social construction of technology approaches adopt the view that innovation is a dynamic social process through which technological artefacts are shaped and interpreted by social actors in the particular social contexts into which they are introduced (Bijker et al., 1987). Similarly, organizational theorists have emphasized structuration (Spender, this volume), as a dynamic process through which social and technical systems are (re)produced, rather than structure as a relatively stable entity (Barley, 1986). These approaches define technological innovation as a dynamic, iterative process whereby new technologies allow new social systems to emerge which in turn shape new organizing processes and new ideas about technological innovation. Accordingly, people design technology and organization in keeping with their own perceptions and explanatory frameworks (Weick, 1979, 1990). Thus the cognitions of principal actors, and the social transactions in which they involve themselves, both shape and are shaped by the emergence of new technologies.

A similar view is taken by Clark and Staunton (1989) who see technology as knowledge which is embedded in technical systems (hardware and software systems, and the physical layout of factories, and in organizational systems (patterns of social order evident in languages, organizational procedures and structures, and so on). Technological innovations are dynamic configurations which appear to potential users as a complex bundle of elements. Some system elements will appear as more relevant than others, contingent on the existing features of the adopting organization. To appropriate an innovation requires it be unpacked so that its implications, such as the revision of supplier specifications to match the specific demands of the user, can be worked out. Users may introduce pivotal modifications that reshape the original innovation. For example, in the late nineteenth century American players reshaped the British games of association football and rugby union into a new configuration – American football (Clark, 1987). This view emphasizes the importance of both the choices on the part of the user about the design of the innovation configuration and the organizational context in which design decisions are made. Failures with technological innovation often occur because users make inappropriate choices at the design stage (Clark, 1987; Clark and Staunton, 1989).

Clark and Staunton also criticize diffusion of innovation perspective (Rogers, 1983) because they treat technology as an entity with well-defined and fixed parameters which can be slotted into firms. When there is but a single 'best practice', there is no choice about design, so the active part played by users, as they make decisions about innovative solutions to their unique problems, is underemphasized. Diffusion perspectives measure innovation by the rates at which firms buy technologies, but this may be a poor measure. There are plenty of examples of users who buy technologies that they then fail fully to implement (Cox and Clark, 1984; Waterlow and Monniot, 1986). These failures have been attributed, at least in part, to the users' decision-making processes.

Even though these speculations emphasize the importance of managerial cognitions, empirical research on the role of knowledge and cognition is still fairly limited (Clark and Staunton, 1989). The contribution has been modest in spite of the huge amount of research by cognitive psychologists and cognitive scientists in the latter half of the twentieth century (Bartlett, 1932; Tolman, 1948; Rummelhart and Ortony, 1977; Schank and Abelson, 1977). The reasons for this shortfall remain unclear. It might be a problem of different units of analysis, with psychologists focusing on how individuals represent knowledge, while innovation and management researchers seek solutions that relate to organizational knowledge and actions (Swan and Newell, 1994). Another problem has been the emphasis on normative rational models of decision-making, both in the psychology and the management of technology literature, wherein decision-makers are seen as rational actors engaged in a careful evaluation of alternatives and arriving at statistically optimal solutions. Technological innovation has also been treated as a sequential and linear process of problem solving, and research has sought to offer prescriptive best practice solutions. However, linear and normative approaches have limited relevance, demonstrating the need for descriptive models that better capture the ways in which managers operating on complex problems within particular organizational contexts bring their own mental models to bear in order to frame and simplify problems and to make decisions. Clearly managers' interpretations of technological solutions have consequences for the ways in which technologies are used in organizations.

Another problem has been the lack of appropriate methods and tools with which to explore and describe managerial cognition in their decisions about technological innovation (Stubbart, 1989). New cognitive mapping techniques (Bougon et al., 1977; Huff, 1990; Weick and Bougon, 1986) allow researchers to identify and describe individual managers' mental maps, and have been used to try to understand why managers make particular strategic choices (Huff, 1990; Narayanan and Fahey, 1990). They can also be used to construct organizational maps which aggregate individual maps into a collective representation (Bougon et al., 1977; Weick and Bougon, 1986; Eden, 1989). A collective map reveals the beliefs which are shared by organizational members and these may be more likely to impact organizational decisions than would beliefs that are held by particular individuals and not shared by others (Schwenk, 1988). But empirical work is still needed to substantiate this assumption and the research to date has suggested that political factors, such as the influence of particular actors in setting agendas for decision-making, also need to be taken into account (Schwenk, 1989; Hosking and Morley, 1991).

Cognitive mapping techniques may be useful for understanding the ways in which managers make choices about technological innovation, especially given the importance of such choices in determining the outcomes of the innovation process. However, a potential drawback of such techniques is that they tend to isolate features of managerial cognition, in the form of maps, from their social and organizational context. However, social construction theorists see cognitions as dynamically interacting with and inseparable from the organizational environment. This suggests the need for research that can describe and explain the process of innovation and the dynamic relation between managerial cognitions and organizational knowledge which becomes codified and embedded in technical and organizational procedures and practices (Clark and Staunton, 1989). Detailed case studies may offer insights here and the remainder of the chapter looks at examples of how these two rather different approaches have been used in our research on technological innovation. We describe both methods and consider the advantages and limitations of each.

Case studies of innovation with CAPM

This section describes case study research investigating the adoption of CAPM. Case studies offer the opportunity to understand and unravel complex processes that emerge in organizations over time. This is important, given the dynamic and contextualized nature of the relationship between cognitions and technological innovation. The relative advantages of the type of process-oriented research used here are considered later.

Production and operations managers attempt to sequence and plan material flows and production runs so that materials are available for production without holding unnecessarily high levels of inventory. Recently there have been major technological developments in this area with the introduction of information technologies to formalize the process. These technologies are referred to collectively as computer-aided production management systems (CAPM). Although originally presented as a technology with fixed parameters (Corke, 1985), it is now apparent that different variants of CAPM exist. Users face complex problems of choosing technological solutions that they can then appropriate within their own organizations. Appropriation may require dual modification of both the presented technology and organizational practices and thus entails both technical and organizational knowledge (Waterlow and Monniot, 1986; Clark, 1987; Clark and Staunton, 1989). CAPM technologies have the potential to integrate data used across functions with manufacturing strategy and objectives although, in reality, many organizations do not reach high levels of integration and manage only to implement a few isolated computer modules.

Our research analysed seven cases of medium-sized manufacturing firms that had attempted to adopt CAPM systems and were at similar points in the decision. At this stage the firms had all attempted to implement CAPM and therefore the cases were retrospective – the data were derived from secondary sources and from interviews with key managers within each firm that addressed their views of their firms' attempts to adopt CAPM. These managers were reflecting on events that had already occurred, as well as making suggestions about likely consequences. The focus of the analysis was on understanding cognitive dimensions of the innovation process and whether or not these dimensions were important for the success of firms' attempts to implement CAPM.

In conjunction with these case investigations the research examined the existing literatures which addressed cognitive issues in decisions about technological innovation (for example, Schwenk, 1988, 1989; Hosking and Morley, 1991). From this, and from the case study investigations, it became clear that political variables were also needed to contextualize the innovation process. Relevant cognitive and political dimensions were identified from these rather diverse literatures and drawn together in a single taxonomy (Table 7.1) then used to describe the cases. Comparisons of the cases could then be made along these dimensions and in relation to outcomes of the innovation process in order to identify patterns that could help to explain the outcomes. The analysis and the description of the variables in Table 7.1 are presented more fully elsewhere (Swan and Clark, 1992). The analysis is summarized here in order to demonstrate that it provided interesting insights into the cognitive and political dimensions that emerged as important for innovation with CAPM. In particular, decisions about the adoption and design of CAPM were influenced by managerial cognitions in the firms concerned, but this influence was mediated by organizational politics because some managers had relatively more power to influence the decision process than others.

The headings shown in Table 7.1 were not exhaustive but did provide a basis for comparison of firms along important dimensions with respect to outcomes of their attempts to adopt CAPM technologies. Outcomes were described in terms of appropriation (Clark, 1987) and integration (Waterlow and Monniot, 1986). From this it could be seen that firms 3, 4 and 7 had been relatively more successful in their attempts to implement

Table 7.1 Cognitive and political dimensions of seven firms adopting a CAPM system

Cognitive	Firm 1	Firm 2	Firm 3	Firm 4	Firm 5	Firm 6	Firm 7
Knowledge – technical							
Internal	Medium (e.g. UNIVAC)	Low (mostly manual)	Low (mostly manual)	High (e.g. CNC, MAPICS)	Medium (some computing)	Medium (bespoke package)	High (inhouse s/ware)
External	Software house	Consultant	Parent firm	None	Consultant	None	Software house
Innovation compatible?	No	No	Yes	Yes	No	Yes	Partly
Innovation understood?	No	No	Yes	Yes	No	Partly	Yes
organisational							
Training	Limited	Limited	Extensive	Extensive	Limited	Mgmt only	Extensive
Problem defined?	Not clear	No	Yes	Yes	No	No	Yes
Solution defined?	Partly	No	Yes	Yes	No	Yes	Yes
Alternative solutions evaluated?	Yes (but overruled)	No	No	Yes	No	Yes (but overruled)	Yes
Strategy	Ill-defined short-term direct control	Not defined short-term autonomy	Well-defined long-term direct control	Well-defined long-term autonomy	Ill-defined short-term autonomy	Ill-defined short-term direct control	Well-defined long-term autonomy
Communication	Poor	Very poor	Good	Good	Poor	Poor	Fair
Innovation altering/entrenching?	Altering	Altering	Entrenching	Entrenching	Altering	Altering	Altering
Restructuring?	Limited	None	None	None (done earlier)	None	Decentralize	Decentralize
Schemata-cognitive maps							
Beliefs shared re CAPM	No	No	Yes	Yes	No	No	Yes
Variations admitted	No	No	Yes	Yes	Some	Yes	Yes

Table 7.1   Cognitive and political dimensions of seven firms adopting a CAPM system – contd

Cognitive	Firm 1	Firm 2	Firm 3	Firm 4	Firm 5	Firm 6	Firm 7
– heuristics	Many	Many	Few	Few	Many	Many	Not enough info
– analogies	Many	Many	Not evident	Some	Some	Many	Few
Political							
Problem owned / shared?	Owned by data processing	Owned by parent firm	Shared	Shared	Owned by parent firm	Owned by manufacturing	Shared
Solution imposed / shared?	Imposed by parent firm	Imposed by parent firm	Imposed by top mgmt	Shared	Imposed	Imposed	Shared
Confidence in project leaders	Very low	Low	High	Unknown	Low	Medium	High
Intra-organizational conflict	High	High	Medium	Low	High	High	High
Outcomes							
Degree of appropriation	Failure	Reproduction only	Small-scale modification	Appropriation	Reproduction only	Reproduction only	Appropriation
Level of integration (start level – finish level)	0/1 – 1	0 – 1	0 – 3	2 – 4	0/1 – 2	1 – 2	1 – 3

Source: Swan and Clark, 1992

CAPM than had firms 1, 2, 5 and 6. The latter firms had failed to configure the technical and organizational features of the technology so that it met their unique requirements. They had also failed to establish any integration of the technology across different functional areas despite having attempted to do so. This appeared to be, in part, because the people in those different functions (for example, sales, production, finance) had very different understandings of the chosen technological solution and of the problems it was intended to solve (Bessant et al., 1989; Swan and Clark, 1992).

The cognitive dimension

First a distinction was made between knowledge bases, which referred to existing competencies that were socially recognized within the firms (Berniker, 1989), and schemata which referred to the mental models and commonsense social theories (Rummelhart and Ortony, 1977) that individuals used in their judgements about technological innovation. The breakdown of schemata into cognitive maps, analogies and heuristics followed from Schwenk's (1988) description of cognition in strategic problem solving. The distinction between knowledge bases and schemata represents a distinction between knowledge at the level of the organization which is recognized, codified and embedded in organizational and technical systems, and knowledge at the level of the individual, which is based on an individual's past experiences and used to formulate their expectations about future events. The distinction is somewhat arbitrary, however, given the social constructionist view that the two are intertwined. This suggests that managerial cognitions both shape and are shaped by organizational and technical knowledge bases. Nonetheless, for the purposes of description the distinction proved useful.

The research revealed that both technical and organizational knowledge bases were important for the innovation process. Technical knowledge (specialist knowledge about hardware and software) could exist internally embedded in current technical systems, but also externally in the form of advice from suppliers and consultants. Problems occurred when new technologies were chosen that were poorly understood and incompatible with existing technical systems (for example, Firms 1, 2 and 5). Compatibility of technologies with existing organizational knowledge bases (organizational rules, procedures, structures, languages and so forth) was also important. Firms experienced more problems when they failed to recognize that the CAPM solution required a change in their existing ways of operating. These are referred to in Table 7.1 as 'altering innovations', as opposed to 'entrenching innovations' where the chosen technology is compatible with existing organizational knowledge bases (Clark and Staunton, 1989). Major problems occurred in the firms that tried to introduce these altering innovations without attempting to change their existing infrastructure (Firms 1, 2 and 5). For example, Firm 1 had a very traditional functional structure such that each function used its own software and databases and there were few mechanisms for horizontal interaction across functions. CAPM, however, requires that different functions share data and enter the same kind of data with very high accuracy, otherwise the system cannot be integrated. This firm failed to recognize this. In contrast, Firm 3 had a production system that already integrated different functions in the organization, albeit manually. Therefore adopting CAPM was easier as the technology entrenched their existing methods of organization.

Other features of organizational knowledge bases that were important were the extent to which firms had a clearly defined technology strategy with a long-term time horizon. Firm strategy has also been found to be important for adoption of other types of integrating manufacturing systems (Gerwin, 1988). Management in the relatively successful firms had spent time identifying short- and long-term problems and in defining solutions and communicating these to other members of the firm. In part this communication was achieved through extensive training programmes that encompassed individuals across functions and different levels of the hierarchy. However, in general, the decision-making process did not closely resemble the kind of normative-rational approach of collecting data, defining problems, analysing alternatives, proposing solutions and so on portrayed in the literature (Glass and Holyoak, 1986). Frequently problem definitions chased solutions, initial decisions were made with little data, little consideration of alternatives, and so on. The decision process was iterative circular, and encompassed changes in problem ownership as the innovation process unfolded (Clark et al., 1992). The important element seemed to be that different individuals saw themselves as understanding the problems and solutions in similar ways so that they had a fairly clear sense of the problems that CAPM was intended to solve.

In firms that had attempted to define problems and solutions (Firms 3, 4 and 7) it was more likely that individuals across functions shared similar beliefs about CAPM. These shared schemata were reflected in statements about CAPM as an appropriate solution, that CAPM was probably going to be complex, that it had the potential to improve existing competencies. Of course, these statements were made with the benefit of hindsight, although at least some interviewees in these relatively successful firms also reported that they, or others, had concerns about CAPM but that these variations in beliefs had been recognized and discussed at the time. Where beliefs were not shared, firms experienced political infighting, delays and disruptions, especially where individuals that did not believe CAPM to be an appropriate solution had tacit knowledge and expertise that was needed to implement the system.

Where decision-makers deal with complex problems they will typically simplify them by drawing upon heuristics and analogies with past and present situations (Tversky and Kahneman, 1974; Schwenk, 1988). These can provide useful short cuts to the decision-maker but can also result in distortions or biases if used inappropriately. Although the decision-making process rarely follows the rational problem-solving route in any of the firms, some did appear to place greater emphasis on the use of heuristics and analogies to understand and justify their choices, and these also tended to experience more problems. For example, key decision-makers in Firm 1 saw CAPM as a quick-fix technical solution and used analogies of successes in other firms to explain and justify their choice in written and verbal statements. Given that CAPM is a complex configuration of both organizational and technical knowledge and that its use is highly context dependent, these analogies, with highly dissimilar manufacturing firms, represented an oversimplification of the technology (Clark and Staunton, 1989). This also illustrates a heuristic of 'wishful thinking' – the probability of desired outcomes being judged as inappropriately high. Other examples of heuristics were illusions of control, hindsight biases, and availability heuristics (Swan and Clark, 1992). These cases suggested that the schemata which individuals used to frame and simplify problems were an important feature of decisions about CAPM. However, idiosyncratic beliefs of particular individuals were only relevant to the innovation process to the extent that they had the opportunity to influence decisions in the firm (Swan and Clark, 1992). This political dimension is considered in the next section.

The political dimension

The cases indicated that one important dimension of the analysis was that of the political interdependencies between different interest groups in the organizations and their power to enter the decision arena. These are summarized in Table 7.1. Degree of commitment to the CAPM solution among users at all levels of the organization hierarchy was given as a reason for success or failure with CAPM. In general, commitment was higher and firms had more success with CAPM when lower level users felt that they were involved early in the decision process, that is, in agenda formation, when decisions about the nature of the problems and potential solutions were being considered, and when solutions were not imposed upon them. One exception was Firm 3, where lower level managers had the solution imposed upon them but nonetheless remained committed to the solution. Another important feature was confidence in the project leaders. In Firm 3 implementation was handled by a project champion who was not aligned to a particular function and perceived as politically neutral. This person was well respected and in a position of power from which he managed to convince users in different functions that the solution was relevant for their particular problems. Thus, even though the solution was imposed by senior management via the data processing function, users saw the problem as an organizational one and not one that was aligned to a particular function. This reduced the level of political infighting about the relevance of the technological solution for particular groups in the organization. In contrast, in Firm 1, many users viewed the project as owned by the data processing department and treated this department with suspicion. The extent to which beliefs of particular managers mediated outcomes depended crucially on their ability to influence the innovation process. In the example given earlier (Firm 1), the purchasing manager's negative beliefs about CAPM were able to disrupt outcomes because without the cooperation of his function implementation plans could not proceed.

These comparisons provided some empirical support for the idea that outcomes of decisions to adopt technological innovation were mediated by cognitive and political dimensions involved in choosing and implementing the solution. The approach allowed managerial cognitions (their beliefs and expectations) to be studied in the context of organizational and technical knowledge. While the case study analysis was useful in identifying broad patterns, we felt that the descriptions of managers' cognitions were generalized and superficial. To investigate managerial cognitions in more detail a second study used a cognitive mapping methodology to explore managers' beliefs about factors that relate causally to innovation in the production and inventory control (PIC) area (Swan and Newell, 1994). This is reviewed next.

Using cognitive mapping

There are now numerous cognitive mapping methodologies to choose from (Huff, 1990). We chose an adaptation of the matrix technique developed by Bougon et al. (1977) which allowed us to identify managers' beliefs about the causes and effects of innovation in the production and inventory control area. The details of the methodology are presented elsewhere (Swan and Newell, 1994). The sample in this study was 16 executive members of the Canadian Association of Production and Inventory Control (CAPIC) who were also experienced production and inventory control practitioners. The participants were involved in the organization of CAPIC on a voluntary basis, in addition to carrying out their regular jobs in industry. CAPIC is the largest association for production and inventory controllers in Canada. We were interested to discover what these managers believed to be important factors affecting a firm's adoption of technological innovations in the production and inventory control area, and to discover whether they saw professional associations as playing a prominent role in this process. From this sample, eight provided data for our study. This is a small sample but not unusual for this kind of cognitive mapping research which focuses on individuals or on small groups.

We used the mapping methodology to test these managers' beliefs about the factors that were causally related to adoption of innovation in the production and inventory control area. Participants were guided through a two-dimensional grid with thirteen variables listed in rows and repeated in columns. For each cell in the grid participants were asked to indicate the predominant relationship between the row variable (A) and the column variable (B). Thus there were five possible responses: A causes an increase in B; A causes a decrease in B; B causes an increase in A; B causes a decrease in A; and no causal relationship exists between A and B. Participants were encouraged to assign only one type of relationship to each cell, although in some cases they found this impossible as they felt that a reciprocal relationship existed.

Group maps were constructed from the individual responses which produced some interesting patterns in managers' understandings about the factors that were causally related to innovation in the PIC function and also suggested that these understandings were not always consistent with those presented in the academic literature. A full discussion of the analysis can be found in Swan and Newell (1994). The analysis involves the calculation of indegrees (the number of paths leading to a particular variable from other variables) and outdegrees (the number of paths leading from a particular variable to other variables). Indegrees is a measure of how much one variable is influenced by the other variables while outdegrees indicate how much a variable causes change in other variables (Eden and Ackermann; Laukkanen, this volume). Table 7.2 summarizes these data, showing the variables ranked by outdegree (Table 2a) and by indegree (Table 2b). Looking first at the outdegree scores, as predicted by the academic literature, some variables such as firm size and ratio of professional and technical staff in the firm were seen to cause change in many other variables (Gerwin, 1988). Others, such as uncertainty, were seen not to cause change in other variables. However, these data were confusing, with innovation in production and inventory control emerging as primarily causal rather than, as we had expected, being a result of changes in other variables. Thus these data did not give us much information about these managers' beliefs about the factors that cause innovation. This finding is in keeping with that of Bougon et al. (1977) who also commented that ranking outdegree scores shows little pattern and is conceptually difficult to understand.

The ranking by indegree showed an interesting and meaningful pattern. Variables with high indegree scores (uncertainty, innovation, sophistication of the infrastructure) are typically those regarded as organizational goals. Those variables with the lowest indegree scores can be seen as the givens of the situation (size, competitors, vendor activities) and those in the middle range can be understood as the means through which organizations can achieve certain goals. These means, then, include delegation, training, having relatively more professional or technical people, networking, involvement in professional associations, and having longer time horizons of strategies.

Table 7.3 summarizes the nature of these managers' beliefs about the causes and effect of the focal variable in the study: innovation in production and inventory control. The relationships noted were the ones for which over half the sample agreed and the numbers in brackets indicate the proportion that agreed in each case. These managers saw involvement in professional associations as an important causal factor in innovation in production and inventory control, and also believed that such involvement

Table 7.2   *Ranking of variables by (a) outdegree score and (b) indegree score*

(a) Outdegree score

Variables	Score	Rank	
Firm size	6.78	13	
Ratio professional and technical staff/others	6.15	12	
Innovation in PIC	5.53	11	
Involvement in professional associations	5.03	10	
Commitment to training	4.91	9	
Sophistication of firm infrastructure	4.65	7	
Competitors' level of technology	4.65	7	
Time horizon of strategies	4.54	6	
Integration of technical/organizational strategies	4.53	5	
Involvement in collaborative networks	4.15	4	
Vendors' knowledge promotion activities	3.79	3	
Delegation of decision-making	3.52	2	
Uncertainty about PIC systems	3.03	1	

(b) Indegree score

Variables	Score	Rank	
Uncertainty about PIC systems	6.79	13	g
Integration of tech/org strategies	6.41	12	o
Innovation in PIC	5.56	11	a
Sophistication of firm infrastructure	5.53	10	l
Commitment to training	5.52	9	
Involvement in collaborative networks	5.03	8	m
Involvement in professional associations	4.91	7	e
Time horizon of strategies	4.78	6	a
Ratio professional and technical staff/others	4.29	5	n
Delegation of decision-making	4.28	4	
Vendors' knowledge promotion activities	3.65	3	s
Competitors' level of technology	2.40	2	i
Firm size	2.02	1	t

Source: Swan and Newell, 1994

is more likely to occur in larger companies with a high commitment to training and a high proportion of professional technical staff. Interestingly, size per se was not seen as an important cause of innovation. The relationship between increased size and increased innovation was indirect, with size being seen as leading to greater involvement in professional associations in the firm and a higher proportion of professional and technical staff, with these factors in turn leading to innovation. The academic literature on innovation largely neglects the role played by professional associations but these managers, at least, believed that this was important.

Other factors seen to be direct causes of innovation were the ratio of professional and technical staff to others in the firm, the promotion activities of vendors, and the competitors' levels of technology. Factors which, according to the academic literature, increase the likelihood of innovation (for example, increased time horizon of strategies, increased size,

Table 7.3   *Causal relationships for innovation where more than half the*
sample agreed

Innovation in PIC causes	Proportion of sample that agreed
* increased time horizon of strategies	(.75)
* increased sophistication of infrastructure	(.75)
* increased collaborative networks	(.63)
* reduced uncertainty about PIC systems	(.63)
Innovation in PIC caused by	
* greater proportion of professional/tech personnel	(.75)
* greater involvement in professional associations	(.63)
* greater vendors' knowledge promotion	(.63)
* greater competitors' level of technology	(.63)

collaborative networks) were not believed to be important direct causes by these managers. Thus there were some incongruities between the beliefs of these managers and the conclusions drawn by academics in the field. These might have important implications if the academic research is to be believed. For example, some academic research has demonstrated that firms are more likely to achieve high levels of technological integration in production and inventory control if they have a fairly sophisticated infra-structure in place before the innovation is introduced (Swan and Clark, 1992). However, these managers believed that sophistication of the infra-structure was more likely to be an outcome of increased innovation rather than a cause. Thus the lessons learned from academic research may, for some reason, be failing to reach those in industry. Alternatively, the expe-riences of those in industry may be incongruent with the academic research. Either way, such discrepancies between these managers' beliefs and the academic literature reveal potential areas for further research.

Discussion

The two rather different methodologies discussed above provide oppor-tunities for exploring the role of managerial cognition in the process of innovation. The comparisons of case studies provide empirical support for the view that managers' cognitions are important in mediating the out-comes of the innovation process. This is because there are choices to be made in the design of technological innovation that are important in deter-mining whether or not an innovation will be appropriated. Managers bring their own beliefs to bear when making judgements about particular tech-nologies, although the extent to which these judgements mediate outcomes with innovation will be constrained by the degree of influence that partic-ular managers have in the political infrastructure of their firms. Other research also supports this view. For example, research investigating the roles of professional associations in diffusion of technologies has shown that members of professional associations may act as boundary spanners who are able to learn about the latest technological developments in their area and then translate this knowledge into their firms so that it can be used for innovation (Tushman and Scanlan, 1981; Swan and Newell, 1993). However, boundary spanning is a two-step process, requiring first that individuals have access to sources of knowledge which are outside their organization's boundaries, second that those individuals then have sufficient influence within their own organizations to ensure that this knowledge is used in the innovation process.

The case studies also highlight the importance of knowledge bases in the innovation process and attempt to relate cognitive processes to organizational outcomes. This is an area in which more research is necessary. However, the cases did not provide detailed descriptions of the types of mental models that managers may use to frame problems surrounding their decisions about technological innovation. This kind of detail might be provided by using cognitive mapping techniques. It is difficult to claim that cognitive mapping techniques could be used to model and predict managerial thought because the very process of eliciting the map would involve the manager in some new kind of sensemaking (Eden, 1992). However, cognitive mapping techniques may be useful for presenting subjective, descriptive data in a meaningful way, so that discussion about differences in the beliefs of different managers (using maps for individuals) and different interest groups (using group maps) is possible. This may then facilitate negotiation and decisions about technological innovation, especially when the proposed innovation is likely to impact people in different areas of the firm with different interests and different expectations.

The cases indicated that knowledge bases, both organizational and technical, could constrain or facilitate innovation. The relationship between managerial cognition and knowledge bases requires further clarification. An initial attempt to do this, based on the theoretical approaches (Löwstedt, 1985; Clark and Staunton, 1989; Weick, 1990) and empirical findings outlined above, suggests that knowledge at the level of the organization is socially recognized, codified and embedded in organizational systems as rules, procedures for communication, strategies, and so on, and in technical systems as hardware, software, and the technical information derived from a variety of external sources. Individuals in organizations access this knowledge but may emphasize some elements over others in making sense of particular problems such as choices about design of technologies. For example, they may overemphasize information from system suppliers, and underemphasize their existing technical systems. The process of sensemaking depends, to some extent, on the individuals' own experience within and beyond their organization's boundaries, for example, from their boundary-spanning activities. The results may be decisions to adopt particular innovative solutions which, if implemented, then shape their organization's knowledge bases.

Figure 7.1 implies that knowledge bases at the level of the organization

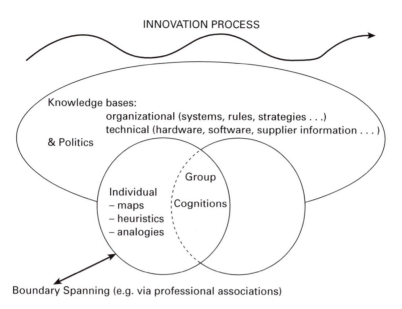

Figure 7.1   *Knowledge and cognitions in the innovation process*

and cognitions at the level of the individual are in a dynamic relation and change over time as innovations are introduced. However, individuals also interact socially in groups within organizations and may share beliefs about important concepts and relationships with other group members. Beliefs that are shared by group members (illustrated as the area of overlap between individual cognitions in Figure 7.1), may be more likely to influence the innovation process than are beliefs that are held by only one individual, although this will depend on the power relations between individuals and groups in organizations. Cognitive mapping methodologies may therefore be useful in describing the subjective beliefs of individuals and groups of individuals. Cognitive maps may also be useful to chart organizations (Weick and Bougon, 1986). However, it is more difficult for maps to describe the dynamic nature of the relationship between individual sensemaking, organizational knowledge and outcomes of the innovation process, especially since organizational knowledge is embedded in a variety of ways that a map may not capture. Process research could be used in conjunction with mapping techniques to unravel these complex interdependencies between cognition, knowledge at the organizational level, and outcomes of the innovation process over time.

Case studies: process research

The first study described in the chapter used case studies which are a form of process research, aimed at developing descriptive accounts and explanations through looking at patterns and sequences of events over time

(Pettigrew, 1993). Process research relates antecedents (in our cases in terms of cognitive and political dimensions) to outcomes (in our cases in terms of integration and appropriation of CAPM). The aim is to develop descriptive accounts of events that are interconnected in time and then to use these to develop explanations (Pettigrew, 1993). Longitudinal studies are a form of process research carried out in 'real time' over a period of months or years and allow events to be examined as they unfold, and accounts to be generated. That is not to say that these provide a truly objective explanation of events because the emergence of the process and the explanatory accounts will be subject to shaping by the research itself (Weick, 1979). Longitudinal research into cases of CAPM adoption would be difficult because this technology typically takes up to two years to implement fully so research funding and access would need to be secured over this length of time.

Often a more practical alternative to longitudinal studies is retrospective accounts based on case studies of the kind used here. These use interviews where interviewees provide accounts of events that precede particular outcomes, the researcher's own observations of the firm over a shorter time period, and secondary data on the firm as and when available (company reports, minutes of meetings, and so forth). The explanatory power of these accounts comes when different cases are compared and meaningful patterns observed (Pettigrew, 1993). This was possible here using a comparison of seven cases along the same cognitive and political dimensions. However, comparing cases raises critical issues surrounding the similarity of the firms and the point of entry of the research project in each case. Given the importance of organizational context for the adoption of complex, multifaceted innovations like CAPM, the case firms would need to have some degree of comparability, for example, in size, availability of resources for investment in technology, the type of technological solution chosen, industrial sector and so forth.

It would be very difficult to draw meaningful comparisons in terms of antecedents from, say, a large chemical process production firm with huge capacity for investment with a small electronics batch production firm. Here the firms were all medium sized (around 300 employees) and were components manufacturers in the UK, mostly using batch-type production. Each firm had chosen to implement an MRP2 system (Manufacturing Resource Planning) and were around two years into the process at the point of entry of the research (with the exception of Firm 6 which was somewhat less far down the MRP2 route). Again, it would be very difficult to compare outcomes in a firm that had decided to implement MRP2, say, a month ago with one that was two years into the process. The researcher needs to decide on a broad set of parameters for the selection of cases so that some degree of comparison is possible and patterns can be observed. The relevant parameters will depend on the type of innovation being considered. A related point is that an explanation derived from one set of accounts (or cases) will not necessarily apply to another. The cognitive and political dimensions which were relevant to outcomes in our seven cases may not translate well to other types of innovation or to firms in other countries. For example, sharing beliefs about the advantages of the technology may be less relevant if the firm were making decisions about adopting an information technology that did not cut across established areas of expertise. This is important because innovations are contextually embedded (Bijker et al., 1987).

The comparisons were useful in providing empirical support for the idea that outcomes of decisions to adopt technological innovation were mediated by cognitive and political dimensions involved in choosing and implementing the solution. The approach allowed managerial cognitions to be studied in the context of organizational and technical knowledge and in the political environment. Cognitions could be explored in relation to antecedents and consequences. The drawbacks of this approach were, first, that much of the data collection involved interviewing people after the events had occurred. Thus managers' explanations of events leading up to adoption decisions and reasons for particular choices were given with the benefit of hindsight. Such post facto explanations may have been liable to assume a rationality that they did not have in reality. To some extent this is inevitable since even the very act of interviewing may lead interviewees to engage in sensemaking so that accounts given in response to the interviewer's questions are, in part, a product of this sensemaking process and in part an account of the original episode (Bartlett, 1932), a problem that Bougon (1983) addresses with his 'self-Q' method of elicitation during interviews. However, the advantage of retrospective accounts is that interviewees may feel more comfortable in giving accounts because the event is over (Pettigrew, 1993). In these cases, for example, interviewees freely admitted to problems that may have been unlikely to be admitted at the time, for example, that they made decisions on the basis of limited data and little understanding of the technology. Another drawback was that descriptions of managerial cognitions were quite broad and general, being drawn rather loosely from semi-structured interview data. To investigate managerial cognitions systematically and in more detail a cognitive mapping methodology could be used. This methodology was used here to explore managers' beliefs about factors that relate causally to innovation in the PIC area.

Causal grid: cognitive mapping research

The second study reported in this chapter used a cognitive mapping methodology. In psychology, a cognitive map refers to a mental model which allows a particular problem domain to be framed and simplified so that it can be understood (Tolman, 1948). This understanding enables decisions to be made about a solution or set of potential solutions to the problem. Cognitive maps incorporate representations of concepts and relationships among concepts. A mapping methodology aims to uncover important features of a person's internal representations and to externalize them. It is important for the researcher using cognitive mapping to recognize that the revealed maps are only a reconstruction of the internally represented events, though this does not negate their usefulness as a research tool (see Eden, 1992). Cognitive maps can be elicited in a variety of ways (see Huff, 1990; Jenkins and Laukkanen, this volume). The content of the revealed map will, to some extent, be bounded by the particular technique chosen. There are critical research design issues in the choice of which technique to adopt. Cause–effect maps of the type selected here have attracted particular attention from strategy researchers because they form the basis for predicting the likelihood of future occurrences from past events and are thus believed to be closely tied to strategy formulation and decision-making. It is worth pointing out that this assumption is not shared by all authors (Ginsberg, 1989). It is probably simplistic to think that there is a direct relationship between an individual's cognitions and organizational decisions because it is likely that there will be other contextual features that mediate such a relationship. For example, our own research into CAPM adoption using case studies revealed that the power and influence of individuals moderated the degree to which their beliefs were reflected in organizational decisions (Swan and Clark, 1992).

The methodology we chose allowed us to look at cause–effect relationships which, as was mentioned earlier, are probably more likely to affect strategic decision-making. Second, it allowed us to combine individual maps and get a group's representation of their beliefs about the causes and effects of innovation in production and inventory control. This would give us a better insight into the kinds of shared beliefs that may have mediated the outcomes of the innovation process. Third, we were interested in discovering whether the factors indicated to be important for outcomes of innovation by research in this area were also felt by practitioners to be important. Finally, the method's development was well documented and accessible. It had been used in earlier studies to obtain representations for groups of a similar size to our own, with interesting results (Bougon et al., 1977). From a practical point of view it was also relatively fast and appropriate, given the time we had available with the participants.

The causal grid used in our study (Swan and Newell, 1994) showed only the cells to the top right of the diagonal line of the matrix. This technique therefore differed somewhat from that used by Bougon et al. (1977) in which a complete matrix was used such that the relationships which represented the cells to the top right of the diagonal line were repeated in the bottom left.. The advantage of our 'half-grid' was that participants considered each relationship between the row variable and the column variable only once, reducing the amount of time taken to complete the grid. This encouraged subjects to indicate the main direction of causality (for example, uncertainty causes innovation) rather than to take what might have been the easier option of indicating reciprocal relationships (see also 'implication grids' – Armstrong and Eden, 1979). However, this may also carry costs if such reciprocal relationships were important. An example might be the relationship between innovation in PIC and integration of technology and corporate strategies, where innovation might be a cause as well as a consequence of integration of strategies. Although these managers were permitted to indicate reciprocal relationships, the technique did not encourage it. The process of completing grids can be problematic for managers because of the length of time it can take (Brown, 1992).

The variables listed in the grid were drawn from the academic literature and from discussions with key academics where these variables were identified as particularly important to the innovation process. The only variable which is not given much consideration in the academic literature on innovation is 'involvement in professional associations' (Hage, 1980). This variable was added because it was of focal interest to our study at the time, one aim of which was to explore the role of professional associations in innovation diffusion. Using the same variables for each individual allowed us to construct fairly simply a group map. It also allowed us to assess whether the understandings of this group of practitioners differed from those espoused in the academic literature about factors that precede and result from technological innovation in PIC. A disadvantage of providing the elements is that it may have precluded other variables which these managers considered important. Spaces were provided on the grid for the managers to enter additional variables but none of them were used. This may have been an artefact of the technique rather than a real indication that all pertinent variables had been included. Other mapping techniques, for example, repertory grids (Kelly, 1955) or cognitive mapping with COPE (Bood, this volume; Eden, 1988), derive elements from the participants themselves and probably reveal a map that is much closer to the idiosyncratic schemata for the individuals concerned. The problem then, however, is that it is difficult to compare the importance of particular concepts for different individuals and groups, because each map is unique (see Eden and Ackermann, this volume).

References

Armstrong, T. and Eden, C. (1979) An exploration of occupational role – an exercise in team development, *Personnel Review*, Winter.

Barley, S.R. (1986) Technology as an occasion for structuring: evidence from observations of CT scanners and the social order of radiology departments, *Administrative Science Quarterly*, 31: 78–108.

Bartlett, F.C. (1932) *Remembering*. Cambridge: Cambridge University Press.

Berniker, E. (1989) Understanding technical systems. Symposium on Management Training Programs: Implications of New Technologies, Geneva.

Bessant, J., Buckingham, J. and Lamming, R. (1989) *Organizational Learning for Effective Implementation of Computer-aided Production Management*. Report for ACME, Science and Engineering Research Council, Swindon, UK.

Bijker, W.E., Hughes, T.P. and Pinch, T.J. (1987) *The Social Construction of Technological Systems*. Cambridge, MA: MIT Press.

Bougon, M. (1983) Uncovering cognitive maps: the Self-Q technique, in G. Morgan (ed.), *Beyond Method: Strategies for Social Research*. Beverley Hills, CA: Sage.

Bougon, M., Weick, K. and Binkhorst, D. (1977) Cognition in organizations: an analysis of the Utrecht Jazz Orchestra, *Administrative Science Quarterly*, 22: 606–39.

Brown, S.M. (1992) Cognitive mapping and repertory grids for qualitative survey research: some comparative observations, *Journal of Management Studies*, 29: 287–308.

Clark, P.A. (1987) *Anglo-American Innovation*. New York: De Gruyter.

Clark, P.A., Bennett, D., Burcher, P., Newell, S., Swan, J. and Sharifi, S. (1992) The decision-episode framework and computer-aided production management (CAPM), *International Studies of Management and Organization*, 22: 69–80.

Clark, P.A. and Staunton, N. (1989) *Innovation in Technology and Organization*. London: Routledge.

Corke, D. (1985) *A Guide to CAPM*. London: Institute of Production Engineers.

Cox, J.F. and Clark, S.L. (1984) Problems in implementing and operating a manufacturing resource planning information system, *Journal of Management Information Systems*, 1: 81–101.

Eden, C. (1988) Cognitive mapping: a review, *European Journal of Operational Research*, 36: 1–13.

Eden, C. (1989) Using cognitive mapping for strategic options development and analysis (SODA), in J. Rosenhead (ed.), *Rational Analysis for a Problematic World*. Chichester: John Wiley.

Eden, C. (1992) On the nature of cognitive maps, *Journal of Management Studies*, 29: 261–5.

Gerwin, D. (1988) A theory of innovation processes for computer-aided manufacturing, *IEEE Transactions on Engineering Management*, 35: 90–100.

Ginsberg, A. (1989) Construing the business portfolio: a cognitive model of diversification, *Journal of Management Studies*, 26: 417–38.

Glass, A.L. and Holyoak, K.J. (1986) *Cognition*, 2nd edn. New York: Random House.

Hage, J. (1980) *Theories on Organization: Form, Process, and Transformation*. New York: John Wiley.

Hayes, R.H. and Wheelwright, S. (1984) *Restoring Our Competitive Edge: Competing Through Manufacturing*. New York: John Wiley.

Hosking, D.M. and Morley, I.E. (1991) *A Social Psychology of Organizing: People, Processes and Contexts*. New York: Harvester-Wheatsheaf.

Huff, A. (1990) *Mapping Strategic Thought*. Chichester: John Wiley.

Isenberg, D.J. (1988) How senior mangers think, in D. Bell, H. Raiffa and A. Tversky, *Decision-Making*. Cambridge: Cambridge University Press.

Kelly, G.A. (1955) *The Psychology of Personal Constructs*. New York: Norton.

Löwstedt, J. (1985) Contingencies or cognitions? Two paths for research on organization and technology, *Scandinavian Journal of Management Studies*, 1: 207–25.

Narayanan, V. and Fahey, L. (1990) Evolution of revealed causal maps during decline: a case study of admiral, in A. Huff (ed.), *Mapping Strategic Thought*. Chichester: John Wiley.

Pettigrew, A. (1993) Doing qualitative research. Paper presented at the British Academy of Management Conference, Milton Keynes.

Rogers, E.M. (1983) *Diffusion of Innovations*, 3rd edn. New York: Free Press.

Rummelhart, D.E. and Ortony, A. (1977) The representation of knowledge in memory, in R.C. Anderson, R.J. Spiro and W.E. Montague (eds), *Schooling and the Acquisition of Knowledge*. Hillsdale, NJ: Erlbaum.

Schank, R.C. and Abelson, R.P. (1977) *Scripts, Plans, Goals, and Understanding.* Hillsdale, NJ: Erlbaum.

Schwenk, C. (1988) The cognitive perspective on strategic decision making, *Journal of Management Studies*, 25: 41–55.

Schwenk, C. (1989) Linking cognitive, organizational and political factors in explaining strategic change, *Journal of Management Studies*, 26: 177–87.

Stubbart, C.I. (1989) Managerial cognition: a missing link in strategic management research, *Journal of Management Studies*, 26: 325–47.

Swan, J.A. (1995) Exploring knowledge and cognitions in decisions about technological innovation: mapping managerial cognitions, *Human Relations*, 48: 1241–70.

Swan, J.A. and Clark, P.A. (1992) Organizational decision making in the diffusion and appropriation of technological innovation: cognitive and political dimensions, *European Work and Organizational Psychologist*, 2: 103–27.

Swan, J.A. and Newell, S. (1993) The role of professional associations in the diffusion and shaping of production management technologies: a comparison of Britain and North America, in A. Bramley and T. Mileham (eds), *Advances in Manufacturing Technology VII*. Bath: Bath University Press. pp. 191–95.

Swan, J.A. and Newell, S. (1994) Managers' beliefs about factors affecting the adoption of technological innovation: a study using cognitive maps, *Journal of Managerial Psychology*, 9: 3–11.

Tolman, E. (1948) Cognitive maps in rats and men, *Psychological Review*, 55: 189–208.

Trist, E.L. and Bamforth, K.W. (1951) Some social and psychological consequences of the longwall method of coal-getting, *Human Relations*, 4: 3–38.

Tushman, M.L. and Moore, W.L. (eds) (1988) *Readings in the Management of Innovation*. New York: HarperCollins.

Tushman, M.L. and Scanlan, T. (1981) Boundary spanning individuals and their role in information transfer and their antecedents, *Academy of Management Journal*, 24: 289–305.

Tversky, A. and Khaneman, D. (1974) Judgement under uncertainty: heuristics and biases, *Science*, 185: 1124–31.

Van de Ven, A.H. (1986) Central problems in the management of innovation, *Management Science*, 32.

Waterlow, G. and Monniot, J. (1986) *A Study of the State of the Art in Computer-aided Production Management*. Report for ACME, Science and Engineering Research Council, Swindon.

Weick, K.E. (1979) *The Social Psychology of Organizing*. Reading, MA: Addison and Wesley.

Weick, K.E. (1990) Technology as an equivoque: sensemaking in new technologies, in P. Goodman and L. Sproull, *Technology and Organizations*. San Francisco, CA: Jossey Bass.

Weick, K.E. and Bougon, M.G. (1986) Organizations as cognitive maps: charting ways to success and failure, in D. Sims and D. Gioia (eds), *The Thinking Organization: Dynamics of Organizational Social Cognition*. San Francisco, CA: Jossey-Bass.

8

MENTAL MODELS OF COMPETITION

Phyllis Johnson, Kevin Daniels and Rachel Asch

The primary aim of this chapter is to identify the level at which managerial cognition of competitive environments is held, either at the group or individual level. Its secondary aim is to test the impact of organizational and environmental contingencies on the diversity of the knowledge structures developed by a group of managers as they consider their competitive environment. We begin by outlining an argument to support the notion that individual managers have diverse mental models of their competitive environments. The next section describes testing four specific hypotheses in three international automobile manufacturers and retailers. In the last section the academic and practical implications of the findings are discussed.

Diverse mental models

Recent research within organizational theory has began to use the cognitive metaphor as an innovative tool to account for management activity. It has become apparent, at least within strategic management research, that the element of individual choice inherent within the strategic decision-making process has an effect on an organization's performance (Child, 1972). This leads to a critique of the assumptions that have dominated strategy research for the past decade; the economists' rational decision-maker (Porter, 1980). Traditional theories that minimized the importance of the interaction of individual managers and strategic choice were unable to cope with the idea of the complex manager. Rational decision-making implies that managers deal with vast quantities of information and perform complex strategic analyses in a manner that is free from inherent bias and gives each piece of information equal attention. It also implies that the managers in a decision-making unit have the same perfect knowledge of the issue in question that enables them to carry out these complex analyses in a logical manner (Quinn, 1980).

This view has been discredited by developments in cognitive psychology (Neisser, 1967; Baddeley and Hitch, 1974; Fiske and Taylor, 1991) which provide some support for the idea of the bounded rationality of an individual decision-maker's information processing ability (Simon, 1957; Weick, 1979). This top-down information processing theory suggests that decision-makers in an incomplete and complex informational environment, such as when making strategic decisions, will resort to theory-driven processing of information. An individual will attend to, process and represent only the information relevant to the theories adopted and created by past experience. Managers would therefore be unable to carry out decision-making in the manner prescribed by economic theory and some earlier perspectives of the strategic decision-making process, such as the logical incrementalist approach, that rely heavily on the assumption of rationality (Quinn, 1980).

Managers are naturally drawn to concentrate intellectual activity, and consequently decision-making, on certain pieces of information. As a result they are able to cope quickly with their potentially vast information environment to allow them to reach satisfactory strategic decisions. The particular sections of new strategic information on which managers are likely to focus their attention become entrenched in terms of how they approached similar situations in the past. Essentially this is a learning process in which the expert manager will collect a growing number of entrenched approaches to strategic scenarios. The rapid application of well-rehearsed approaches to new strategic issues is the hallmark of expert information processing (Lurgio and Carroll, 1985; Gilhooly, 1990) and evidence of individual and organizational learning (Corner et al., 1994). However, the worrying paradox that exists within this mode of information processing (Walsh, 1995) is that managers seriously limit the information accessed during decision-making (Gioia, 1986). Recognition of this paradox has promoted a stream of research concerned with managerial cognition that has attempted to describe not only the content and structure of managers' knowledge structures, but also to comment on how particular structures develop and how they impact on decision-making behaviour.

The cognitive perspective, when applied directly to investigation of strategic decision-making, has produced a number of studies that have attempted to clarify the content and structure of managers' knowledge structures of their competitive environment. One particular subset of research has taken as its subject matter knowledge of competition. The specific interest in managers' knowledge structures of their competitive environment has two origins. First, the definition of an organization's competitive environment is an axiomatic first step in the function of strategic analysis (Porter, 1980; Porac et al., 1987; Johnson and Scholes, 1993). It would therefore seem an appropriately widespread information processing task to study. Second, certain benefits are gained within exploratory academic work if researchers coordinate their findings; the investigation of the same phenomena from a number of different angles allows an embryonic subject to evolve through the testing of validity and reliability of research findings in a variety of organizational and environmental contexts.

The aim of this chapter is to add further detail to this particular vein of research concerning the structure and content of managers' knowledge about competition. A second aim is to add unique information concerning the effect that particular environmental and organizational contingencies have on the development of such competitor knowledge structures. The particular research questions of this chapter have been largely determined by the findings of a subset of six pieces of closely related research investigating managers' competitor knowledge (Huff, 1982; Porac et al., 1987; Reger, 1988; Porac et al., 1989; Daniels et al., 1994; Hodgkinson and Johnson, 1994). These authors have attempted to describe and characterize the content and structure of managers' competitor knowledge. Huff (1982) made the initial suggestion that managers may represent knowledge of their competitive environment in a manner that reflects the structure of phenomena within that environment. She suggested that managers arrange competitors into strategic groups.

The first exploratory work describing managers' knowledge structures of their competitive environment (Porac et al., 1987) was designed to test the primary assumption that such knowledge is simplified and categorized according to the hierarchical principles of cognitive psychology. Evidence was indeed found to support the claim that managers simplify their competitive environment. Porac et al. (1987) based their research methodology on the a priori assumption grounded in experimental psychology (Kempton, 1978) that individuals all organize their knowledge in the same way. The issue of individual differences is not prioritized. Consequently the technique employed to elicit managers' knowledge structures of their competitive environment was based on aggregating the responses of a number of managers into one group structure. The conclusions drawn from this work suggest that managers do arrange their knowledge according to the principles of cognitive psychology and in addition that those knowledge structures demonstrate considerable homogeneity in both structure and content at the group level (Porac et al., 1987). These findings were supported in later work (Porac et al., 1989).

As a reaction to the findings of this early work, later studies set out to remove the a priori assumption of homogeneity that dominated research designs. Hodgkinson and Johnson (1994) modified the aggregative technique of Porac et al. and allowed individual managers to complete their own taxonomic structure of their competitive environment. A comparative analysis of the resulting taxonomies indicated that although there was evidence of diverse content of managers' knowledge of their competitive environment, there was also evidence to suggest similarities in the structure of this knowledge that was the result of organizational and environmental contingencies. In particular Hodgkinson and Johnson found that managers from the same organization were likely to structure their knowledge in a more similar way than those from different organizations. Evidence supported the same effect occurring as a result of a managers' functional position. Those managers from similar functions were likely to share similarities in their knowledge structures of the competitive environment. The work of Hodgkinson and Johnson, although overcoming the problem introduced by Porac et al. of imposing a group level structure of response on participating managers, did remain to a large extent context dependent on the a priori assumption that managers structure their knowledge in a taxonomy that allowed them to respond only within its context.

Another development of research methodology in this area came with the work of Daniels et al. (1994). They designed a research methodology that made minimal assumptions concerning the structure and content of managers' knowledge structures of competition. When this context-independent elicitation was implemented, little evidence of homogeneity was found between participating managers. However, as with the work of Hodgkinson and Johnson (1994), there was evidence to suggest that certain organizational and environmental contingencies, when common to a group of managers, caused knowledge structures to be significantly more similar than for those who did not share the group characteristics. The contingencies that were found to have an effect were managerial function and the organization to which a manager belonged. Those managers from the same company and same function were more similar. These findings can be extended into a tentative social proximity theory of similarity shown in Figure 8.1.

In summary, the literature appears to suggest that managers do indeed simplify their informational environment as implied by organizational theory and cognitive psychology. However, empirical work suggests that managers do not share perfectly homogeneous knowledge structures of their competitive environment as economic theories of strategic decision-making would assume. In addition it would also appear that there are certain environmental and organizational contingencies that have a common effect on the development of managers' knowledge structures.

Exploring knowledge structures about competition

The research questions of this chapter specifically address these issues. First, the elicitation methodology used by Daniels et al. (1994) is employed in a different industry context in order to test the finding that managers have diverse knowledge structures of their competitive environment. Second, by stratifying the industry sample the chapter intends to examine the impact of previously tested and untested organizational and environmental contingencies on the development of diversity in managers' knowledge structures. The specific organizational and environmental

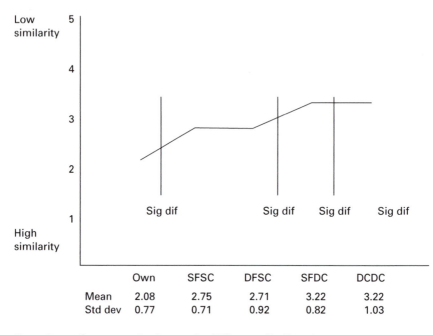

	Own	SFSC	DFSC	SFDC	DCDC
Mean	2.08	2.75	2.71	3.22	3.22
Std dev	0.77	0.71	0.92	0.82	1.03

Key Own = Own map   S = Same   D = Different   F = Function
       C = Company   Sig dif = Significant difference

Figure 8.1   *The relationship between increasing social distance and decreasing similarity in managers' knowledge structures of their competitive environment (adapted from Daniels et al., 1994)*

contingencies selected for exploration were the organization to which managers belong and the functional positions that managers hold. These contingencies were chosen in order to test further the findings of Hodgkinson and Johnson (1994) and Daniels et al. (1994). These pretested contingencies form H1 and H2.

H1 Managers from the same organization will possess knowledge structures that are significantly similar in comparison with knowledge structures of managers from different organizations. (Daniels et al., 1994; Hodgkinson and Johnson, 1994)

H2 Managers who share a common functional position will hold models that are significantly similar in comparison with those managers holding different functional positions. (Dearborn and Simon, 1958; Daniels et al., 1994; Hodgkinson and Johnson, 1994)

The previously untested contingencies that are expected to have an impact on the development of managers' knowledge structures of their competitive environment are the national base in which a manager operates and the level of the parent organization at which a manager works. The nationality contingency is anticipated to have an effect based on evidence of cross-cultural differences in managerial attitudes and perception (Hofstede, 1989; Calori et al., 1992; Kakabadse, 1994; Trompenars, 1993) and is operationalized in H3.

> H3 Managers from organizations with the same national base will possess significantly more similar models in comparison with those managers from different national bases.

Finally, the organizational level at which a manager operates is anticipated to have an effect based on an extension of the findings of Daniels et al. (1994) to support a social proximity theory (Figure 8.1). In addition the work of Ireland et al. (1987) provides support for the view that managers placed at different levels of the organizational hierarchy tend to have apparent differences in perception. This anticipation of this effect is operationalized in H4.

> H4 Managers from the same level will hold models that are significantly similar in comparison with managers from different organizational levels. (Ireland et al., 1987)

The industry selected for investigation was the international automotive industry as it is made up of predominantly multinational organizations and therefore allowed sampling from more than one national base. In addition, this industry has clear strata of organizational levels between automobile retail dealers and automobile manufacturers that allowed for a test of H4.

Research method

The participants in this study were selected from a total of three organizations that operate in the international automotive industry. These were selected for study because from among the organizations approached they all had a comparable level of operations within one specific market – Europe. As all three organizations A, B and C had interests in both the manufacturing and retail dealership of automobiles they were suitable to test H4 (organizational level effect). Two of the three organizations (A and B) were based in country 1 while organization C was based in country 2, therefore allowing for a test of H3 (nationality effect). However, all the managers interviewed from the retail dealership level were from country 2. In order to test H2, the managerial function effect, the dealership sample was matched on the basis of interviewing both a managing director and a sales manager from each organization.

The total number of managers interviewed was 22, of these 21 were male with 1 female participant. The average length of tenure for a manager's current position was 5.5 years (sd = 9.3). The average length of tenure in the industry was 10.7 years (sd = 9.6). The profile of the sample is broken down in Table 8.1.

Table 8.1   *Profile of managers sampled*

Organization	Manufacturer level	Dealership level	Managing director	Sales manager
A	3 – country 1	4 – country 2	2	2
B	3 – country 1	4 – country 2	2	2
C	4 – country 2	4 – country 2	2	2

A semi-structured interview was undertaken with each participant. The interviews lasted approximately half an hour. During this period their knowledge structures were elicited of the competitive environment in which their organization operated. The elicitation technique used was the Visual Card Sort Technique (Daniels et al., 1995). This technique was selected as it makes minimal a priori assumptions concerning the characteristics of managers' knowledge. The construct validity of this technique was tested against the Repertory Grid Technique (Kelly, 1955) and achieved convergent results (Daniels et al., 1995). The Visual Card Sort Technique is administered by asking each participant to think about the international automotive industry as a whole and name all those organizations that they perceive as competitors to their organization. The names of these organizations (including their own) are written on small cards. These are then handed back to the managers who are asked to arrange them on the table in front of them to reflect the manner in which those organizations compete with each other.

This first structure is taken as the most salient knowledge of their competitive environment. The managers are allowed to remap as many times as required. They are asked to explain the knowledge structures/maps they have just created. The justifications they verbalize are again written on small cards. This final set of cards, once given back to the manager and arranged, is considered to make up the construct map. This construct map is a spatial representation of the categorization principles that each manager uses to generate competitor maps. The construct maps commonly contained categorizing principles such as market share, market segmentation, manufacturing efficiency. The first map that the managers create of their competitive environment is considered the most salient and is taken forward for data analysis along with the final construct map.

To test the hypotheses, the maps elicited from each manager required comparative analysis. The comparative analysis of idiosyncratic data proves a problematic issue (Eden and Ackermann, this volume). The solution taken by this chapter was to apply statistical analysis to the competitors and constructs named by each manager in order to group the

A Internal issues	B External issues	C Product issues	D Promotion issues	E Sales issues	F Specific sales issues	G Personal issues
Financial position	State policies	Image	Launch	National sales vol.	Retail not fleet sales	Personal preference
Strategic direction	EC policies	Quality	Marketing	Local sales	Fleet sales	Franchise interests
Culture	Monetary changes	Production costs	Pricing	Local sales enviro.	Diesel sales	
Chosen markets	Nationality	Design	Distribution network		After-sales service	
Inter-firm agreements		Technology				
Top managers		New model launch				

Figure 8.2   *Strategic issues continuum*

most similar maps together and test the resulting grouping according to those expected. The nature of the data specified that the statistical technique used to group the data should be binary squared Euclidean distance cluster analysis. The reasoning behind this choice was twofold. First, in order to arrive at a data set that could be clustered each participant's response set (the competitors and constructs they named) had to be coded. This was achieved by listing all the competitors and constructs named by the total number of managers and awarding each manager 1 or 0 if they used or did not use each competitor or construct in their elicited map. The coding strategy resulted in a binary data set, hence binary cluster analysis was used. Second, when the squared Euclidean distance measure was used as in a pilot comparison with the simple proximates measure the same cluster solutions were achieved. The standard Euclidean distance was therefore selected based on this cross-validation.

Three separate cluster analyses were carried out on the total group of 22 managers. The first cluster analysis grouped managers purely on the basis of competitors they named. The second cluster analysis grouped managers on the basis of the constructs they used. The final clustering added an element of further analysis to the data. In this final cluster analysis the total number of constructs used by the managers was categorized according to their position on a Strategic Issues Continuum developed during the research. This continuum is shown in Figure 8.2 and categorized the constructs used by managers according to their focus. This ranged from a focus on the internal issues of the manufacturing organization through to those issues that were focused on the personal opinions of individual sales people.

The total number of constructs named was placed in the strategic issues continuum by two members of the research team. The inter-rater reliability, tested using Cohen's Kappa, was found to be acceptable (K = 0.75). The coded responses were then clustered.

Research results

The results will be reported in three sections pertaining to the cluster analyses of the competitors named by managers, the constructs used by managers and their position on the strategic issues continuum. The total number of competitors named collectively by all 22 managers was 35 (mean = 10.136, sd = 11.365). Each manager's response set of competitors was binary coded in terms of the total response set of all 22 managers. This data set was then grouped using binary squared Euclidean distance cluster analysis. By analysing large jumps in the agglomeration schedule and the dendogram, a taxonomy of respondents emerged as shown in Figure 8.3.

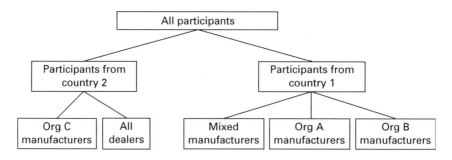

Figure 8.3   *Group hierarchy of managers according to the competitors named*

The group hierarchy shown in Figure 8.3 demonstrates clearly that the first and most predominant effect on the group formation was that of the national base of the participants. This evidence strongly supports H3, the nationality effect. The result implies that differences in national base of an organization's operations lead to greater diversity in managers' knowledge structures of their competitive environment. There was equivocal evidence in support of H1, the organizational effect. This result requires further investigation.

The total number of constructs named collectively by all 22 managers was 59 (mean = 9.4, sd = 9.09). Each manager's response set of constructs named was binary coded in terms of the total response set of all 22 managers. This data set was then grouped using binary squared Euclidean distance cluster analysis. By analysing large jumps in the agglomeration schedule and the dendogram, a taxonomy of respondents emerged as shown in Figure 8.4.

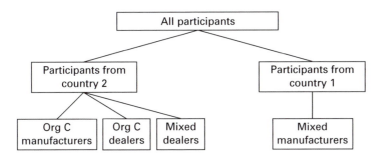

Figure 8.4   *Group hierarchy of managers according to the constructs named*

The hierarchy shown in Figure 8.5 clearly demonstrates support for H3, the nationality effect, as national base was the only basis upon which managers were grouped. There is also some weak and equivocal evidence of an organizational level effect H4; this also requires further investigation.

The total of 59 constructs named by all 22 managers was categorized according to their specific focus. These categories were developed into a continuum of strategic issues (see Figure 8.2). This data set was then grouped using binary squared Euclidean distance cluster analysis. By analysing large jumps in the agglomeration schedule and the dendogram, a taxonomy of respondents emerged as shown in Figure 8.5.

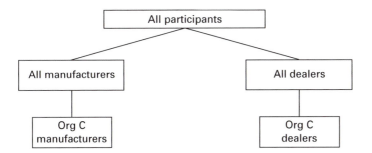

Figure 8.5   *Group hierarchy of managers according to the constructs named and their position on the strategic issues continuum*

The results from this final analysis indicated strong support for H4, the organizational level effect. The level status of managers was the first and only variable to group participants together based on the qualitative differences in the constructs used to describe their maps of competition with the industry. The constructs used by managers from retail dealership concentrated on the sales end of the continuum: Promotion, Sales, Specific Sales and Personal Issues. Managers from this level rarely concentrated their conversation on the strategic issues of the manufacturing organization. This situation also applied to the managers from the manufacturing level. The constructs they used were concentrated at the manufacturing end of the continuum: Internal, External, Product, Promotion Issues.

The evidence from the comparison of visual card sort maps suggests that there is indeed diversity between managers on the issue of their competitive environment. With very little commonality occurring between maps, this is displayed through the highly skewed mean and standard deviations of the competitors named and the constructs used by managers. However, the cluster analyses carried out indicated that there is a pull towards similarity from the variables of nationality and organizational level. Therefore both H3 and H4 are supported. The strongest effect to occur was that managers fell into national groups, that is those managers from the same national base used more similar competitors and constructs than those from different countries. A secondary effect that was strongly supported from the strategic issues continuum was that of organizational level H4. Those managers from the same organizational level were more likely to use constructs that fell in the same area on the strategic issues continuum than those participants from different levels. There was only weak evidence to support H1, the proposition that managers from the same organization will have similar knowledge structures of their competitive environment relative to managers from other organizations. Finally, there was no evidence to support H2, the functional position of the manager. Again this would indicate that managers who share the same functional position across the industry do not share more homogeneous knowledge structures of that industry's competitive environment.

Discussion

The results of this study indicate the following. First, within the sample of 22 managers from the international automotive industry, there is little evidence of industry, organization or even group level homogeneity in the knowledge structures that managers hold of their competitive environment. However, managers did share a certain level of similarity. The variables that were identified as inductive of this limited similarity were first nationality and second organizational level. There was little evidence to support an effect from the organization to which a manager belonged, and no evidence to suggest that managers in the same function had any tendency towards more similar mental models. An additional point to note is that it was possible to make a qualitative differentiation between a manager's organizational level in terms of constructs named. If the results of this study are applied to the research cited in the introductory section of this chapter, there are several statements of note to be made.

First, there is evidence to support the claims of the cognitive perspective of management studies that individuals simplify their competitive environment. Of a total of 35 competitors named the mean identified by each manager as a competitor was only 10.1 (mode = 5). This indicates that individual managers are considering only a specialized subsection of the total information available to them. Second, when considering the issue of the level to which managers' knowledge structures can be considered commonly held, the findings of this chapter support a high degree of idiosyncrasy and therefore subscribe to the individual level perspective. That is, managers failed to demonstrate sufficient homogeneity to group together at the organization level or even the functional level. This finding questions the propositions made by Porac et al. (1987, 1989), and Reger and Huff (1993) that managers' knowledge structures demonstrate commonality at the strategic group and organizational level. The finding that managers' knowledge structures are to a large extent idiosyncratic in nature concurs with the overall conclusions of Hodgkinson and Johnson (1994) and Daniels et al. (1994).

However, Hodgkinson and Johnson and Daniels et al. found evidence that managers from the same organization and functional position shared a tendency towards similarity. This chapter found only minimal evidence to support the organizational effect and no evidence to support the functional effect. This divergence is undoubtedly due to variance in analytic focus. The two earlier studies analysed both the content and structure of managers' knowledge whereas this chapter focused purely on the content of managers' knowledge. Much of the evidence of organizational and functional homogeneity in Hodgkinson and Johnson's work came from the structure and not the content of managers' knowledge. The final point of note in this section is that the two unique variables added to the chapter (nationality and organizational level) were found to have much the largest effect on the development of diversity in managers' knowledge structures. This would suggest that future work which assumes idiosyncrasy in the study of managers should take these variables into consideration during research design.

Theoretical implications of this work

Placing these findings back into the wider context not only of managerial cognition theory but also wider management theory raises two issues worthy of comment. First, future work on managerial cognition cannot blindly assume homogeneity in the knowledge structures held within the strategic decision-making unit of an organization. Second, if it is accepted that managers hold diverse knowledge structures of a particular organizational phenomena – in this case knowledge structures of the competitive environment – then how is this diversity mediated in order for the eventual consensus required by the decision-making process to be achieved? In order to answer this question researchers need to progress to another phase of analysis of the problematic that is managerial cognition. It would seem that researchers need to move from addressing questions that describe the nature of managerial cognition and take on the task of using cognitive metaphor forward to explain problems that exist within organization theory. The results of this study suggest that one such project would be to examine the relationship between idiosyncratic knowledge structures and decision-making behaviour in top management teams, thus answering the research question of how is diversity mediated (Walsh et al., 1988; Corner et al., 1994; Hughes et al., 1995).

A brief review of the relevant literature suggests that such diversity may be mediated through the filter of several organizational phenomena. These include: social cognition (Asch, 1951; Tversky and Kahneman, 1974; Brecker and Greenwald, 1986; Fiske and Taylor, 1991); group decision-making processes (Hall, 1987; Weldon and Weingart, 1993); power and political influence (French and Raven, 1959; Walsh et al., 1988; Sackman, 1991; Hughes et al., 1995); and personality (Hughes et al., 1995) . An investigation of the relationships between these phenomena and managerial cognition may lead to a fuller and more integrated model of strategy formulation and the strategic decision-making process.

Practical implications of this work

There are at least two immediate practical concerns that arise from the findings of this chapter. First, the finding that the national base of a manager influences managerial knowledge structures has important implications for multinational organizations which operate on the principle of strategy shared across nations. Managers based in different nations within the multinational organization may well have entirely different mental models of their major competitors. This implies that strategy developed with a particular competitive group in mind could be misdirected across nations to subsets of different competitors. Organizations wishing to apply global strategy would have to address specifically this issue as part of their strategy implementation processes. The second practical implication raised by this chapter is that managers from different levels of the organizational hierarchy cannot be assumed to be operating with the same model of competition. The possibility exists that strategy implementation at high levels in the parent organization will be unrecognizable when filtered to lower level for direct implementation.

Conclusions

The overall conclusions of this chapter can be summarized as follows:

1   Managers do operate under conditions of bounded rationality as suggested by the cognitive perspective. The study of management activity should consider this view in its methodological approach to research.
2   The knowledge structures held by managers of certain organizational phenomena cannot be assumed to be commonly held at any level above that of the individual. Future data concerning managerial cognition should be collected at this level.
3   Nationality and organizational level are variables that can account for at least some of this individual diversity. This finding has implications for both future research and practical management of multinational and multilevel organizations.
4   If individual level diversity of managers' knowledge structures is accepted, then research must concern itself with the question of how cognition is translated into action or are diverse cognitions mediated by other organizational phenomena? In order to answer such questions researchers need to address the interaction between cognition and behaviour in detail.

Critical issues and key phases of research design

As researchers it is critical that we be aware of and justify our fundamental assumptions as we begin the research design. The first of these deals with our epistemological view – what we take to be the nature of knowledge and reality. One stance is to assume there is an objective reality that can be measured, commented on and generalized. The alternative stance is to suggest that reality is in fact socially constructed. The acceptance of either of these standpoints will lead later research design to seek either broad generalizations to construct objective reality or to spend time prioritizing individual difference and building up a picture of themes that construct a social reality. We adopted the view that reality is socially constructed, that is, it is a function of individual perception. The notion of individual difference was therefore prioritized as a central issue in a review of the literature. An assumption was made of diversity rather than homogeneity in the knowledge structures of top management teams. The implication for the research design was to guide the selection of an appropriate elicitation technique that allowed for the demonstration of individual difference. Therefore it was decided to use the Visual Card Sort Technique (Daniels et al., 1994).

The key phases in the research design for this work were all at the early stages. There was a number of characteristics of research in the field of managerial cognition of which this particular design had to be aware and to anticipate the effect. First, the field of managerial cognition is very imprecise. There is little agreement concerning what we are studying, how we should be studying it and why, or what end product we are aiming for. The selection of this topic, and within that a research question, requires precision and clarity as to exactly what assumptions were made about the what, how and why. What at first glance may seem a narrow issue, competitor cognitions, is well grounded to theory development in the field as a whole. Second, when operationalizing the chosen research question it was important to be aware that sampling was going to be a problem. This work focused on top management teams and access was therefore an issue. Convenience sampling in this and many other studies in managerial cognition is the well-disguised norm. In addition, as senior and busy managers were the source of data, time constraints were important in the selection of interviewing and elicitation techniques. Lengthy techniques can and do lead quickly to uncooperative responses. Finally, this work was based on a small sample size and used qualitative analyses. This made it necessary to pay attention to rigour during both data collection and data reduction, and also to be interpretative in drawing conclusions. In this young field of research it is a real opportunity to use insightful interpretation during qualitative analysis to arrive at stimulating findings.

References

Asch, S.E. (1951) Effect of group pressure on the modification and distortion of judgment, in H. Guetzkow (ed.), *Group Leadership and Men*. Pittsburgh, PA: Carnegie Press.

Baddeley, A.D. and Hitch, G. (1974) Working memory, in G. Bower (ed.), *The Psychology of Learning and Motivation*, vol. 8. London: Academic Press. pp. 151–2.

Brecker, L.J. and Greenwald, A. (1986) Motivational facets of the self, in R. Sorentino and T. Higgins (eds), *Handbook of Motivation and Cognition*. New York: Guilford. pp 145–64.

Calori, R., Johnson, G. and Sarnin, P. (1992) French and British top managers' understanding of the structure and the dynamics of their industries: a cognitive analysis and comparison, *British Journal of Management*, 3: 61–78.

Child, J. (1972) Organization structure, environment and performance. The role of strategic choice, *Sociology*, 6: 1–22.

Corner, P.D., Kinicki, A.J. and Keats, B.W. (1994) Integrating organizational and individual information processing perspective on choice, *Organization Science*, 5 (3), August, 294–308.

Daniels, K., De Chernatony, L. and Johnson, G. (1994) Differences in the cognitive models of buyers and sellers, *British Journal of Management*, 5: S21–S30.

Daniels, K., De Chernatony, L. and Johnson, G. (1995) Validating a method for mapping managers' mental models of competition, *Human Relations*, 48 (9): 975–91.

Dearborn, D.C. and Simon, H.A. (1958) Selective perception: a note of departmental identification of executives, *Sociometry*, 21: 140–44.

Fiske, S.T. and Taylor, S.E. (1991) *Social Cognition*, 2nd edn. Maidenhead: McGraw Hill

French, J.R.P. and Raven, B.H. (1959) The bases of social power, in D. Cartwright (ed.), *Studies in Social Power*. Ann Arbour, MA: University of Michigan Press.

Gilhooly, K.J. (1990) Cognitive psychology and medical diagnosis, *Applied Cognitive Psychology*, 4: 261–72.

Gioia, D.A. (1986) Conclusion: the state of the art in organization social cognition. A personal view, in H.P. Sims and D.A. Gioia (eds), *The Thinking Organization: Dynamics of Organizational and Social Cognition*. San Francisco, CA: Jossey-Bass. pp. 336–56.

Hall, R.H. (1987) *Organizations. Structures, Processes and Outcomes*. Englewood Cliffs, NJ: Prentice-Hall.

Hodgkinson, G. and Johnson, G. (1994) Exploring the mental models of competitive strategists: the case for a processual approach, *Journal Of Management Studies*, 31: 4 July, 525–51.

Hofstede, G. (1989) *Cultures Consequences: International Differences in Work Related Issues*, abridged edition. London: Sage.

Huff, A.S. (1982) Industry influences on strategy reformulation, *Strategic Management Journal*, 3: 119–31.

Hughes, P., Daniels, K. and Johnson, G. (1995) The transition of individual to collective cognition: the strategic decision making process. Paper presented at EGOS, Istanbul.

Ireland, R.D., Hitt, M.A., Bettis, R.A. and de Porras, D.A. (1987) Strategy formulation processes: differences in perceptions of strength and weaknesses indicators and environmental uncertainty by managerial level, *Strategic Management Journal*, 8: 469–85.

Johnson, G. and Scholes, K. (1993) *Exploring Corporate Strategy*, 3rd edn. Englewood Cliffs, NJ: Prentice-Hall.

Kakabadse, A., McMahon, J.T. and Myers, A. (1994) Universalism and individualism: a cross cultural investigation with managerial prescriptions. Cranfield University School of Management Working Paper Series.

Kelly, G.A. (1955) *The Psychology of Personal Construct*, vols. 1 and 2. New York: W.W. Norton.

Kempton, W. (1978) Category grading and taxonomic relations: a mug is sort of a cup, *American Ethnologist*, 5: 44–65.

Leiberson, S. and O'Connor, J.F. (1972) Leadership and organizational performance. A study of large corporations, *American Sociological Review*, 37: 117–30.

Lurgio, A.J. and Carroll, J.S. (1985) Probation officers schemata of offenders: content development and impact on treatment decisions, *Journal of Personality and Social Psychology*, 48 (5): 1112–26.

Neisser, U. (1967) *Cognitive Psychology*. New York: Appelton Century Crofts.

Porac, J.F., Thomas, H. and Baden Fuller, C. (1989) Competitive groups as cognitive communities, *Journal of Management Studies*, July: 398–416.

Porac, J.F., Thomas, H. and Emme, B. (1987) Knowing the competition: the mental models of retailing strategists, in G. Johnson (ed.), *Strategy In Retailing*. Chichester: John Wiley.

Porter, M.E. (1980) *Competitive Strategy*. New York: Free Press.

Quinn, J.B. (1980) *Strategies for Change. Logical Incrementalism*. New York: Richard Irwin.

Reger, R.K. (1988) Competitive positioning in the Chicago banking market. Mapping the mind of a strategist. PhD thesis, University of Illinois.

Reger, R.K. and Huff, A.S. (1993) Strategic groups a cognitive perspective, *Strategic Management Journal*, 14: 103–24.

Sackman, S. (1991) *Cultural Knowledge in Organizations, Exploring the Collective Mind*. London: Sage.

Simon, H.A. (1957) *Models of Man*. New York: Wiley.

Trompenars, F. (1993) *Riding on the Waves of Culture*. London: Economist Books.

Tversky, A. and Kahneman, D. (1974) Judgment under uncertainty: heuristics and biases, *Science*, 185: 1124–31.

Walsh, J.P. (1995) Managerial and organizational cognition: notes from a trip down memory lane, *Organization Science*, 6 (3): 280–321.

Walsh, J.P., Henderson, C.A. and Deighton, J. (1988) Negotiated belief structures and decision performance: an empirical investigation, *Organizational Behavior and Human Decision Processes*, 42: 194–216.

Weick, K.E. (1979) Cognitive processes in organizations, in B. Staw (ed.), *Research in Organizational Behavior*, vol. 1. Greenwich, CT: JAI Press. pp. 41–74.

Weldon, E. and Weingart, L.R. (1993) Group goals and group performance, *British Journal of Social Psychology*, 32: 307–34.

9

THE DEVELOPMENT OF NATIONAL COLLECTIVE KNOWLEDGE IN MANAGEMENT

Roland Calori, Michael Lubatkin and Philippe Very

In the global competition, ethnocentrism (Perlmutter, 1969) and the lack of adaptation to foreign contexts (Kogut, 1991) hinder the international development of firms and the adoption of the transnational solution (Bartlett and Ghoshal, 1989). These authors point out the persistence of national administrative heritages, defined as sets of administrative practices embedded in the culture of the home country.

The administrative heritage shared by the firms of the same nation is a concrete manifestation of explicit and implicit collective knowledge. For instance, there is some empirical evidence of national administrative heritages in the ways French and British firms manage their enterprises. French firms exercise a high level of control whereas British firms follow a 'hands-off' approach (Granick, 1972; Horovitz, 1980; Calori et al., 1993). In this chapter we explain such differences through a historical institutional analysis. We argue that today's differences are rooted in different philosophies and systems of government (kingdoms, colonial empires) and different industrialization processes. Educational institutions (school, family and church) play a major role in the socialization of new generations. They transmit explicit and implicit knowledge directly (content) and indirectly (through their methods). Knowledge is collective when it is shared by the members of a given social group (a nation, profession, organization). Implicit knowledge is tacit, taken for granted and unconscious; explicit knowledge is conscious and communicated. Thus Spender (1994) distinguishes between 'science' (explicit collective knowledge) and 'culture' (implicit collective knowledge).

The concept of national administrative heritage is close to the concept of national culture in the workplace. Hofstede (1980, 1991) wrote about national culture in the workplace as a 'collective programming of the mind'. National culture is an abstract unobservable phenomenon, the members themselves may be unconscious of their preferences. However, national culture prescribes the bounds of acceptable practices. In turn, practices strengthen culture over time; they can be viewed as tangible surface representations of collective knowledge. Throughout the history of a social group successful administrative practices become institution-alized (Argyris and Schön, 1978) and they are passed through generations as a heritage. Indeed, they are learned by the new genera-tions within educational institutions (the family, the church, the school). Particularly the school is at the core of primary and early secondary socialization of individuals (Berger and Luckmann, 1967). Nation-states design educational systems and instil some national character into the programmes and methods. Consequently managers carry an often unconscious collective knowledge, a nationally bound heritage which slows down the learning process across borders during their professional career.

The national layer of mental programming is one among several other layers: ethnic, religious, gender, generation, social class, professional, orga-nizational. Hofstede (1980) focused on cross-national comparisons of conscious preferences in the workplace: 'how things ought to be'. He com-mented upon management practices that may be related to preferences but he did not observe the practices themselves. Moreover his question-naire surveys only scratched the surface of managerial cognitive structures. In the field of managerial and organizational cognition (MOC) a few studies provided international comparisons. Several compared Japanese and North American managers, their perceptions of events as threats or opportunities (Dutton and Jackson, 1987) or their thinking modes (Keegan, 1983). Calori et al. (1992) elicited differences between French and British managers' mental maps of their industries. The prob-lem with these studies is that they did not provide thorough explanations of the empirical differences found between national groups. Particularly the influence of nationally bound educational systems has been over-looked. In his latest book, Hofstede suggested some guidelines for further research: 'The sources of one's mental programs lie within the social envi-ronment in which one grew up and collected one's life experiences . . . it starts with the family . . . it continues within the neighborhood . . . at school . . . in youth groups . . . at the workplace, and in the living com-munity. . . . A customary term for such mental software is culture' (Hofstede, 1991: 4). As far as the 'national layer' of mental programming is concerned, in order to understand explicit and implicit collective knowl-edge, we argue that the comparative analysis of administrative practices complemented by a historical analysis of institutions is more adequate than (naively) asking individuals about their perceptions of their own preferences and knowledge. Our purpose is to raise managers' awareness of their own biases which often are unconscious. For this, a concrete evi-dence should be surfaced (the existence of specific administrative practices) and explanations should be provided (the influence of specific historical institutional factors).

In this chapter we adopt such a perspective and propose a framework to explain the persistence of nationally bound administrative heritages. The framework is based on Berger and Luckmann's theory of knowledge

(1967): background educational institutions transmit nationally bound collective knowledge from generation to generation. The framework is applied to explain the differences found between French and British integration practices following acquisitions (Calori et al., 1993).

Eliciting national administrative heritages in French and British firms

Three main research perspectives can be identified in the field of comparative management: comparing cultural preferences, comparing practices, and comparing institutional systems formed during the history of a nation. The first two perspectives aim at eliciting cultural differences, the third aims at explaining cultural differences. In the first perspective individuals are surveyed as to their preferences: 'how things ought to be in the workplace'. Scholars adopting this approach expect to identify the preferred values and norms of behaviour; they use questionnaires and generally come out with some sort of quantitative measurement (scores). Comparisons are made between social groups: nations, organizations, industries, professions. The research by Hofstede (1980) falls into this category, as do the European value systems study by Harding and Phillips (1986), and the work by Hampden et al. (1993). As far as comparisons between nations are concerned such studies elicit a few broad dimensions along which nations may differ. For instance, Hofstede (1980) empirically identified four dimensions:

- Power distance refers to the degree to which power differences are deemed acceptable by society.
- Uncertainty avoidance refers to the degree of discomfort that a society feels about ambiguity and risk.
- Masculinity, and its opposite femininity, refer to the degree to which a society values traditional masculine values such as competitiveness, assertiveness and ambition, as opposed to feminine values such as harmony and quality of life.
- Individualism, and its opposite, collectivism, refer to the degree to which a society emphasizes the role of the individual versus the role of the group.

Later on, thanks to Bond and his Chinese value survey (quoted in Hofstede, 1991), a fifth dimension was added: the time orientation in life, long-term versus short-term. Hofstede (1980) found that the French scored higher than the British on power distance and uncertainty avoidance. In high power distance societies individuals should expect more formal hierarchical controls and respect hierarchy; planning and controlling systems should be more centralized with top-down decision-making processes. In high uncertainty avoidance societies there should be a tendency towards more tightly managed control systems. Top managers will not feel secure about delegating the responsibilities for key business decisions. Consequently French firms should demonstrate higher levels of structural control and systems control than the British. The British were found to have higher needs for masculinity than the French (Hofstede, 1980); corroborating evidence was found in several empirical studies (Kluckhohn and Strodtbeck, 1961; Sirota and Greenwood, 1971; Very et al., 1993). Such an emphasis on performance may lead the British to tighter controls of individual and financial performance. Concerning individualism and its opposite collectivism the evidence is mixed. Hofstede found the British to have slightly higher needs for individualism, but other studies suggest the opposite. According to Laurent (1983) the French see organizations as hierarchies subject to power struggles, whereas the British see organizations as networks of relationships. According to Very et al. (1993) the French are less cooperative among themselves than the British. These contradictory results may come from the ambiguity of the concept of individualism. As far as 'time orientation' is concerned, Hofstede did not have the opportunity to compare the French and British. Another study (Very et al., 1993) showed that the French have a long-term perspective as compared to British short-termism. Such cultural analyses often lead to vague descriptions of a nation's cultural profile. There are several problems with this approach:

- Implicit collective knowledge may not be surfaced, as individuals may not be aware of it.
- The practical consequences of cultural differences are not systematically assessed.
- Even when cultural analyses capture real divergence, they often leave it unexplained.

In order to conclude about the existence of a nationally bound administrative heritage, research should analyse the consequences (practices) and the causes. It should identify the factors which have contributed to the formation and transmission of nationally bound collective knowledge in the field of administration. In doing so, research would help to predict future administrative action by managers and guide learning priorities.

Comparing practices

The comparison of management practices across nations represents a rich body of research, with useful implications for practitioners involved in international business. Some comparisons are focused, for instance, on negotiation behaviour (Harnett and Cummings, 1980) or on human resource management (Price Waterhouse–Cranfield, 1991). Some studies take a broader perspective and compare aspects of the manager's job (for instance, Barsoux and Lawrence, 1990) or organizational structures (for instance, Pugh et al., 1993).

A few studies have compared management in France and the UK. As far as organizational characteristics are concerned, Granick (1972) and Horovitz (1980) reached similar conclusions. French companies tended to be organized by functions whereas British companies were often organized by product–market profit centres and controlled their operations through financial procedures. The French tended to centralize decisions more than the British and to develop tighter relationships between the centre and the periphery. British corporations often adopted a holding form of organization.

During the 1980s organizational structures evolved under a globalization effect (Pugh et al., 1993; Mueller, 1994). For this reason it is important to refer to recent studies. Calori et al. (1993) surveyed top managers of French and British firms which were acquired by either British or French firms in the period 1987–9. Mergers and acquisitions are particularly relevant phenomena for studying administrative heritage associated with headquarters–subsidiary relations. International acquisitions provide opportunities to compare the practices of different national groups. As Grant (1988) noted, individuals may not be fully cognizant of their organization's administrative practices which have become a matter of automatic routine. By asking the managers of acquired firms to describe the administrative mechanisms exercised by the buying firm, one may have a more accurate view of such integration mechanisms.

The results of the study show that French buying firms exercise more control of strategy than their British counterparts, both in domestic and cross-national mergers. More precisely the French centralize decisions concerning goals, portfolios of businesses and competitive strategies (there is no significant difference between the two countries as far as decisions about financial and human resources are concerned). Also, more than their British counterparts, French companies transfer managers from the buying firm to the acquired firm. This practice is a way to control the organization both by taking over power and by socializing. The results of these empirical studies are consistent with each other: the French headquarters exercise high control over the organizational units, whereas the British are satisfied with a 'hands-off' style of management. These differences in management practices are consistent with the differences found when comparing preferences. The high control exercised by the French is consistent with the combination of high power distance and high uncertainty avoidance found by Hofstede (1980).

Our main objective is to explain such differences: their origins, the transmission of collective knowledge over time, and the reproduction of administrative practices which are concrete manifestations of knowledge. A historical institutional approach should highlight the mechanisms through which collective knowledge has been transmitted and national administrative recipes have been frozen.

Explaining national administrative heritages

The system of institutions of a given country forms the context in which firms develop. This context produces a 'societal effect' which influences companies' strategies and organizational practices (Sorge and Maurice, 1990; Sorge, 1991). Whitley (1992: 6) analyses 'business systems', 'configurations of hierarchy–market relations that become institutionalized', in terms of the nature of the firm, market organization and authoritative coordination and control systems. He distinguishes 'background social institutions' (such as the family, religious organizations and educational system) that structure general patterns of trust, cooperation, identity and subordination, from 'proximate institutions' (such as the political system, legal system, role of the state, financial system, labour market and training system) which directly influence firms and markets.

Many studies are limited to one period in the history of a country. For instance, Albert (1991) analysed the confrontation between 'Anglo-Saxon capitalism' and the 'Rhine model' during the 1970s and 1980s. He showed the influence of the two societal contexts on the management of firms. A few researchers take a historical approach. For example, Daalder (1974) argued that the strength of the Dutch democracy and the consensual management style in Dutch enterprises are based on centuries of practice at the level of townships. D'Iribarne (1989) took a historical perspective in order to explain the 'honor principle' which he had observed in a French firm. According to this view, the modern enterprises which emerged at the beginning of the nineteenth century were influenced by administrative practices developed in the government of states and local authorities. The historical analysis of entries in a new socio-economical paradigm also helps understanding of today's practices, successes and failures. For instance, Chandler (1990) showed that the relatively poor performance of British industrial firms during the second half of the twentieth century was partly explained by the relatively low level of investment during the second industrial revolution and, basically, by the governance system adopted by British firms during the first industrial revolution. A historical perspective helps to understand long-term effects and inertia. Due to recent institutional changes at the EEC level, some institutions may now look more and more similar across Europe. However, some differences may persist as they are ingrained in implicit collective knowledge that cannot be rubbed out in a few years.

We adopt a historical perspective since this is the only way to understand the transmission of heritages from one generation (of managers) to another (Kieser, 1994). We focus on background institutions that structure knowledge and general patterns of behaviour. Among background institutions, family structures have been shown to influence political ideologies in terms of authority and equality (Todd, 1985). France and the UK differ in their dominant family structures. However, several types of family structures coexist on the French territory (Todd, 1985). Religious institutions also contribute to shaping collective values and beliefs which influence administrative behaviour (Weber, 1964). France and the UK are dominated by different religious ethos (Protestant vs. Catholic), but national boundaries do not coincide perfectly with religious boundaries. For these reasons we will focus on the third background educational institution: school.

School has a particular double role in the 'fabric' of collective knowledge: the role of selecting and transmitting knowledge from one generation to another (good theories and practices), and the role of shaping thinking processes. In doing so, it fulfils its socialization function (Berger and Luckmann, 1967). Some knowledge is explicit and some is implicit. Information is processed directly by communicating the right knowledge and the right behaviour (normative acquisition) and indirectly by imprinting the desired behaviour (mimetism). Previous research (Locke, 1985) has shown the influence of educational institutions on management practices. Here we do not limit the argument to management education. Kindergarten, primary and secondary schools are more influential than business schools because they achieve primary and early secondary socialization (Berger and Luckmann, 1967). Schools are in the hands of states which take a domestic perspective in designing programmes and methods. As a consequence, national biases are maintained, and, as far as the management of firms is concerned, nationally bound administrative heritages are preserved. The general framework is summarized in Figure 9.1.

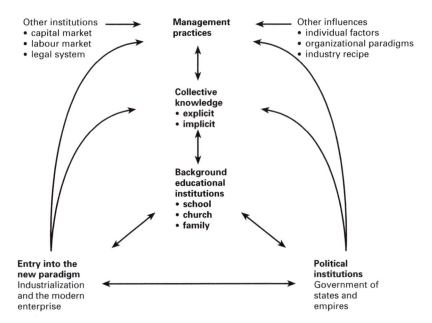

Figure 9.1   *The development of national collective knowledge in management*

In the next sections we use the model shown in Figure 9.1 to explain the differences between French and British management practices, for instance, the high control (centralization) in French firms versus low control ('hands-off' attitude) in British firms. We suggest that:

1   Managing an international company is analogous to pre-industrial activities such as governing a country. Previous research (D'Iribarne, 1989) suggested that the management of firms learned something from political institutions: the government of states, empires or local authorities.
2   The conditions in which the industrialization took place may also explain some of today's management practices (Chandler, 1990).
3   The educational system is the main vector for the transmission of explicit and implicit collective knowledge (Berger and Luckmann, 1967), including managerial knowledge (Locke, 1985).

Learning from the government of states and empires

Successful government systems become myths which are taught to the following generations and contribute to collective (explicit and implicit) knowledge. Philosophers and historians strengthen the myth which is transmitted through the educational system and permeates similar institutions and organizations over time. Most of the European kingdoms were governed according to absolutist principles during the sixteenth century, including England, during the reigns of Henry VIII, Elizabeth I and James I. However, the French seemed to be the most absolutists of all. According to Emperor Maximilien I (1493–1519), 'the king of France is the king of animals, he commands strict obedience, like man commands the animals'. French absolutism started during the reign of François I with his court in Chambord, Fontainebleau and the Louvre and continued under Henri II, Henri III and Henri IV (1553–1610). According to Elias (1975) it was stimulated by the threat of invasions such as the Hundred Years War against the British (1338–1453) and the war against the Spanish at the end of the sixteenth century. Indeed, given its relatively large territory and large penetrable land frontiers, France suffered from many invasions during its history. On the other hand, after the Norman invasion (1066), England could preserve its relatively small territory protected by the sea. In order to balance the centrifugal forces and reduce the threat from invasions, French sovereigns tried to increase their control over the territory and the nobility (Elias, 1975). But still the difference with the British monarchy was not significant at the beginning of the seventeenth century. The Stuarts claimed to be absolute kings by divine right. They were supported by theoreticians such as Thomas Hobbes (1651) who argued that the people can secure peace only by delegating their powers to a sovereign who then enforces order by fear and strength if necessary. The divergence between French and British government principles increased in the second half of the seventeenth century.

During the Thirty Years War between the Bourbons and the Habsburg, Louis XIII strengthened his authority over the provinces. Starvation and taxes led to a popular uprising, the Fronde, which ended in complete chaos and created a need for stability. From the chaos emerged the 'Sun King', Louis XIV, whose reign was the most successful in French history. Between 1661 and 1715 France dominated Europe on the battlefields and in the arts. During 'Le Grand Siècle' the French enjoyed relative peace and wealth (Duby, 1987). The absolutism of Louis XIV and the interventionist economic policy of his minister Colbert strengthened the French tendency toward centralization. The king had absolute authority; he was assisted by several councils but he did not need a prime minister. Louis XIV developed the court and attracted nobles to Versailles. He created a Catholic Gallican Church independent from the Pope and legislated through edicts. In each province an 'intendant' represented the central authority and new provinces (Alsace, Artois, Roussillon) were placed under their authority. The new 'Contrôleur Général des Finances', Colbert (1661), developed a mercantilist policy: more state intervention encouraging production and exports and raising of import custom rates. The state started to get involved in industry, particularly the sector of luxury products, through the 'manufactures du roi' (state owned) and the 'manufactures royales' (both privately and state owned). The French government was also directly involved in the creation of the colonial companies in the West and East Indies, in Senegal and Guinea (in contrast, the Dutch and the British colonial companies were private). Under Louis XIV an effective centralized administration was established and its principles and several of its institutions were maintained throughout the turbulent centuries to follow.

The National Assembly deprived Louis XVI of his sovereignty in July 1789 and the 'Déclaration des Droits de l'Homme et du Citoyen' was promulgated in August. However the egalitarian ideology of the Jacobins went hand in hand with centralization. The 'Comité de Salut Public' and the 'Comité de Sûreté Générale' held the executive power and the government was a collective dictatorship at war with its enemies. Centralization was further developed under Napoléon I. The parliament was overshadowed, a 'Conseil d'Etat' was established (similar to the king's council), the central and local bureaucracy were increased and powerful 'préfets' were named in the 'départements' in order to manage local affairs and represent the Emperor (Duby, 1987). More recent signs of centralization were shown during the 'Trente Glorieuses' (1945–75). Nationalization and state economic planning were achieved during this period, particularly under the leadership of Général de Gaulle who personified the 'régime présidentiel', in which the French 'Président de la République' dominates parliament. A law on decentralization was voted in 1982, giving a little more power to local authorities but, at the beginning of the 1980s, the French government style was still characterized by high central control, both political and economic.

The divergence between the French and British government systems increased in the second half of the seventeenth century but the basic principles of the English monarchy were established long before. In June 1215, at Runnymede, King John was compelled to sign the Magna Carta, which confirmed the rights of the Lords, the Church and the freemen of England. Article 61 even granted subjects the right to revolt against the King in case he should not abide by his promise. The Magna Carta was to become a myth, the symbol of English liberties, the foundation of a parliamentary monarchy, with a sovereign under control of parliament (Halimi, 1994). Wales was annexed in 1282 and Scotland was invaded in 1296. When Henry VII ascended the throne he strove to re-establish the authority of the crown: the Star Chamber (a sort of supreme court) was established in 1487. After a period of relative harmony under Elizabeth I, relations between king and parliament again deteriorated as the early Stuarts adopted an authoritarian policy. The revolution led by Cromwell and the parliament began in 1642. In 1648 Charles I was sentenced to death and Cromwell became the Lord Protector of the Commonwealth of England, Scotland and Ireland. He was helped by a council and a parliament elected by property owners. After his death, parliament proclaimed the restoration of Charles II's rights to the throne (1660), but with the restored monarchy under its control. The King accepted the Habeas Corpus Act, a charter of the inviolable rights of his subjects (1679). His successor, James II, dissolved parliament in 1687 and provoked the Glorious Revolution. After the Glorious Revolution (1688), William of Orange was compelled to accept the Bill of Rights (1689) which asserted the liberties of the English people and established a constitutional monarchy with a strict control of parliament (mainly the House of Commons) over the sovereign. These pillars of the English system were discussed by John Locke in his *Treatises of Civil Government* (1690), explaining the theories of natural rights, the social contract, constitutional government and the division of powers (Oakland, 1989). Compared to France, the British government system was less centralized, considering the relative power of the parliament (which indirectly represented local communities). Also the late integration of Scotland and Ireland preserved some regional autonomy, whereas the new French provinces were assimilated within a more homogeneous system (although ethnically they were very heterogeneous).

Several arguments have been put forward to explain the low control exercised by British governments as compared to the high control exercised by the French. We have already mentioned the threat of invasions, higher in France than in the UK. High control also developed in order to balance ethnic diversity resulting from high rates of immigration to France as compared to the UK, particularly during the period 1850 to 1945 (Noiriel, 1992). A third explanation should be pointed out: the probable influence of the dominant religion in each country. The Catholic Church is based on a hierarchy with the infallible Pope at the top, whereas the Protestant Church gives more importance and responsibility to the individual (Weber, 1964). Interestingly, periods of absolutism in England corresponded to sovereigns having sympathies for the Catholic religion: the Stuarts, James II. Also several French Catholic governments demonstrated little tolerance to alternative religious ideologies (for example, the Massacre of St Bartholomew and the Revocation of the Edict of Nantes). Moreover religious institutions had a direct influence on education; schools were in the hands of the Catholic Church in France and in the hands of the Protestant Anglican Church in the UK for centuries.

Finally, family structures may have influenced the political ideologies and institutions (Todd, 1985). Several types of family structures coexisted in France: the 'egalitarian nuclear family', the 'exogamous community family', and the 'authoritarian family', whereas the 'absolute nuclear family' dominated the UK (Todd, 1985). Family relations in France were favourable to authoritarian and egalitarian modes of government. The same patterns of control can be found in the French and British colonial empires. The administrative recipes learned in the home country were extended to the colonies during the eighteenth century.

The French executive power generally centralized decisions by means of decrees and edicts, in the old colonies (Antilles, La Réunion, Saint Pierre et Miquelon) as well as in the new colonies (Algeria, Madagascar, Côte d'Ivoire, Gabon, Dahomey, Tahiti, New Caledonia, and Indo-China). The French parliament did not make legislation before 1870. Even in the 'protectorates' (Tunisia and Morocco) the French were tempted to control the local affairs by naming influential top civil servants. The Brazzaville conference held in 1944 started with this principle: 'We refuse, even in the far future, the idea of self-government in the French colonies.'

After the loss of the North American colony (1777) the British tended to decentralize the administration of their populating colonies: Australia, Canada and South Africa. The presence of strong European populations in two of these countries (the French in Canada and the Boers in South Africa) forced them to respect some local autonomy. These countries became white dominions at the end of the nineteenth century and, with the UK, formed the Commonwealth in 1926: 'a club of white nations'. In their other colonies (West Indies, India, Africa and the Far East) the British exercised more control but, in general, they adopted the principles of 'local self-government' and 'indirect rule'. British governors were assisted by legislative and executive local councils. The native princes and authorities were involved in the local administration (as long as they acknowledged the British system). According to the system of indirect rule the British authority exercised control a posteriori (Walker, 1943; Barker, 1944). In India, local unions and political forces (the Indian National Congress) were accepted earlier than in any French colony. The British colonial legislation respected the home country principles whereas the French home country legislation was adapted for the colonies. This subtle difference shows the French policy of 'assimilation' and the British policy of 'association' (Guillaume, 1994). Finally, in the twentieth century France only kept

control over some small territories which were assimilated as 'départements' and 'Territoires d'Outre Mer'. British colonies became independent
and joined the Commonwealth as freely associated members. The French
and British colonial experiences institutionalized different administrative
practices in managing foreign activities: the French high control and the
British 'hands-off' attitude.

Industrialization and the modern enterprise

The modern enterprise emerged at the end of the eighteenth century. The
UK led the first industrial revolution in textiles, food, and steel. The high
productivity of the agricultural sector (since the policy of enclosures), the
technological skills and extensive British colonial empire contributed to
this early leadership. Given their dominant position, the British implemented a liberal economic policy. The type of industries and the nature of
the competition at the time gave birth to a form of 'personal capitalism'
and later on to loose federations of firms as a result of acquisition strategies
(Chandler, 1990). The industrialization of France was much slower. The
French did not perform well in the first and second industrial revolutions.
The industrialization of France took off after World War II, during the
'Trente Glorieuses' (thirty years of high growth). Late industrialization
required more state intervention (as in the case of Italy), in order to protect
domestic production in its early years and to support development. The
concentration of firms came late and required the formation of industrial
groups (Asselain, 1984).

In *The Wealth of Nations* Adam Smith questioned mercantilist theories
and was convinced that free trade would be beneficial to consumers and
producers and lead to a specialization of countries (which was a condition
for peace). The Manchester School of Economists took up and developed
these arguments in the early decades of the nineteenth century. The leading British economy had by far the highest share of world trade. In 1842 the
UK began reducing custom duties on imports, including agricultural products. Robert Peel repealed the Corn Laws in 1846 and the Navigation Acts
in 1849. The industrial revolution went hand in hand with liberalism. By
1850 agriculture's share of the GNP had reduced to 20 per cent and the
political influence of the traditionally protectionist agricultural sector had
dramatically decreased. France had a protectionist policy during the eighteenth century (with the exception of the 1861–80 period of the free trade
agreement between France and the UK). As a consequence of the great economic depression in France, a protectionist coalition led by Meline won the
1890 elections and was strongly supported by the rural population
(Braudel, 1986).

Until the 1950s protectionism became the rule. The weaknesses of French
industry (except in luxury products, automobiles and aluminium) and the
importance of the rural population (which still represented 48 per cent of

the total in 1936) fostered this attitude toward foreign competition. Late industrialization generally requires some form of state intervention (Asselain, 1984). There have been multiple signs of the involvement of the French state in the economy: the organization of the 'expositions universelles'; the creation of the 'Office National du Commerce Extérieur' (1898); the role of the state in railways since 1840 and with the Freycinet plan (1880); the attitude toward cartels in the 1920s; nationalization under the 'Front Populaire' (1936); nationalization between 1944 and 1948, the original French system of state 'planification' set up in 1946, 'l'économie dirigée', and the organization of industrial concentration (for instance, in electronics, 1967, and aeronautics, 1971). After World War II some nationalization also occurred in the UK, but in the area of industrial policy the philosophy of 'laisser-faire' dominated (with the exception of the late 1960s and early 1970s) and reached its apex during the 1980s with the idea of a minimalist state (Lane, 1992). In France state intervention institutionalized high control in business. State-owned firms were managed according to the principles of government already described. When civil servants were appointed to senior management positions in state-owned companies, a French system known as 'pantouflage' (Barsoux and Lawrence, 1990), they carried their administrative science with them. The late industrialization of France and state intervention influenced the process of concentration. With some exceptions (chemicals and car manufacturing), the concentration of the French industry took place after World War II, under the pressure of European competition within the EEC. Several mergers were arranged by the state which sometimes organized monopolies. Industrial consolidation and new investments had to be achieved in order to benefit from scale economies and to catch up with foreign competition.

After being leaders in the first industrial revolution, British entrepreneurs continued to commit themselves to 'personal capitalism' (Chandler, 1990), whereas Germany and the USA led the second industrial revolution with a new form of 'managerial capitalism' based on high investments. The first wave of mergers and acquisitions took place in the late 1880s and early 1900s. British owner-managers preferred to form loose federations of small firms, each legally controlling its small personally managed operating subsidiaries. The industries in which mergers took place (textiles, food, cement) offered little potential for rationalization and economies of scale. The logic was more to control price and output than to reap scale economies. In this context the federal form was adequate and little coordination or consolidation was implemented in British holdings. Chandler (1990) argues that 'the British style through mergers and acquisitions' started to create problems when the context changed in the twentieth century and required consolidation, high investments, research and development efforts, and professional managers. During the second wave of capital concentration in the 1960s, mergers and acquisitions were more frequently followed by structural modernization. However, the loose holding company structure persisted in many of the large British corporations

(Hannah, 1976). In summary, the UK and France differed in the way in which they entered the new paradigm of the modern enterprise. The British 'personal capitalism' maintained low control from the top management, whereas the French 'dirigisme' (joint action of the state and private entrepreneurs) established high levels of control. Also, these respective administrative recipes were consistent with the principles of government established long before. The successive generations were linked by the educational system.

Educational systems create nationally bound collective knowledge

The frontiers between the family, the church and the school were not clear at the time when the family and/or the church handled education (until the beginning of the nineteenth century). The Catholic Church passed on the Catholic ethos and the Protestant Church passed on the Protestant ethos. The British 'absolute nuclear family' emphasized freedom and competition, whereas the French families taught the respect of authority and the sense of community to their children (Todd, 1985). When independent mass education emerged and developed, the school progressively became the main source of collective knowledge. A comparative study of the French and the British educational systems shows that contents and methods are different. At the end of the twentieth century school history programmes remain very ethnocentric, both in the proportion of time dedicated to the history of the nation and in the emphasis put on the glorious eras of the home country (for instance, the Grand Siècle, the 1789 Revolution and the Empire in France as compared to Magna Carta, the Glorious Revolution and the Constitutional Monarchy in the UK). History syllabuses communicate strong symbols in the early education of children. School programmes in literature and philosophy are also strongly biased towards national authors and the dominant philosophies of science: for instance, René Descartes and Jean-Jacques Rousseau in France as compared to Francis Bacon and John Locke in the UK. Descartes wanted to find the metaphysical foundations of the effectiveness of reason. He applied the rationality of mathematics to all the phenomena in the universe (Descartes, *Le Discours de la Méthode*, 1637). On the British side, Bacon argued that experimentation is the only way to discover the secrets of nature and a necessary step in theory building (Bacon, *Novum Organum*, 1620). Locke emphasized the role of sensation in understanding the world (Locke, *An Essay Concerning Human Understanding*, 1689) and defended the status of experimental empiricism against rationalism.

This is of course a simplified comparison which overlooks several authors who converged during the Enlightenment and after. However it shows the French preference for deductive thinking (abstraction, theory building) and the British preference for inductive thinking (intuition, pragmatism, learning by doing). 'L'Ecole Républicaine' (founded in the 1880s) based its course content on the dominant positivist philosophy of the end of the nineteenth century, adopting the hierarchy of knowledge established by Auguste Comte: theory at the top, practice at the bottom (Comte, *Cours de Philosophie Positive*, 1850). A simple comparison between British and French textbooks shows that the French developed deductive thinking whereas the British developed inductive thinking (OCDE, 1986). Both French and British education systems gave a priority to 'general education' over professional education (a major difference with the German system), but the French gave priority to mathematics and hard sciences whereas the British gave priority to humanities and the training of character, an ideal inherited from Victorian times. The French education system showed a tendency to dominate and control nature and events, whereas the British system showed a tendency to shape critical judgement and develop flexibility. French and British education methods also differ. Typically in a French school the teacher begins with the presentation of a model, then application to a concrete case and debate follows. In British schools the teachers often prefer to begin with issues, debates and eventually come to some model afterwards. The French approach is analytical and rationalistic: all variables should be controlled before a solution is constructed. The British approach is more action oriented and intuitive (Weinshall, 1978; Revans, 1980). The relationships between teachers and pupils also shape and reflect two different attitudes towards authority and control: the frequent use of 'tutoring' in the UK as opposed to the preference for 'lecturing' in France (Weinshall, 1971; Jallade, 1991). Differences start in the kindergarten and primary school which achieve the 'primary socialization' of individuals. Differences are still marked in the curriculum of secondary schools and in most institutions of higher education which achieve the 'secondary socialization' of citizens.

Educational institutions were developed in harmony with other national institutions. Napoléon Bonaparte wanted to take education out of the hands of the Church. He created the 'lycées' (secondary schools) and the French University was founded in 1806 (after the 'Grandes Ecoles' of engineering) in order to foster national unity. 'L'Ecole Républicaine' aimed at strengthening patriotism based on an egalitarian ideology. The whole French educational system (including the private sector) was centralized under the 'Ministère de l'Education Nationale'. The persistence of personal capitalism in the UK went together with distrust and indifference in the relationships between the university and the business world (25 per cent of British managers have a university degree, against 60 per cent of French managers). The French Grandes Ecoles provided the elite of civil servants needed in state-owned companies. They communicated the principles of 'administration générale' established by the French pioneer Henri Fayol (1918): the virtues of planning and control. There are signs of a recent and slow convergence between the two educational systems, but diversity still remains (Dufour, 1994). Moreover, the top managers who design today's organizational structures went to school before the globalizing twirl of the 1980s. It may be hard for them to question their administrative heritage.

Discussion and conclusion

In the field of managerial and organizational cognition research has paid a lot more attention to individual and small groups' explicit knowledge (conscious) than to collective implicit knowledge in large social groups such as organizations, nations. In other words, a psychological perspective has been preferred to a sociological approach, at least until recently. When dealing with collective implicit knowledge, research in managerial cognition gets closer to research on organizational culture and closer to anthropological, historical or institutional theories and methods.

In this chapter we tried to link the conscious preferences of a social group (about 'how things ought to be in the workplace') to their consequences (the actual practices consistent with the preferences) and to their causes (the transmission of collective knowledge through education). We constructed a framework explaining the development of nationally bound administrative knowledge. A historical institutional analysis proved to be useful in explaining today's practices and cognitive structures, particularly when several theories are combined: political history, the historical analysis of business systems 'à la Chandler', and the theory of socialization by Berger and Luckmann (1967). The application of this framework to a comparison of two national groups, the French and the British, showed the benefits we can draw from teaching comparative history and reflecting on our educational systems. The framework aims at explaining the creation and transmission of nationally bound administrative heritages, but we suggest that it may be transposed to study collective knowledge at the organizational level. By analogy, a research design should be comparative, identify specific management practices, try to find the roots of such practices in the history of the organization (glorious times and crises, entries into new paradigms: the creation of the organization and periods of transition), and analyse the content and the process of socialization of new members (education). Many firms and consultants work hard to surface organizational 'identities'. In this purpose, historical analysis can help to uncover tacit knowledge and can provide a dynamic perspective.

In spite of recent globalization trends, empirical studies still find evidence of national biases in the management of firms. The differences found between French and British firms – the high control exercised by French headquarters as compared to the hands-off attitude of British corporations – can be explained by the transmission of a nationally bound administrative heritage. The transmission is achieved by nationally bound educational systems which fulfil their socialization role. Kindergartens, primary and secondary schools are particularly influential as they contribute to the primary and early secondary socialization of citizens. The origins of national biases in the management of firms can be traced in the history of the country: the recipes learned in the government of states and empires and the administrative formulae adopted in the early phases of industrialization. The cases of France and the UK show that administrative recipes were formed during glorious times: the 'Grand Siècle' and the 'Trente Glorieuses' in France, the 'Glorious Revolution' and the world leadership of the UK during the first industrial revolution. These typically national experiences took place in different religious and philosophical contexts, which still impregnate today's educational institutions.

The imprint of primary and early secondary socialization at school is so strong that late secondary socialization, in business schools and on the job, hardly corrects the cognitive structure formed in childhood. Managers exposed to the teaching of global frameworks and international job experiences have to resolve the cognitive (and emotional) conflicts which may arise from discrepancies with their primary socialization. The transformation of the structures constructed in primary socialization ('alternation', according to Berger and Luckmann, 1967) is relatively rare. Individuals may not even be aware of their (national) biases; most of this collective knowledge is implicit and taken for granted. Thus, raising awareness of implicit collective knowledge is one of the first steps in the learning process. In order to raise awareness, the evidence of differences in practices should be provided first; then historical institutional explanations should be sought for and discussed. Management development programmes that follow such a process have an emancipatory effect. They help individuals to understand the relativity of knowledge and increase their tolerance of foreign biases. Indeed research in managerial cognition should pay more attention to the influence of basic education on implicit collective knowledge and to historical perspectives.

APPENDIX CRITICAL RESEARCH ISSUES IN THIS TYPE OF STUDY

This study, as well as others comparing managerial frames of references across nations, underlines the relativity of management theories and the limits of empirical studies performed in a single cultural context. Theories should be tested in different cultural settings before pretending to be universal (often by omission of their cultural bounds). The awareness of differences in managerial behaviour and cognition across nations is not new, but with a few exceptions it has been overlooked in previous Managerial and Organizational Cognition (MOC) research. One reason for this is the difficulty in conducting international research: travel expenses, language differences, cost of translations and ethnocentric biases of the researchers themselves. Such difficulties can be reduced by setting up an international research team, ideally one composed of members of the main nations (or cultures) under study. This principle is particularly important when institutional and historical analyses have to be conducted in two or more countries, in order to guarantee access to the relevant documentation.

The analysis of educational systems embraces several domains: education science (stricto sensu), sociology, anthropology and philosophy. A single individual (or a small research team) can hardly master all these disciplines. As a consequence it is crucial to rely on experts who can help in the selection and interpretation of previous work on the subject. Most universities and some business schools have a department of education that may provide data, but unfortunately international comparisons are seldom available. Some fundamental contributions help in the understanding of basic anthropological differences, for example, Weber's (1964) work on religious ethics and Todd's (1985) work on the influence of family structures on political ideologies. When one tries to understand the dominant philosophies in a given country (for instance, Hegelian dialectics in Germany) it is certainly more relevant to refer to several interpretations of the original work. In brief, eliciting and explaining institutional differences between nations and their impact on collective knowledge requires motivation and skill for an eclectic piece of research.

Historical analysis should be revitalized within organizational research: 'Structures of and behavior in present organizations reflect culture-specific historical developments. Differences between organizations in different cultures can only be explained if the historical dimension is included in the comparison' (Kieser, 1994). The historical analysis of national institutions and/or an organization requires several precautions in order to reduce biases. The selection bias is the most problematic; historical events and references are selected in order to prove the theory. It is probably always possible to select historical facts that fit any general model, but one can never be sure that the researcher is not leaving out important elements which contradict it. Several methods help to reduce selection biases:

● Rely on well-established references.
● Look for several sources of information and references and cross-check their consistency.
● Check for counter-factuals and inflexion points.

For instance, in the present study it was important to balance the references from French and British (or Anglo-Saxon) historians. It was also crucial to corroborate the main historical arguments and try to explain the facts and events which may contradict these arguments (for example, the 'Commune de Paris' may contradict the French tendency to centralize). Kieser (1994) suggests several other strategies in order to reduce the selection bias: compare historical cases with each other and with ideal types; maintain a constant dialogue with the historical data; adopt an inductive research strategy; accept the multiplicity of causes. In any case, historical analyses are extremely time-consuming and require a great deal of patience from the researcher.

In order to surface collective knowledge shared by the members of an organization and/or the people educated in a given nation, eclectic historical research designs are necessary. The methodological constraints of such methods have to be accepted. They provide new opportunities to learn for the researchers themselves and sometimes reveal the researchers' own biases.

References

Albert, M. (1991) *Capitalisme contre capitalisme*. Paris: Editions de Seuil.

Argyris, C. and Schön, D. (1978) *Organizational Learning*. Reading, MA: Addison Wesley.

Asselain, J.C. (1984) *Histoire économique de la France du XVIIIième siècle à nos jours*. Paris: Editions du Seuil.

Barker, E. (1944) *Ideas and Ideals of the British Empire*, in P. Guillaume (ed.), *Le Monde colonial XIXième–XXième siecle*. Paris: Armand Colin. pp. 118–79.

Barsoux, J.L. and Lawrence, P. (1990) *Management in France*. London: Cassell.

Bartlett, C.A. and Ghoshal, S. (1989) *Managing Across Borders: The Transnational Solution*. Boston: Harvard Business School Press.

Berger, P.L. and Luckmann, T. (1967) *The Social Construction of Reality, A Treatise in the Sociology of Knowledge*. London: Penguin.

Calori, R., Johnson, G. and Sarnin, P. (1992) French and British managers' understanding of the structure and the dynamics of their industries: a cognitive analysis and comparison, *British Journal of Management*, 3 (2): 61–78.

Calori, R., Lubatkin, M. and Very, P. (1993) Managing mergers across borders: a test of administrative heritage and administrative rigidity. Paper presented at the Academy of Management meeting, Atlanta, August.

Chandler, A.D. (1990) *Scale and Scope, The Dynamics of Industrial Capitalism*. Cambridge, MA: Belknap Press.

Daalder, H. (1974) On building consociational nations: the cases of the Netherlands and Switzerland, in K. McRae (ed.), *Consociational Democracy: Political Accommodation in Segmented Societies*. Toronto: McClelland and Stewart. pp. 107–24.

D'Iribarne, P. (1989) *La Logique de l'honneur, gestion des entreprises et traditions nationales*. Paris: Editions du Seuil.

Duby, G. (1987) *Histoire de la France de 1348 à 1852*. Paris: Larousse.

Dufour, B. (1994) Changes in management education and development: a European perspective, in R. Calori and P. de Woot (eds), *A European Management Model, Beyond Diversity*. London: Prentice Hall. pp. 236–57.

Dutton, J.E. and Jackson, S.E. (1987) Categorizing strategic issues: links to organizational action, *Academy of Management Review*, 12: 76–90.

Elias, N. (1975) *La Dynamique de l'Occident*. Paris: Calmann Levy.

Granick, D. (1972) *Managerial Comparisons of Four Developed Countries*. Cambridge, MA: MIT Press.

Grant, R. (1988) On dominant logic, relatedness, and the link between diversity and performance, *Strategic Management Journal*, 9: 639–42.

Guillaume, P. (1994) *Le Monde colonial XIXième–XXième siècle*. Paris: Armand Colin.

Halimi, S. (1994) *La Grande Bretagne, histoire et civilisation*. Nancy: Presses Universitaires de Nancy.

Hampden Turner, C. and Trompenaars, F. (1993) *The Seven Cultures of Capitalism*. New York: Doubleday.

Hannah, L. (1976) *Management Strategy and Business Development*. London: Macmillan.

Harding, S. and Phillips, D. with Fogarty, M. (1986) *Contrasting Values in Western Europe*. London: Macmillan.

Harnett, D.L. and Cummings, L.L. (1980) *Bargaining Behavior: An International Study*. Houston, TX: Dame Publications.

Hofstede, G. (1980) *Culture's Consequences: International Differences in Work-related Values*. London: Sage.

Hofstede, G. (1991) *Cultures and Organizations, Software of the Mind*. Maidenhead: McGraw-Hill.

Horovitz, J.H. (1980) *Top Management Control in Europe*. London: Macmillan.

Jallade, J.P. (1991) L'Enseignement supérieur en Europe, *Notes et Etudes Documentaires*, 4929.

Keegan, W.J. (1983) Strategic market planning: the Japanese approach, *International Marketing Review*, 1: 5–15.

Kieser, A. (1994) Why organization theory needs historical analyses – and how this should be performed, *Organization Science*, 5 (4): 608–20.

Kluckhohn, F.R. and Strodtbeck, F.L. (1961) *Variations in Value Orientations*. New York: Row, Peterson.

Kogut, B. (1991) Country capabilities and the permeability of borders, *Strategic Management Journal*, 12 (special issue): 33–48.

Lane, C. (1992) European business systems: Britain and Germany compared, in R. Whitley (ed.), *European Business Systems*. London: Sage. pp. 64–97.

Laurent, A. (1983) The cultural diversity of western conceptions of management, *International Studies of Management and Organizations*, 13 (1–2): 75–96.

Lawrence, P. (1984) *Management in Action*. London: Routledge and Kegan Paul.

Locke, R. (1985) The relationship between higher educational and management cultures in Britain and West Germany: a comparative analysis of higher education from an historical perspective, in P. Joynt and M. Warner (eds), *Managing in Different Cultures*. Oslo: Universitets forlaget. pp. 96–127.

Mueller, F. (1994) Societal effect, organizational effect and globalization, *Organization Studies*, 15 (3): 407–28.

Noiriel, G. (1992) *Population, immigration et identité nationale en France XIXième–XXième siècle*. Paris: Hachette.

Oakland, J. (1989) *British Civilization*. London: Routledge.

OCDE (1986) Le système de formation, in *La Politique d'innovation en France*. Paris: Economica et OCDE.

Perlmutter, H. (1969) The tortuous evolution of the multinational corporation, *Columbia Journal of World Business*, 4: 9–18.

Price Waterhouse–Cranfield (1991) *The Price Waterhouse–Cranfield Project on International Strategic Human Resource Management Report*. Cranfield: Cranfield School of Management.

Pugh, D., Clark, T. and Mallory, G. (1993) Organizational structure and structural change in European manufacturing organizations: a preliminary report on a comparative study. Paper presented at the 7th British Academy of Management Conference, Milton Keynes, England, September.

Revans, R. (1980) *Action Learning*. London: Blond and Briggs.

Sirota, D. and Greenwood, M. (1971) Understanding your overseas workforce, *Harvard Business Review*, Jan–Feb: 53–60.

Sorge, A. (1991) Strategic fit and the societal effect: interpreting cross-national comparisons of technology, organization and human resources, *Organization Studies*, 12 (2): 161–90.

Sorge, A. and Maurice, M. (1990) The societal effect in strategies and competitiveness of machine tool manufacturers in France and West Germany, *International Journal of Human Resource Management*, 1–2: 141–72.

Spender, J.-C. (1994) Workplace knowledge: the individual and collective dimensions, *2nd International Workshop on Managerial and Organizational Cognition Proceedings*, Brussels, EIASM: 567–99.

Todd, E. (1985) *The Explanation of Ideology, Family Structures and Social Systems*. Oxford: Basil Blackwell.

Tribalat, M. (1991) Cent ans d'immigration, etrangers d'hier, français d'aujourd'hui. Apports démographiques, dynamique familiale et économique de l'immigration étrangère, INED, *Travaux et Documents*, 131, PUF.

Very, P., Calori, R. and Lubatkin, M. (1993) An investigation of national and organizational culture influences in recent European Mergers, in P. Shrivastava, A. Huff and J. Dutton (eds), *Advances in Strategic Management*. Greenwich: JAI Press. pp. 323–46.

Walker, E.A. (1943) *The British Empire; Its Structure and Spirit*, Oxford: Oxford University Press.

Weber, M. (1964) *L'Ethique protestante et l'esprit du capitalisme*. Paris: Plon.

Weinshall, T.D. (1971) Multinational business education-research methodology and attitude study, *Management International Review*, II (1): 70–87.

Whitley, R. (ed.) (1992) *European Business Systems, Firms and Markets in their National Contexts*. London: Sage.

10

CONDUCTING CAUSAL MAPPING RESEARCH: OPPORTUNITIES AND CHALLENGES

Mauri Laukkanen

Let us assume that we need to describe the subjective causal knowledge or belief systems of a set of organizational actors for some critical action domains and, further, that we have to compare them in order to locate the shared and non-shared belief elements. A number of management and organization cognition (MOC) studies could imply such a situation. For example, we might want to trace the evolution of the strategic thinking of a dominant coalition, or to locate and compare the core beliefs within a set of organizational units whose levels of performance differ. This chapter discusses some of the method-related problems involved in such cross-sectional or longitudinal MOC research tasks and, specifically, how they can be solved using comparative causal (cognitive) mapping (CCM). The techniques we discuss are largely content and theory free, applicable to different types or traditions of studies, not only the cognitively oriented. Accordingly, there is no need to advocate some specific social or cognitive theories or methodological stances. In addition, many researchers have explicit, sometimes tacit, a priori positions about such issues and would not really be interested in challenging or changing them. The chapter will address the following subtopics: research design and CM; raw data acquisition for CCM; computerized data processing for comparative causal mapping; achieving comparability; standardizing natural language; and analysis and presenting evidence in CCM.

Research design issues in causal mapping

Assessing causal mapping (CM) as a research method involves a number of issues. Perhaps the primary question is for what target phenomena and thus research problems causal mapping could be a feasible technique. In addition, there are concerns of a more pragmatic character. As to the target phenomena, there are at least three broad classes, which could be described and subsequently analysed using causal maps, rather the causal map metaphor:

1   A social or physical system, mechanism or process, some real domain.
2   A person's or group's knowledge or beliefs relative to such a system or about a real domain (1).
3   The patterns of natural communication or discourse, emanating from a set of actors, relative to a real system (1) or the actors' beliefs about it (2).

Of the above items, the first two are most typical in management and organization research. Therefore, we will emphasize them, especially the second (cognitive) category. As the list implies, we reject the notion that causal mapping should be necessarily linked with the psychological construct of cognitive maps. To be sure, causal maps have often been used to represent, overtly model or describe some inherently unobservable human cognitive contents. Causal maps do enable a manifest mode of description and analysis, which is sometimes more practical and powerful than, say, a text-based analysis of the same data/phenomenon. However, the field of application is broader than this.

First, CMs can model real causal systems in a way that helps to understand and analyse their underlying mechanisms and structures. When used to describe real-world systems, causal maps are sometimes called influence diagrams. Target phenomena on this type could range, for example, from how an electromechanical device works to how a social system like a business organization operates in a given strategic field. CMs can be used to present the structure of the target system and the critical interrelationships within it. They support a visual, mental imagery based simulation of the system's behaviour and also social communication about it. However, CMs are not good for modelling and tracking the actual dynamics of such systems or even people's knowledge about the dynamics in a formal, quantitatively useful sense. To do that we need to augment substantially the causal maps, for example, by using additional texts or a series of successive CMs. Preferably, dedicated software should be used that is capable of really simulating the system's dynamics. Such programs[1] are becoming increasingly affordable, probably mainly caused by the emergence of various process-oriented management practices such as 're-engineering'. When the target phenomenon is a real system, the data on which the respective causal maps are eventually based can be acquired following an engineering type of logic, that is, by trying to maximize valid information content while paying careful attention to the marginal value of each additional piece of information. Therefore, in these cases, the data can and probably should come from different, simultaneous sources such as textbooks, domain documents, observations and local experts. Also, testing and at least quasi-simulation of the models is recommended.

Second, causal maps can serve as a cognitive research technique. In this case, the logic is to use CMs for describing the single elements and patterns in which social actors like managers are found to think (know, believe, etc.) about some issue or phenomena. This is based on the characteristic of action-oriented knowledge being to a large extent causal and system oriented. For instance, to control or adapt to the strategic or operative situations they face, business managers, almost by definition, need to understand cognitively those phenomena, to explain and to predict their behaviour with adequate validity. Such capabilities, a key component in all professional domain knowledge, are a good example of the cognitive type of target phenomena. What are the phenomena to be represented or, rather, how they are conceptualized, will be influenced by the theoretical orientation of the researcher. Thus, some would indeed prefer the term cognitive maps, whereas others might conceptualize the mapped cognitive contents as mental models, ideology, belief systems or simply as operative knowledge.

Causal mapping is inherently neutral as far as the cognitive phenomena are concerned. However, the applicability and usefulness of causal mapping, idiosyncratic or comparative, is not, but varies depending on a number of factors. Perhaps the most important of them can be called coverage, that is, whether the causal map metaphor adequately corresponds to the key dimensions of the target phenomenon, for example, the research-relevant cognitive substance of the managers. This is a relative problem whose solution involves both sides of the equation. In particular, it is necessary to recognize what aspects and elements causal maps can and cannot represent relative to the target phenomenon. Studying any causal map shows that they cover, at least, the phenomenological beliefs (that 'A, B, etc. exist') and causal notions (that 'A leads to B, C is an outcome of B') within an interlinked, systemic pattern. For the technique it is not relevant if the subjective notions have the status of subjective beliefs of questionable validity or are regarded as established, corroborated facts or as something in between. The key is that we are dealing with a system of variables or individual phenomena which have or are assumed to have causal or some other connections such as time succession or hierarchical relations with each other as an interlinked system. Another implication is that applicable phenomena are cognitive substance and contents, not cognitive processing or styles, that is, structural elements, not dynamic.

It is possible to add information to the nodes and causal links of the basic causal map to specify further the minimalist description. The added data could be about types of links (causal, temporal, etc.), the direction of the causal assertions $(+/-)$, or some other qualifying information such as subjective certainty, triggering clauses, etc. Obviously, such additions expand the coverage relative to the real domain or the theoretic cognitive substance we want to represent. However, the benefits also incur trade-offs which the researcher must weigh carefully. A highly grained representation needs a more detailed data acquisition. This in turn affects the number of domains that can be covered, the number of managers and time requirements. When pondering these issues, it is important to observe that causal maps, even if augmented considerably, will still remain only partial and structurally oriented representations of the cognitive target phenomena. To use an analogue, a photograph is a pale replica of the original target, for example, a heavy traffic junction, yet its information content about the target can be most adequate, especially depending on previous knowledge. Thus, the answers will depend on the purpose and research at hand.

In addition to the relevance of the causal map metaphor itself, there are criteria which are linked with the research context and situation. It is obvious that if the task requires just the description of a single actor's causal thinking, perhaps about rather simple small domains, there is probably no point in using CM. Such tasks are probably better served by traditional text-based descriptions of the target, considering the different resource requirements. However, there is a number of research situations where causal mapping of cognitions is an efficient, even critical approach.

First, causal maps can be very valuable if the studied action domain or system of knowledge is extensive and it is specifically the subjective, causal element in the knowledge that is most research relevant. A good example of this is the well-documented Strategic Options Development Analysis (SODA) by Eden and his associates. In such cases, the borderline between studying cognitions or some real systems may naturally become quite fuzzy. Second, if there are several domains or issues and/or several persons or time points which must be analysed and compared, comparative causal mapping (CCM) may be an increasingly useful descriptive and analytic technique. The reason is that such research typically uses rich, interview-based data or multiple documentary sources. Both will generate a large data volume to process. In addition, the number of details and observation units soon grows beyond any researcher's capabilities of comparing them and observing patterns therein. In addition to their objectives and theoretical questions, study projects imply decisions, implicit or by conscious planning, about a number of other issues. In causal mapping studies (Figure 10.1), these include:

- What is the study's context, for example, a given industry or type of organization?
- What is the level and unit of analysis, for example, firms, manager group, organizational subunit or individual entrepreneur?
- What target systems or domains of action do we address, for example, corporate-level aggregate phenomena or some critical action processes in the firm set studied?
- What types of data should or can we use, for example, interview-elicited or archival data or observations?

The context and the units of analysis in the study, for example, the industry and the types of organizations or subjects studied, also define the action context of the subjects studied. Ideally, these would be decided by the research objectives and thus by the underlying theoretical broad thrust, paradigm base, and the more focused research interests and questions. There are, however, other pragmatic criteria which may be more relevant.

For example, access to data, available time and other resources are important design criteria. In CCM, the needs in this respect are mostly a function
of the cognitive (action) domains covered and of the number of managers
or other distinct raw data sources. Perhaps less acceptable yet real criteria
in some cases are constituted by paradigm pressure. For example, interesting problems in MOC studies are sometimes examined best in small
firms. Yet that may not be possible because it is considered 'not done' or, at
worst, because it is believed to imply some stigma. Thus, instead,
researchers may revert to corporate settings only to be subsequently ham-
pered by serious problems of data access or validity.

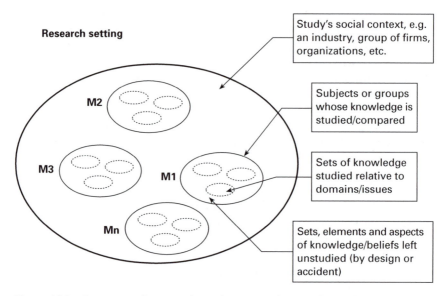

Figure 10.1   *Some research context issues in comparative causal mapping*
studies

   Whether modelling a real world phenomenon or representing people's
cognitive substance about them, there will be focal areas of study creating
a foreground and a background. In the case of real systems, such focal
areas may be called target systems or systems within the context. In the
case of representing cognitions, I would use the term domains of action,
which refers to substance areas within the context, that is, local phenomena or systems about which our subjects presumably have subjective
knowledge or beliefs. In both cases, their definition depends primarily on
the objectives and the theoretic base of the research. In cognitive studies,
action domains parallel an important feature of action-related knowledge,
that is, its local and domain-specific character (Lave, 1991; Hirschfeld
and Gelman, 1994). This implies that people's knowledge or beliefs are
about some finite areas in the situation and of real-world systems, with

large relatively blank areas. Typically, what people know or do not know will be governed by their real-life needs regulated by their profession and social and organizational position, in addition to the experiential and social learning processes to which they have been exposed during their lives. Expertise is an example.

It is a good idea to spend some time on the above issues, even if they seem too obvious or could be decided implicitly a priori. For example, this author may be inclined to think in pragmatic, reductionist terms. This means, among other things, that relative primacy is inherently given to individual actors as controllers and operators in and of action domains like the strategic management of a firm or a core process like customer service or new product development. Also, at the outset, I may be more optimistic about the chances of obtaining valid and useful data by direct elicitation such as interviewing, as opposed to researcher-based observation or indirect interpretation which, of course, would preclude an approach like causal mapping in the normal sense.

Data and data acquisition in causal mapping

In a technical sense, CM/CCM data are various types of documents or of locally elicited, natural communication such as interviews and experiment protocols. From a processing viewpoint, the initial form of the data is not very critical. For example, interviews are usually converted into a suitable documentary form, often by using interviewer notes or transcripts of tapes. Sometimes data are acquired by inducing subjects like managers to respond in writing in an experimental setting. Thus, in most cases we will usually be handling texts. In causal mapping studies there is no direct objective access to the neuro-physiological representations of the subjects' knowledge or thinking, irrespective of whether we call them cognitive or mental maps, rule systems, ideology or knowledge systems. The medium of natural language must serve as a proxy and provide the raw data of the unseen target phenomena. In such data we look for causal assertions that are of the general type A influences B or B follows from A. Here A and B indicate phenomena that the subjects discern in the domain. In most cases, other types of natural expressions in the data will be redundant. When eliciting local natural data, we can control the acquisition so that it produces a high yield of relevant causal material with a low level of noise. When documents are used, there is usually a corresponding coding process (Wrightson, 1976) which distils, as reliably as possible, the wanted kind of data of the background noise.

Documentary data

Historically, documents such as published corporate reports, CEO interviews, minutes of meetings or internal memos are an important data category in MOC studies. Typically these data are created for other objectives than the research project at hand. This can be problematic, especially if we compare cognitive contents of people, even in the special case where they can be shown to have produced the very documents. The reason is the low level of data control. The researcher cannot usually know the purposes of the communications or how and in which context they were born and, thus, how far they do coincide with the relevant cognitions of the actors. In many cases, secondary data may therefore be very questionable. There should at least exist strong converging evidence such as sets of other documentary data which were born in close linkage with the internal organizational processes. At the same time one should recognize the positive features of archival data.

First, as noted above, the research may not really be about cognitions at all. The target phenomenon can be some real system or even the discourse itself, for example, the causal contents and their changes in a series of documents like CEOs' letters to shareholders. Second, if used for data on managers' cognitions, it is sometimes defensible to assume links between the data and the underlying cognitions. With several converging observations, based on the former, our ability to say something about the latter will usually grow. Of course, we may also have some direct evidence of such links as, for example, in the case where we make our managers produce the documentary data in a controlled situation. Third, there may be simply a choice between doing less than ideal research or no research at all. Some important types of MOC research, especially longitudinal, could not be done without documentary data. The obvious reasons include factors like non-accessibility of key actors, living or long passed away, unobtrusiveness of data acquisition, types of research question and resource and data availability, even the personal inclinations of the researcher.

Locally elicited data

There are many studies, including probably some of the most important and innovative ones, where the data need to be elicited locally and specifically for the research project needs. This is typical of contexts which do not rely on or produce written communications such as top management groups, small firms or organizational subunits. It is also usual in comparative causal mapping studies where the data must validly cover the studied domains. Let us therefore assume that we must acquire data for comparative causal mapping of the thinking of several subjects such as managers with respect to a critical action domain. What should be observed?

Obviously, the data must cover the relevant domain thinking. This is the elementary dimension of validity, that is, measuring what we want and need to measure. In other words, our data should be relevant and ideally tap exactly those cognitive contents that the managers do use when thinking about or managing their action domains. We do not want beliefs that may be held but are not usually operative. Validity also requires that the elicited assertions of the respondents reflect their true beliefs or operant knowledge bases instead of espoused notions (Argyris, 1993). Furthermore, data should be satisfactory in terms of reliability. In CCM this refers to satisfactory consistency and stability over all managers during the data's acquisition. This is largely a question of careful, uniform probing techniques. Ideally, the data should, at least in principle, be replicable by researchers having similar resources. To sum up, high-quality data are reliable and authentic, sincere (Axelrod, 1976) and, moreover, pragmatically relevant, not marginal or espoused academic wisdom.

It is only commonsense to observe that acquiring good data is not easy and, disturbingly, we can seldom know how far we have come in any specific case. The difficulties are most salient in studies of very sophisticated high-level managers or with subjects where there is no consistent, good rapport. In most benevolent settings, any normal subject will not, for many good reasons, tell us all they believe in or think they know, even if they feel safe to do so. Some items will be shielded for various cultural or personal reasons. No one can recall at will everything that is stored in the memory, even if they want to or may be able to in typical operative situations. Finally, we cannot have unlimited access to our subjects and must therefore do less probing than might be optimal. More items could be added to the list. It is possible that sometimes the problem factors work at random or cancel each other out, especially over several domains and persons. Again, we cannot usually know if this is so and to what extent. The pragmatic conclusion is to do one's best to enhance data quality by acting on areas that are obviously critical and controllable. This starts with the choice of optimal subjects and the time and place of data acquisition. We should plan and prepare for the probing, for example, by knowing as much as possible about the situation and by testing our instruments in benevolent, predictable circumstances. In the field, we should increase the likelihood that our subjects do know what we want to tap and, second, that they feel relatively committed to produce as valid data as possible. Also, the interviewing should observe commonsense rules, which have been tested and are explained in most qualitative research guides.

Techniques in CCM interviewing

When eliciting data for comparative causal mapping, the first hurdle may be that there is not adequate a priori information about the studied context, domains and topics that are most critical, the terminology to use with the managers, etc. It may therefore be necessary to adopt a stagewise approach (Bougon et al., 1990; Laukkanen, 1992). Typically, a first round of sessions is used to acquire good grasp of the key domains and topics. Additional functions are to get background data and to build mutual trust and commitment, a rapport. The causal ideas of natural subjects can be elicited by a number of different techniques (Evans, 1988; Gordon, 1992). As discussed earlier, they will necessarily have in common that the subjects need to be induced to communicate about their thinking or memory contents. When interviewing for CCM data, we can, in addition, focus the probing process so that it produces predominantly only domain-related causal statements. A non-structured, free-flowing process would create lots of redundant data and, for CCM, probably unacceptably low uniformity and reliability. An interviewing approach that has been found to work efficiently is to use semi-structured probing around a set of anchor topics. These are central descriptive terms using domain-typical terminology or jargon, which refer to key phenomena within the studied action domains. To locate relevant anchor topics may require the preliminary interviewing session mentioned above in addition to normal theoretic and exploratory field work.

Figure 10.2 contains two excerpts from anchor-based interviews. The interviewer asks the managers to talk about the antecedents and outcomes of the focal anchor phenomenon as they see them. This will focus the discussion in a way which is meaningful for the managers. Also, it structures the elicitation process so that there will be satisfactory uniformity and thematic or domain coverage. It can also be argued that an anchor-oriented interviewing strategy will elicit richer and more valid data about the respective domains than a less structured approach. At the same time, however, one must guard against eliciting too much espoused, non-valid data. This can happen if the managers feel too much pressure to be productive. Sometimes a harmful competitive situation may emerge, especially between highly trained interviewers and interviewees who for some reason feel inferior. The interviewer's style is critical, but problems are also caused by unclear or lacking instructions. Depending on the number of domains to be covered, there is a corresponding number of subdiscussions. Obviously, this will be reflected in the length of interview. According to a very rough rule of thumb, ten anchor topics could take some one and a half to two hours, but this depends on factors like the inherent density of the domain, the S's expertise and vigilance, the interviewer's style, etc.

There are some practices which foster the production of satisfactory data. As stressed above, the subjects should be given uniform, perhaps example-based, instructions. Besides explaining the type of causal knowledge wanted, it seems necessary to stress obtaining relevant 'in-use' knowledge (Argyris, 1993). This includes things that may appear to the subjects too mundane, obvious or self-evident to be worth mentioning besides avoiding academic book wisdom that the S does not really use or believe in. Of course, such instructing is more or less what we really can do. During the interviews we do not instruct any more. Rather, we gently prod and listen approvingly to whatever the subjects see fit to tell us.

Second, the probing should not be a mechanistic exercise in linear

Transcript excerpts of anchor-based interviews with managers

Manager 1 (R1)

Probe 1: Could you next tell me about the outcomes of a good or weak **liquidity** position in a firm like yours.

Answer: Well, I think there are three things. First, it affects your **buying capacity**. Next, the **cash rebates** depend on that, i.e., whether you can deduct them or not. Finally, it seems to affect strongly the way our distributors feel about us, your **image** kind of, that is.

Second Probe: I see. Is there something else?

Answer: I can't think of any right now.

Probe 2: OK – if something comes to your mind, just tell me. Next, let's talk about on what factors liquidity – good or bad – is mostly dependent. How do you see that?

Answer: That is an important action area. My experience is that the key thing in this business is the level of **inventories**, which in turn depends on your **control systems** and **buying skills**, and of course on the level of **sales**. In an unforeseen tight place, you can patch up liquidity by **short-term credit** operations. In the long run, of course, it is mainly a question of maintaining good **profitability**, that is, a strong positive **cash flow**.

Manager 2 (R2)

Probe 1: as above

Answer: Hmm . . . It determines your **buying ability**. Also, I think it may influence what some distributors **think** of us.

Second Probe: as above

Answer: I guess not.

Probe 2: as above

Answer: I'd say the main things are **inventories** and **sales**. If there are cash problems, I try first to reduce stock by pushing sales. If that does not help, you go to your bank to borrow some **quick money** or you just try to talk a new time **arrangement** with someone of the affected distributors. That's more or less how I do it.

Standardizing with standard vocabulary terms

Standard vocabulary decisions: 'buying ability' = **buying capacity**; 'what they think of us' = **image**; 'short-term credit operations' and 'quick money' = **short-term credit**.

Figure 10.2 *Raw data for comparative cause maps: transcripts of interviews*

memory access. It is critical, for example, to provide the managers with multiple viewpoints when discussing anchor themes. This means, for example, asking them to consider high and low values of the anchor variable, its bad or good situations, their methods of controlling it, etc. instead of just asking and waiting for a linear list of the anchor's causes and effects. Why? Human memory does not work linearly, but uses an associative system of networks for memory search. Some of the elicited data will be produced ad hoc by problem-solving processes triggered by the interviewer's anchors. Therefore different types of probes or 'memory hooks', even if they are variants of the same anchor phenomenon, typically elicit different subjective causal ideas. Finally, we should maintain a high level of uniformity, consistency and relevance over all the interviews and be relatively uniform in allowing production time especially in CCM. The probing should flow naturally and, if possible, without the subjects feeling the need to be somehow unusually productive or eloquent. Often, they will voluntarily augment their causal assertions by giving grounds or providing longish script-like path descriptions of how one thing may lead to another. This adds to data and should normally be allowed. In fact, we could use such additional probes as uniform parts of the subdiscussions. However, they can pose a threat to the uniformity of elicitation, which is crucial in CCM. Therefore, one should not encourage autonomous production. Instead, the subjects need to be moved back to the main track unobtrusively.

To capture the discourse created by the process, the interviewer must use an appropriate technique. In most cases, keeping written notes will be adequate, assuming the researchers can also read their notes later. A simple form, where the anchor theme is located in the paper's centre with empty rows and columns of text boxes around it, has proved useful (Laukkanen, 1992). A tape recorder is recommended as a backup and checking device for the transcription phase.

Depending on the research case, causal maps may contain more information than the concepts and their causal links, such as the direction of the influence links $(+/-)$. Also this must be produced during the elicitation process simultaneously or using a separate phase. Probably the former would produce more valid data, whereas the latter may be more time saving but could imply possibly some non-valid mechanistic responses. However, as suggested above, all information must be task relevant rather than something dictated by tradition. For example, the common link information $(+/-)$ is often obvious and does not really differentiate among the managers in CCM. In this case, the time expended may have a better use. Sometimes rich details of the managers' causal ideas can be crucial, but this could extend far beyond the traditional directional information (Laukkanen, 1994b). This underlines commonsense research design: what are the questions and what do we need to answer them?

Data processing in CCM

Data processing in causal mapping varies depending on the specific approach used. There is a number of reports that describe techniques for producing idiosyncratic (individual or group composite) causal maps (for example, Axelrod, 1976; Eden, 1990; Cossette and Audet, 1992; Eden et al., 1992). Here we will address comparative causal mapping (CCM). Also in CCM there are alternatives in dealing with data. In simple cases, which deal with a single, limited domain of knowledge and with small numbers of managers, manual methods may be feasible and are perhaps the optimal approach (see Ford and Hegarty, 1984). On the other hand, there are many CCM studies where researchers must handle a considerable volume of natural data in the form of original documents or/and interview transcripts. These may carry very large numbers of relevant causal assertions, among varying amounts of largely redundant information. Also, there may be several persons and groups to compare for many action domains with an unpredictable number of concepts. All such elements make computerized techniques more and more necessary. Alternatively, computerized methods may enable researchers to tackle more demanding tasks or to extend the analysis further than would be possible with manual methods.

There are few specialized programs for causal mapping, if we exclude generic drawing software. An example of a computer technique that was designed specifically for natural data based CCM, CMAP2,[2] is a set of PC software tools which supports a number of typical CCM research tasks and phases (Figure 10.3). The raw data used in CMAP2 may be acquired by interviewing in the manner described above, but the data can be also document based, distilled data. Moreover, in CMAP2 the data do not have to comply to a definite a priori format such as a predefined or limited number of causal map nodes or type of raw data.

CMAP2 is based on the observation that causal maps can be decomposed into the constituent causal units, that is, concept-concept pairs, assumed to be causally (or otherwise) linked to each other. These units can then be processed by the computer as semi-independent data entities (table records) using sets of interlinked files which will hold each study project's natural terms, causal link information, standard term vocabulary, etc. To explain the operative logic of CMAP2, Figure 10.4 presents three informationally equivalent modes of representing the phenomenological and causal information of the interview transcripts in Figure 10.2. Thus, in addition to a textual form we have a traditional graphical map mode, a causal matrix and, finally, a data table form. Because the managers' (or other observation units) phenomenological (A, B) and causal expressions (A->B) will be available as data table records, we can also link them to other information about the owner/s (managers) of each unit (Figure 10.4c). The various technical aspects and phases of the program cannot be discussed in detail here (see Laukkanen, 1992, 1994c). Let us just note that

```
┌─────────────────────────────────────────────────────────────────┐
│                   ***   C M A P 2   v . 2 . 0 ß   ***             │
├─────────────────────────────────────────────────────────────────┤
│                                                                   │
│  NATURAL LANGUAGE UNIT Input … A    STANDARD TERM Input/Editor … B│
│                                                                   │
│  NLU-FILE Editor … C                NLU-TAGGING/S-TERM Editor … D  │
│                                                                   │
│  NATURAL CAUSAL UNIT Input … E      NCU-FILE Editor … F           │
│                                                                   │
│  SNT- and SCU-File Generator … G    FOCAL/DOMAIN SCU-Set-Analysis … H│
│                                                                   │
│  SNT-Base List/Analysis … I         LISTING Modules … L          │
│                                                                   │
│  PRINTING Modules … P               DBF/ASCII-TXT-file copy … T   │
│                                                                   │
│  PROJECT Manager … S                QUIT to System … X            │
│                                                                   │
│  ACTIVE Project Code … P1           CHOICE … □                    │
│                                                                   │
└─────────────────────────────────────────────────────────────────┘
```

Figure 10.3   *The main menu screen of CMAP2 v.2.0 β*

before data are input the first step is to transcribe them, that is, the causal discourse elements or relevant causal expressions found in documents, using dedicated data sheets (Laukkanen, 1992). This supports the data collection and possible distillation of the source, such as interviewing notes and/or tapes or documents. Importantly, doing so links the computer's databases with the input data elements and thus with the source. There will be an audit trail from the source to the final standardized concepts and causal units.

Besides modules for the input of raw data, that is, the natural language terms and causal assertions of the subjects, the program has tools for creating and inputting the standard language vocabulary (see below) necessary for achieving comparability over the managers and for coding the natural language expressions. There are also modules for editing all input data and for the generation of analysable databases. Finally, there are tools for CCM-oriented analysis and output, including the calculation of numerical measures for the distances between the map systems of individual subjects or clusters of subjects.

The present version of CMAP2 (v. 2.0) supports maximum 40 observation units. In addition, the researcher can use a virtual subject (S00) as, for example, a theoretical or an optimal base, against which the real managers are compared. Furthermore, the subjects can be grouped into five a priori defined Clusters (C1–C5). In CMAP2, a cluster is defined as a given set of subjects, one cluster accepting maximum 20 subjects. Any subject can be simultaneously a member in several clusters or in none. There is also a C0 cluster available for similar template purposes as the S00.

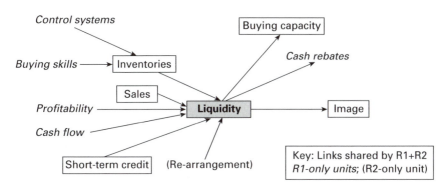

Figure 10.4   *(a) A graphical cause map*

Standard node terms	1.	2.	3.	4.	5.	6.	7.	8.	9.	10.	11.	Od.
1. control systems					1							1
2. buying skills					1							1
3. profitability								1				1
4. cash flow								1				1
5. inventories								1				1
6. sales								1				1
7. short-term credit								1				1
8. liquidity									1	1	1	3
9. buying capacity												0
10. cash rebates												0
11. image												0
Indegree (Id)	0	0	0	0	2	0	0	5	1	1	1	

Figure 10.4   *(b) Cause matrix of R1*

Respondent ownership/
non-ownership

Cause term	Effect term	TF	R1	R2
Control systems	Inventories	1	1	
Buying skills	Inventories	1	1	
Cash flow	Liquidity	1	1	
Inventories	Liquidity	2	1	1
Sales	Liquidity	2	1	1
Short-term credit	Liquidity	2	1	1
Re-arrangement	Liquidity	1		1
Liquidity	Buying capacity	2	1	1
Liquidity	Image	2	1	1
Liquidity	Cash rebates	1	1	

Standardized
causal units =
database records

Standard node
terms

Figure 10.4   *(c) Standard causal unit datatable*

Achieving comparability: standardizing natural language

As shown in Figure 10.2, people typically use different expressions, called natural language units (NLU) in CMAP2, when they talk or write about same referent phenomena. In causal mapping it is usually the phenomena, not the details of language or professional jargon in which we are interested. Therefore, to achieve comparability in the underlying meaning sense, we may have to translate the outwardly different but same denoting NLUs into a common meaning space. This is called standardizing in CMAP2. The primary, and in many CCM studies only, objective of standardizing is to remove the redundancy of the persons' natural language expressions. Synonymous natural terms, words, interpreted as having the same referent are coded as same denoting, that is, assigned to the same meaning category by giving them the respective standard term code tag. Basically, what is done is to adopt a new, more compact vocabulary system of common referents and core meanings into which the natural expressions and their underlying meanings will be mapped. CMAP2 uses a separate data table for the standard term vocabulary (STV). The techniques by which they are created can vary.

For instance, we might first create a rough, tentative STV system. This is done simply by browsing the raw data transcripts and writing down a first-pass list of broad categories of NLUs that are somehow meaningfully related (for example, refer to customers, financing, personnel). Thus, a preliminary ST could cover all NLUs that refer to a firm's accounting based performance. These terms/categories are then input to the STV file, using the respective program module, preferably before the input of NLUs is started. Possible errors of interpretation are not critical at this stage. When all NLUs have been input, including their respective tentative STV codes, the researcher can list or print the NLU table, sorted into the first-pass ST order. This produces a display of the contents (NLUs) of the tentative categories which is very helpful for a second-pass standardization, especially if there are hundreds or thousands of NLUs. This is not uncommon in CCM projects which involve many managers and domains of action. During the creation of a satisfactory STV and coding solution, there may have to be four or five successive iteration rounds where we produce from the larger categories of NLUs smaller, more homogeneous categories in terms of their common referent or core meaning. To facilitate this, we use a successive process of printouts, creation and input of new STs, replacement of the earlier ST coding of the NLUs and new listings, until the coding solution is considered satisfactory.

Obviously, standardizing is a critical phase in a CCM project. It requires much care and always takes some interpretative effort plus plain tenacious and diligent homework by the researchers. They must find out what are the terms and their synonyms and check the consistency and meaning validity of each ST/category. During the research process one's understanding of the context, language, expressions, jargon and the referent phenomena grows, preferably in a documented way. The resulting knowledge will be important in standardizing. In most CCM cases there are no serious problems because the standardizing aims at removing only the synonym-based expressive redundancy, keeping the STV essentially identical with the NLU level. Such standard terms are usually the most common or somehow most descriptive words used by the managers within the respective NLU sets. In addition, if the CCM project needs a highly interpreted ST vocabulary, it seems important that there is also a more basic or primary ST vocabulary, corresponding to the original, natural repository of the managers' referent base.

The standardizing process should use some validation method if there is a risk of misinterpretation and, especially, of producing non-valid findings as a result. Such a risk exists especially in ambiguous, jargon-type NLU expressions and in research contexts which are not a priori familiar or have not been properly preresearched. As to various validation options, the elementary action, of course, is to elicit experienced research colleagues' opinions. A more independent solution is to feed back the individual coding lists, that is, NLU printouts in ST order, to each subject for their comments. Another approach, especially with documentary source data, could be to employ a panel of context experts. They could help to create the STV and check the coding. All such methods could also be combined.

The impact of standardizing becomes visible when the raw data, that is, the input NLUs and the original causal link information (natural causal units, NCUs), are converted into a new set of data tables/files to be used in the actual comparative analysis. The conversion process can begin when both the NLU/NCU input and the standardization of NLUs have been done. The conversion is automatic in CMAP2. It generates a standard causal unit (SCU) table/file and a standard node term (SNT) table/file. The process can be repeated at will if a better solution is found or input errors are detected later. The conversion will, as is intuitively obvious, 'replace' the NLUs by the respective STs, as defined by the ST code given by the researcher. Likewise the NCUs that link a given pair of NLUs will collapse into an SCU. The original NLU and NCU raw data files are hereby not changed. They remain intact and the outcome of the process is the new standardized files. To support the actual comparison of the study's subjects and the defined clusters, the program will also mark, for each created SNT and SCU, their owner incidence. This means that the researchers and the program know exactly which subjects or clusters used them, who expressed the corresponding NLU or corresponding NCU. In addition to this, CMAP2 calculates the user numbers or occurrence frequencies (TF) of the SNTs and SCUs. It will also mark the core SNTs and SCUs, as defined by the researcher when setting the project parameters.

When using CMAP2, it is important to understand the collapsing and distilling effects of standardizing and the way it regulates the manifest, apparent level of sharedness over the subjects or clusters in each study.

These effects depend, *ceteris paribus*, on the coverage of the individual STs vis-à-vis the NLUs, on average. If broad categories (STs = NLU-groups) are used, more NLUs and thus also NCUs will collapse into single SNTs and SCUs. Therefore, wide categories will increase the apparent commonality by hiding and diminishing the subject- and cluster-distinctive features in the SNT and SCU data. Conversely, narrower categories of STs, closer to and more identical with the original NLUs, will reverse the collapsing and apparent sharedness outcomes because more of the original idiosyncrasy will now be left in the analysed standardized files. Because the computer does not mind redoing the conversions into standardized files, the researcher can also experiment with different (valid) solutions.

In a CCM study, besides addressing the synonym problem, we can also create new theoretic meaning and conceptual systems for mapping the NLUs (Laukkanen, 1994b). Technically, this may imply strong interpretation. This can be problematic in terms of validating the results, but it may also be the way to create important theoretic insights. In CMAP2 the researcher can use the same NLU/NCU base data for parallel projects, each having a different ST coding solution with specific implications and research objectives. The program supports several simultaneous projects, letting the researcher copy the NLU and NCU data between projects to save time and to preserve data integrity.

Standardizing and using common standard vocabularies seems annoying to some in the qualitative research community who regard people's natural expressions as something to be understood but not touched. To worry about validity is a good thing and must be observed, but to deny completely their feasibility and need would be unreasonable. For example, let us assume a case where the managers use different languages when responding. Few would object to adopting one language and translating the individual transcripts into that vocabulary base. This mapping is also standardizing. In qualitative method traditions such as discourse or content analysis, some kind of coding and researcher-based interpretation is customary. What is suggested here is not very different compared to those approaches.

Analysis and evidence in CM studies

Causal maps are devices for describing and analysing the target phenomena for findings that help answer the research questions. In addition, researchers face the task of presenting their results in a way which is plausible and effective in terms of communicating the message to the specific audience, besides being scientifically defensible. These involve some very difficult problems. If CM analysis is defined as what CM researchers usually seem to do, there are two overlapping categories of analytic work which might be called a map-oriented approach and a more context-oriented approach, respectively. In map-oriented analysis, the causal maps, using graphical or matrix formats or both, tend to be the focal point. The emphasis is on the information available in the causal map and its constituent structural elements. In real life, however, map-based analysis is seldom pursued in isolation. Typically, it is strongly implied that the causal maps represent some independent object of analysis such as a person's or social group's system of causal beliefs, ideology, etc. Because these refer usually to a real-world domain, there will be some contextual analysis, for example, addressing the issue of truth value or accuracy of the thinking. Furthermore, if the target phenomenon is a non-cognitive entity like a real-world mechanism of which the causal maps are a model, the analysis will be about that system.

Technically, a map-oriented analysis can involve several approaches (Axelrod, 1976; Eden et al., 1992). Thus, the individual causal map nodes and their linkages to each other could be studied. For example, the so-called indegrees and outdegrees[3] of the nodes could be calculated and used as measures of the respective concepts' key features like their centrality or relative weight within the target causal system. Also, the Od/Ids may indicate the nodes' type such as a goal (high Id, low Od) or a means type of variable (both Id and Od significant) or a contextual 'givens' type (low Id, significant Od). Furthermore, employing the matrix format, a common analysis is to examine the causal maps' causal links and especially the influence paths they are assumed to constitute.

Sometimes map-based path analysis may go too far when conclusions about the S's thinking and beliefs are formally deduced using the map link and path data. It should be obvious that causal maps, even if locally elicited and especially if based on archival secondary data, do not necessarily open up, by implication, any special new window to, for example, managers' minds or internal worlds beyond those observations and data that in fact were acquired. Especially the ontological assumptions and objectives of each study should be observed. Thus, if the target phenomenon is a real causal system or mechanism, even speculative path and simulation analyses are perfectly defensible so long as they stay within the system model built of valid data.

There are several kinds of especially cognitive research which would necessitate a context-oriented, substantive analysis. As an example, causal maps can, using some of the equivalent formats, first represent the managers' thinking or knowledge in studies which contrast or measure them against a theoretically meaningful comparison base. One such base could be, depending on the study, other managers or groups of managers in the studied set because they occupy interesting, different strategic or organizational positions and are stakeholders for each other (Laukkanen and Peltoniemi, 1995). Another potential comparative setting would be to use as the comparison base some template or standard pattern of causal thinking, for instance, a 'textbook' or a sophisticated expert level of thinking about the operative domain. As mentioned above, CMAP2 supports this type of analysis by letting the user define and enter the template data using the S00 facility (=C0) in the same way as other raw data are entered, and by calculating numerical index values for the eventual similarity or distance.

Finally, an important type of context-oriented CCM analysis is to contrast the persons' thinking or knowledge against the external context or situation of action and decision-making, including outcomes such as firm performance. This has been the implied design in some CM-based MOC studies (Stubbart and Ramaprasad, 1988; Fahey and Narayanan, 1989). Depending on the study and data, we might compare the causal maps of various individuals, construct group maps and compare them, or trace the changes in the mapped systems over time versus the strategic situational changes that have taken place.

The mechanics of analysis

Using computerized tools like CMAP2, the researcher has a number of options. Technically, we can generate sets of hierarchical causal unit and standard node term lists, using the base tables of standardized terms and causal units as sources, and locate individual or group node terms and causal units, using different combinatorial and cut-off threshold levels. These can define core causal patterns and node terms. Further, there are some quantitative measures available to support the comparative analysis. The underlying theory and research tasks determine what kinds of map systems and analyses are useful for findings.

To describe some examples of CCM techniques, let us first point out that relative numbers of natural terms and causal units calculated by managers can be a useful object of analysis instead of treating them as just raw data. They may serve, for example, as a rough, diluted measure of cognitive complexity at the natural discourse level. In comparative studies they may be useful as indicators of the more high-grained concept base of the managers and of the structure of the STV baskets over the subjects. A further area of analysis is the standardized causal map nodes in use. Assuming a valid primary level standardization, the nodes correspond to the operative referent base and thus mirror the cognitive grip of the managers (Laukkanen, 1994c), using the level of discourse defined by the standardization solution. In CMAP2, it is technically simple to compare the managers or their groups in this respect. If the ST vocabulary has been constructed using logical or theoretical groups of STVs, creating domain-related families of STVs will be illuminating.

A third area is the SCU base, which enables causal map oriented comparative analyses (Figure 10.5). In a typical CCM project, the full SCU system and database is too large to be analysed visually. In addition this would probably not be a valid representation of the subjects' thinking or knowledge base. Instead, it may be cognitively and technically more defensible to study the action-domain related areas of the mapped knowledge

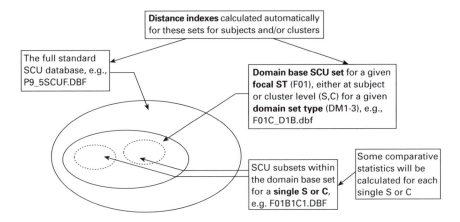

Figure 10.5   *Relationships between the SCU base, domain base files and a domain's S or C subsets*

instead of the whole SCU database. Again, in CMAP2 this is done by creating focal and domain SCU sets to represent the subjects' or the clusters' thinking about relevant key phenomena. Examples of such domains could be a firm's profitability, product development, market position or liquidity maintenance. CMAP2 is oriented towards this type of analysis, allowing the researcher to examine the substantive differences in domain-related causal thinking.

Although causal mapping is predominantly a qualitative research approach, quantitative measures can be useful especially in comparative cognitive analysis. For example, we can calculate distance indexes for the managers and Cs at the full SCU base and any domain SCU-set levels (Figure 10.5). Furthermore, the numbers of NLUs, NCUs, SNTs and SCUs per manager and the relative weight of core terms and core causal units within the domain-related S or C SCU sets can be counted. However, numerical measures should be used with care as bases of comparison in comparative causal mapping and especially as indicators of the degree of actual cognitive substance similarity or dissimilarity of managers. In each case, the origins of the actual comparison base as enabled by the elicited raw data and the role of standardization should be kept in mind.

Being a text-based program, CMAP2 uses lists of standard causal units instead of graphical maps, which correspond to the full base SCU file or, more typically, to some SCU subsets of that base, called domain SCU sets. Although graphical maps are not necessary nor always useful in comparative analysis, traditional graphical maps can be very important, especially in the final reporting stage. They can deliver a visual, holistic view of the domain-related thought patterns, showing the managers' and Cs' domain map systems, their similarities and differences. If necessary, graphical maps can be constructed using the respective SCU lists of CMAP2. A simple option is to print the SCU lists and, based on this information, to draw the causal maps manually or using some drawing software.[4] If CMAP2 is run as a DOS window in the Windows environment, the user can transfer text via Clipboard from the window into a Windows-compatible graphicsdrawing program, saving some retyping.

Conveying the message

When examining published causal mapping studies a general observation seems warranted. There are real difficulties in presenting CM findings and evidence in a manner which is both valid and adequate while retaining plausibility and comprehensibility. Causal maps presented as evidence can be problematic. Sometimes causal maps do not add much net value if compared to textual reporting of the same findings; on the contrary, they may just confuse. It is also too easy to overtax the audience's patience by offering as evidence extensive graphical causal maps or, worse, a series of good-sized causal maps, printed on separate pages, to be compared for the detail changes argued to exist somewhere for the observant eye to detect.

When presenting causal map and comparative causal map findings, the threshold issue is the relative newness of this particular mode of description, really communication, as compared with more traditional modes, notably text-based narratives. Of course, the question of evidence is a relative one and cannot be researcher-dependent alone. For example, when reporting findings produced by established statistical research techniques, it is expected that the audience is at least broadly familiar with them. In the case of reporting causal map and comparative causal map studies, the same general principle should also apply. However, it is only realistic to expect that this is not necessarily so, at least not until these methods have been in use more widely and for a much longer period. Therefore, it is prudent to pay careful attention to presentation and not to overburden one's audiences. Before that, causal mapping studies and their reporting should probably stress much more the substantial findings, assuming that they exist, and not the fancy techniques by which they were generated. There are probably no clear-cut solutions for reporting beyond the general, well-meaning but much too imprecise rule of 'keeping it simple and to the point'. Usually, it is wise to think carefully about the target audience, their likely position in relation to causal maps and their previous knowledge of them. Obviously, the more novel this type of representation is for the audience, the simpler and more focused the graphical maps should probably be. There should also be more traditional textual narrative to support the map-only based messages, with some explanation of the methods applied.

It is sometimes advisable to experiment with the different graphical appearances of the maps one intends to publish, preferably asking for peer comments. This is useful when contemplating alternatives of visually combining information within a single map system. The combination of several managers' or clusters' findings may be important to reduce the visible amount of presented material and to make visual conclusions more feasible. This can be critical when presenting a comparative causal mapping study because of the danger of having too much complexity in the mapped messages. Careful reporting and good appearance are present-day realpolitik. However, we know that the future status and position of causal mapping, comparative or idiosyncratic, will depend mostly on the research uses of the techniques and on the quality of the substantive output rather than on the attitudes of any audience. Fortunately, fields such as the fast-growing MOC community have shown target phenomena and research questions which can beneficially use causal map metaphor-oriented methods. Therefore, we can look forward to new, innovative and sound research within the CM tradition.

Notes

1 See *PC Magazine* (1995), 28 March, 14 (6): 40.

2 CMAP2 is a non-commercial, database-oriented PC program, written by the author and distributed free to interested researchers. It was designed specifically for data processing and analysis for comparative causal mapping in circumstances where the raw data are natural communication and key parameters such as the number of subjects, mapped concepts or causal links must be flexible. There are at least two other causal map metaphor oriented programs that are widely available: Decision Explorer, formerly Graphics COPE (Eden et al., 1992) and DISTRAT (Markoczy and Goldberg, 1993). All these programs differ from each other in several functional areas and design parameters and are therefore good choices in that particular context. Also, some of the functions of CMAP2, especially in raw data processing and conversion, can be accomplished by using relational database software such as Access, dBase or Paradox.

3 The indegree (Id) of a causal map node refers to the number of links that flow into that node from other nodes. Outdegree (Od) is respectively the number of causal links flowing from the node.

4 There are several options for drawing and preparing paper copy of causal maps. Examples of tools that work are the drawing components of recent Windows word processors such as MS Word or presentation packages such as MS PowerPoint 4.0 for Windows. In addition, there are many dedicated drawing programs such as AutoSketch or Visio.

References

Argyris, C. (1993) *Knowledge for Action: A Guide to Overcoming Barriers to Organizational Change.* San Francisco, CA: Jossey-Bass.

Axelrod, R. (ed.) (1976) *Structure of Decision: The Cognitive Maps of Political Elites.* Princeton, NJ: Princeton University Press.

Bougon, M.G., Baird, N., Komocar, J.M. and Ross, W. (1990) Identifying strategic loops: the self-Q interviews, in A.S. Huff (ed.), *Mapping Strategic Thought.* Chichester: John Wiley. pp. 327–54.

Cossette, P. and Audet, M. (1992) Mapping of an idiosyncratic schema, *Journal of Management Studies,* 29 (3): 325–47.

Eden, C. (1990) Using cognitive mapping for strategic options development and analysis (SODA), in Jonathan Rosenhead (ed.), *Rational Analysis for a Problematic World.* Chichester: John Wiley. pp. 21–70.

Eden, C., Ackermann, F. and Cropper, S. (1992) The analysis of cause maps, *Journal of Management Studies,* 29 (3): 309–23.

Evans, J. St B.T. (1988) The knowledge elicitation problem: a psychological perspective, *Behavior and Information Technology,* 7: 111–30.

Fahey, L. and Narayanan, V.K. (1989) Linking changes in revealed causal maps and environmental change: an empirical study, *Journal of Management Studies,* 26: 361–78.

Ford, J.D. and Hegarty, W.H. (1984) Decision makers' beliefs about the causes and effects of structure: an exploratory study, *Academy of Management Journal,* 27: 271–91.

Gordon, S.E. (1992) Implications of cognitive theory for knowledge acquisition, in R.R. Hoffman (ed.), *The Psychology of Expertise: Cognitive Research and Empirical AI.* New York: Springer-Verlag. pp. 99–120.

Hirschfeld, L.A. and Gelman, S.A. (eds) (1994) *Mapping the Mind: Domain Specificity in Cognition and Culture.* Cambridge: Cambridge University Press.

Laukkanen, M. (1992) *Comparative Cause Mapping of Management Cognitions A Computer Database Method for Natural Data.* Helsinki: Helsinki School of Economics.

Laukkanen, M. (1994a) Studying the knowledge base of small business managers. *Proceedings, 8th Nordic Conference on Small Business Research,* vol. 1. Halmstad University, Sweden.

Laukkanen, M. (1994b) Comparative cause mapping of organizational cognitions, *Organization Science,* special issue on managerial and organizational cognition: 322–43.

Laukkanen, M. (1994c) Maps of success and demise: comparing entrepreneur-managers' knowledge-bases. Paper presented at the Academy of Management Annual Meeting, Entrepreneurship Division, Dallas, TX.

Laukkanen, M. and Peltoniemi, J. (1995) Operationalizing stakeholder thinking by comparative cause mapping, in J. Näsi (ed.), *Understanding Stakeholder Thinking.* Helsinki: Gummerus. pp. 259–84.

Lave, J. (1991) Situating learning in communities of practice, in Lauren B. Resnick, John M. Levine and Stephanie D. Teasley (eds) *Perspectives on Socially Shared Cognition.* Washington, DC: American Psychological Association. pp. 63–82.

Levine, M.L. and Teasley, Stephanie D. (eds) (1991) *Perspectives on Socially Shared Cognition.* Washington, DC: American Psychological Association.

Markoczy, L. and Goldberg, J. (1993) A method for eliciting and comparing causal maps. Budapest: Budapest University of Economics. Working Paper 1993/5.

Stubbart, C.I. and Ramaprasad, A. (1988) Probing two chief executives' schematic knowledge of the US steel industry using cognitive maps, *Advances in Strategic Management*, 5: 139–64.

Wrightson, M.T. (1976) The documentary coding method, in R. Axelrod (ed.), *Structure of Decision: The Cognitive Maps of Political Elites*. Princeton, NJ: Princeton University Press.

11

ANALYSING AND COMPARING IDIOGRAPHIC CAUSAL MAPS

Colin Eden and Fran Ackermann

The comparison of cognitive maps which are cause maps or directed graphs is not a new field of study. Many research projects that endeavour to compare cognitive maps across, for example, industries and different countries and between individuals and groups have been undertaken (a recent and excellent example of such a study is Jenkins, 1995). However, other areas of interest abound, apart from those focusing on comparing industrial or national cognitive maps. Research undertaking a comparison of the cognitive structure of an individual both before and after a learning experience has been one such direction (Easterby-Smith, 1980; Pope and Shaw, 1981). This type of research aims to determine the changes in an individual's understanding. It could be used, for example, to yield valuable insights for designers of management training and other instructional practices. Another comparison could involve the study of a group's decision-making/strategy formulation process over time. A comparison could thus be made between a model comprising the amalgamation of individual ideas and one which is dominated by ideas generated during the group's discussion and 'owned' by the group as a whole. Comparisons of this latter type can provide some indication of the movement of the members towards shared meaning or a common understanding. At present there have been too few studies of the dynamics of cognition; indeed many studies presume stability or seek to demonstrate stability of cognition. To some extent this presumption of stability derives from the shallow data which are often collected about cognition which focus on core constructs that are inevitably less permeable. In order to explore the dynamics of cognition there must be reliable methods for working with the comparison of idiographic cognitive maps. This chapter explores ways in which this may be undertaken.

The comparison of cognitive maps can thus satisfy crucial research aims that have a practical importance. The focus of this chapter, however, will be on the general issues of comparing cognitive maps in relation to any type of research data, not just those which have significance within the field of management. The successful attainment of this aim depends upon addressing a number of methodological concerns which will be discussed. The chapter will also introduce some of the ways in which a cognitive map (as a directed graph) can be analysed to reveal properties that can be the basis for comparing idiographic maps. Although several authors (notably Muller-Silva, 1988; Langfield-Smith and Wirth, 1992; Markoczy and Goldberg, 1993) have proposed techniques for comparing cognitive maps, there are nevertheless a number of serious methodological issues that still need to be explored and resolved. Methods that may appear to be suitable for one area of cognitive comparison may be inappropriate for another and while some generic considerations may be tenable, an appreciation of the differences in domain and applicability is important.

The chapter first discusses the status of cognitive maps and goes on to pay attention to issues in capturing individuality. This is followed by a plea for comparisons to be made which attend to differences and similarities in meaning (structural and contextual properties) as well as suggestions about how this might be done when computer software is available to investigate many properties of a map. Finally, the chapter argues for an holistic approach to comparison by declaring the properties of a map as a systemic portfolio of ways of viewing the map.

Reifying cognition

Cognition belongs to individuals, not to organizations; the attribution of cognition to an organization is problematic and depends completely upon the legitimacy of reification. Even if reification can be justified on the practical grounds that doing so allows the research question to be addressed, the source data are dependent upon eliciting material from individuals or small groups, or from documents written by individuals or a team. Documentary evidence is often used as a surrogate for cognition (Axelrod, 1976), but it does not produce maps that can claim to be representations of thinking. At best they are useful surrogates as long as they utilize a theory of cognition as seen through the process of writing documents. Such a theory has yet to be developed, probably because what is written in documents is mediated by considerations of formality, audience and record keeping. The issue of reification is further exacerbated once the relationship between emotion and cognition is recognized; emotion can only belong to an individual.

We accept that cognitive maps which rely upon an interview with an individual are mediated by considerations other than that of a theory of cognition. Interviewing is a process of articulation which is itself a surrogate for thinking. An interview is also a social and political act (Eden, 1992; Eden et al., 1992) focusing thinking in particular directions, considering the implications of options, etc. Furthermore, during the interview the cognitive structure of the individual is likely to change as ideas are explored and understood better: 'how do I know what I think until I see how I act' (Weick, 1979), which translated to the domain of this chapter would be taken as 'how do I know what I think until I see what I say'.

Nevertheless well-run, one-to-one interviews are likely to be the best method for eliciting cognitive maps. Second best are group sessions using well-designed elicitation techniques combined with 'nominal group techniques' (Delbecq et al., 1975), 'Metaplan' (Schnelle, 1979) and 'Domino' or 'Snow-card' techniques (Nutt and Backoff, 1992; Ackermann, 1993). Document analysis (Holsti, 1976) is a very poor third. If we need to establish the cognitive map of an organization then we must aggregate the maps of individuals or groups and so go through a process of comparing individual maps before we can be assured that the aggregated map is stable and so may be compared with aggregated maps of other organizations. This may be achieved by eliciting as many individual cognitive maps as possible and continuously aggregating them until less change/more similarity appears in the shape of the emerging issues. Having made our position on organizational cognition clear, it is worth noting that cause maps of documents are valid models that may have the idiographic properties of cognitive maps. Thus the discussion that follows applies to comparing idiographic cause maps as well as to the comparison of rich cognitive maps. The methods remain similar, although the outcomes are of different theoretical significance.

Working with idiographic data

The ability to elicit, or attend to, idiographic data from respondents is important, so that full recognition is given to the idiosyncratic ways in which each of the research subjects views their world. Many research methods for the analysis of such data depend upon treating it as if it were nomothetic (Markóczy and Goldberg, 1993; Daniels et al., 1994). Thus the difficulties in elicitation and comparison are avoided by having a 'pool' of elements from which research participants select a subset to be included in a cause map. Such an approach limits the extent to which the resulting maps can be personalized, endangering the development of an accurate portrayal of the organization. This is the approach used by Repertory Grid proponents (Fransella and Bannister, 1977), when the elements or constructs are standardized and provided by the researcher.

In some cases the need for direct comparison of individual maps results in the data ignoring the requirement of allowing the idiosyncrasy upon which the research results depend (for example, by restricting the interview schedule to the exploration of only a certain set of constructs). To improve upon this, any method for comparing maps needs to be designed to allow for a comparison of idiographic data without resorting to assumptions about the similarity of individual elements of the data or to the constraints in the collection of the data. Valuable information may be lost if the focus of the interview or other form of data collection restricts the richness and detail. Obviously any interview protocol, even open-ended interviews, will be focused by the interviewer or interviewee. If the interviewer provides no clues as to the expected direction which the interview is to take, then the interviewee will make assumptions about direction. Within the context of this chapter we are interested in the balance to be struck between inviting working with rich data and the pragmatic requirements of ordered research analysis. Laukkanen (this volume) discusses interview protocols and comparison methods that accept some degree of idiography but lean towards ease of direct comparison.

When research participants are given the freedom to add any constructs to the map, the process of comparison becomes fraught with difficulties. It is difficult and time consuming for an analyst manually to compare the elements of many large causal maps, attempting to locate equivalencies. Some form of automated analytic support is essential to ensure fast and accurate detection of synonymous elements. The role of computers in conducting much of this analysis is discussed later.

Comparing across maps or comparing by merging maps?

Most of the existing literature which discusses the comparison of cause maps concentrates on their structural, graph theoretic properties. This ignores the arguably more difficult problem which usually precedes any form of structural comparison, that of identifying synonymous elements (nodes) in the maps being compared. Whether maps are merged or not, the comparison of nodes is important. If maps are to be merged then the merging of synonymous nodes will be the basis for building the merged map, although additional linking between maps where there are taken-for-granted implications is also likely. If not, then comparing the structural properties of each of a number of synonymous nodes across maps will be the basic starting point for comparison. In principle the comparison process can be undertaken using either approach. However, without computer software to support analysis, the comparison of maps after merging into a single map is difficult because of the problems in differentiating construct ownership. With the use of the Decision Explorer (previously known as COPE) software,[1] comparison using a single merged map can be easier. The use of colour and different fonts to depict different categories and different interviewees enables researchers to spot emergent patterns that cannot easily be detected using formal analysis methods. In any event, detecting synonyms is essential for either approach.

Research conducted in an attempt automatically to classify and index scientific documents has achieved some success in matching articles addressing similar topics (Turner et al., 1988). Similarly, standard content analysis methods seek to achieve this end and computer software has been designed for this purpose (for example, NUD.IST; Weitzman and Miles,

1995). However, this is usually accomplished using statistical measures of the co-occurrence of words and phrases in the various documents. While such summary approaches work for comparisons at the document level, they are not sensitive enough to be used for construct comparisons. Constructs are rarely more elaborate than a single sentence. Nevertheless if some form of composite of each idea was examined through building paragraphs from the context immediately around an element and comparing these paragraphs, some automation might be possible. Here the process begins to get closer to an analysis of meaning rather than a study of semantics. Thus the exploration required to compare maps by studying similar verbal tags often finishes up by taking a structural approach designed to determine the extent of shared meaning through the analysis of content (Eden and Vangen, 1995).

This requirement for idiographic data also necessitates that interviewers understand fully the words, language, jargon and shorthand vocabulary of the interviewees. Furthermore, as a number of interviews is likely to be required there is often a need to involve a number of interviewers in such a project, each with a language capability related to each specific sample. This requires developing a method that is likely to produce adequate intercoder reliability without resorting to nomothetic methods in order to simplify and standardize the procedure. Current sets of coding guidelines and interview methods (Bougon, 1983; Ackermann et al., 1990) would need to be refined and tested, particularly if they were to be used in a multilingual or cross-cultural setting.

In one respect, even allowing the researcher to identify synonymous elements is methodologically problematic. Cause maps elicited from an individual or a group only acquire meaning when explored by that individual or group, or the researchers, when they become, in effect, part of the group. Although we argued above that the context of elements will help to illuminate their meaning, the implicit shared background and history of the group will always play a major part in determining the meaning of the map. It would be impossible to embody all of these environmental factors explicitly in a causal map. This suggests that a researcher who, in attempting to compare two causal maps that he was not instrumental in creating, would be reckless to distinguish a pair of elements as synonymous. The only way that this problem can be avoided is to ensure that anyone making use of the maps has been exposed to the climate in which the maps were authored. Some ways in which this could be achieved are:

1 When maps are compared, all the interviewers responsible for eliciting the relevant maps should be involved in the process. Alternatively or additionally the initial merged model/map could be reviewed and explored with the interviewees to ensure reliability.
2 The maps are elicited from groups who have a similar cultural background. This would be difficult to ensure in practice and would almost

certainly conflict with the aims of comparing maps across nationalities or industries.

3   The researchers are acquainted with all the groups (or sites) whose maps they will be asked to compare. However, this may lead to biases being built into the aggregated map as only a single perspective is thus considered.

Comparing meaning

Current measures of similarities and differences in cognitive maps depend upon formulae that assume some degree of agreement about syntactical equivalence. Such an approach is inadequately simplistic and misses the most important aspects of exploring cognition. The issue is one of resolving synonyms on the one hand and shared meaning on the other (Scheper, 1991: 91–146).

Meaning derives from three elements of a cognitive map:

- the words that make up a construct, which may be judged as synonymous with other words or another phrase;
- the contrasting pole in the construct, which in repertory grid work is developed from the use of triads of elements, and in the case of interviews depends upon interviewing skills and appropriate questioning;
- most significantly, the context of the construct within the map; in grids this is developed using an implication grid (Hinkle, 1965) or alternatively by analysis of the repertory grid (Fransella and Bannister, 1977) through factor analysis.

Each of these three elements provides context to a construct and so meaning. Meaning also derives from aspects of thinking that are not easily captured by a cognitive map, for example, non-verbal communication is crucial to communicating meaning. In particular, silences are a significant aspect of non-verbal communications as members of organizations indicate their thinking about issues. The task of the cognitive mapper is not to see the map as a record of what is said, the verbal tags, but rather as a record of a good listener seeking to capture meaning. Thus the map, as a system of verbal tags, will use context and words to signify what was meant by the person being mapped.

This requirement has very significant implications for the way in which interviews are conducted and for the way in which the interview data are used. For most so-called academically respectable research, interviewers are required to record the data source in an explicit and direct manner. This helps other researchers to replicate the analysis of the interview data. Thus it is usual for a series of stages to be undertaken: conduct interview according to prescribed schedule of questions; taperecord interview; transcribe tape into written form; translate transcription into cognitive maps using several coders, so checking intercoder reliability; analyse maps; finally, arrive at robust conclusions. By its very nature each of these steps loses important data, most of which relate to meaning. The significance of the interview as a social event is lost, and so the significance of the nature of that event on the reliable interpretation of the data is also lost. The nature of the power relationship between interviewer and interviewee is an important element in interpreting interview data. The visual nature of the non-verbal is lost when the interview is merely taperecorded. The intonation and silences are lost as the data become a transcript. The subtlety of the data and their meanings is sacrificed to intercoder reliability. If it is important to collect meaning then it becomes important to see the researcher as the research instrument, rather than the data collection and analysis techniques or tools as the research instrument. This is not to argue that audit trails of research are unimportant, on the contrary. However, it does imply that research which seeks to work with meaning needs to establish new methods for providing other researchers with confidence in the research.

Notwithstanding the above commentary on the problems of discovering meaning, the important aspect of research method is the need for the researchers who are concerned with comparing cause maps to be clear about the status of the data they are using. It does not matter that cause maps are not cognitive maps, in the sense of being a depiction of cognition (see Eden, 1992, for concerns about the relationship between cognition and cognitive maps), but rather that the researchers know what they are depicting. Thus, for example, cause maps are useful for comparing the language and arguments embedded in documents (see Axelrod, 1976) or for comparing accounts managers give of their decision-making; but neither of these is an analysis or comparison of meaning or cognition. At the very least the challenge is to identify methods of comparison of idiographic maps which recognize all three of the elements discussed above which can, in relation to any purpose, provide a more subtle and meaningful basis for comparison. The work of Smit (1991) provides some theoretical guidance in the development of computer software so that it can reflect the framework of meaning as well as individual link contexts (Langfield-Smith and Wirth, 1992). The comparison of meaning can also be understood by going beyond an analysis of detail to recognize the holistic properties of each cognitive map, thus allowing exploration and comparison of the emergent properties.

Detecting and comparing emergent properties using computer software aids

Many applications of personal construct theory to understanding organizations (for example, Wacker, 1981) have focused on the semantic content of construct systems rather than structure. The approaches proposed here pay attention to structure, as did the work of Stabell (1978). However, the study of the local structures misses the issues of whether the cognitive structures are monolithic, articulated, or segmented (Norris et al., 1970) and so whether the world is seen in a simple or complex manner. For example, monolithic structures are regarded as rigid and dogmatic because of the existence of a small number of clusters that are highly integrated. In such circumstances impressions formed by people whose constructs are highly interrelated are more likely to be resistant to change, even in the face of large-scale disconfirmation (Crockett, 1965). It is also likely, however, that successive or clear disconfirmation will cause large-scale change in construct systems, a catastrophe theory notion of construct system change. Similarly, highly segmented structures where several clusters are apparent but there is little linkage between them, suggest decisions may be made through a series of jumps across bridges from one cluster to another. The existence of several clusters which are well connected suggests what Norris et al. (1970) called articulated systems where the implication is that these systems are more readily able to change and recategorize, essential to the likelihood of 'unfreezing'. The study of these sorts of emergent characteristics can be more revealing of learning and decision-making behaviour than the analysis of the detail of differences in maps. From an exploration of the structure and its holistic properties it may also be possible to identify particular areas of understanding of the organization which are well elaborated and articulated as opposed to those which are not. Studies of managerial cognition need to uncover such differences between cognitive maps. The methods outlined below, using currently available computer software, provide an easy way of working with cognitive maps in a discovery mode which is likely to encourage treating the data as the source of grounded theory (Glaser and Strauss, 1967; Eden and Huxham, 1996).

Often the most appropriate way to compare maps is dependent upon the researchers immersing themselves in the data, in their detail, and in the data which result from alternative analytical perspectives on the maps. Computer software can provide help when taking this approach because the effort involved in exploration is significantly less than when seeking merely to play at the analysis of the maps using manual techniques. Research conclusions demand the ability to explore differences and similarities rather than simply to go through routine procedures. There are two established computer-based methods for exploring maps: Decision Explorer (Cropper et al., 1990) and CMAP (Laukkanen, 1989; this volume). In contrast to CMAP, Decision Explorer has been used for the analysis of qualitative data for many years (for example Smithin, 1988; Ackermann, 1991; Brown, 1992; Hunter, 1992; Jenkins, 1995) and is now capable of graphics-based display and analysis. Unlike CMAP which is predominantly text/form based, Decision Explorer, through its graphics display can provide insights into the emergent issues from the patterns shown. By revealing the context of the ideas in question through an examination of the data, Decision Explorer can aid the search for shared meaning. In addition the software has been designed so that it can be modified to meet the above requirements without complete reprogramming using its custom fourth generation language (4GL) and interprocess communication facilities. However, CMAP is being continuously adapted to the specific needs of analysing research data whereas Decision Explorer has a history of being used to facilitate group problem-solving. In the rest of this chapter we shall discuss the type of analyses which may be undertaken using Decision Explorer to detect the emergent properties of a single map. These properties can then be compared with the properties of other maps on the same topic.

Categorizing concepts, comparing emergent value systems

The most fundamental property of a cognitive map is the value system embedded within it. Providing that the interview or other elicitation technique has been properly used and coding of interview data has been thorough, then analysis of the map should reveal the value system of the interviewee (the network of values in which each value informs others and is, in turn, informed by others). Values will be defined both by the property of the words making up the construct and by the position of the construct within the hierarchy of a map. Thus analysing the map to find those constructs which are most superordinate, so forming the heads of the map, is the first task. These constructs are the primary candidates as values. If the content of the construct suggests that it is not a valued outcome for the interviewee, then the interviewer should seek an opportunity to conduct a further interview which will explore consequential outcomes using a 'laddering process' (Eden et al., 1979), and so reveal values which will then be coded as hierarchically superordinate to the previous head. Alternatively it may only require additional links to other existing material, thus weaving the head into the model more thoroughly. As each value is affirmed the analysis must continue by moving down the hierarchy and checking each node in turn until no further values are identified. The network of values so defined for each individual can then be compared with one another. When each system of values is large then the methods of comparison identified below become relevant for comparing value systems.

Categorizing concepts, comparing central issues

This can be achieved using two different forms of analysis. The first analysis focuses upon the constructs immediately in the domain of the construct being examined, that is those constructs, possible explanations and consequences which are directly related to it. The analysis is often referred to as determining the extent of indegree and outdegree for each node. Through identifying which of the constructs in the map are the most busy, it is possible to begin to ascertain which areas are of concern to the interviewee as they suggest those constructs which are most cognitively central. This may be due to the interviewee, during the elicitation process, spending considerable amounts of time and energy elaborating the construct, suggesting, for example, possible options open towards the achievement of that value and why it is of critical importance.

The other form of analysis which investigates the relative centrality of constructs within the map is one which examines the wider context of each one within the map. Instead of focusing only on the first level of elaboration, the analysis expands its search to as many levels beyond the construct as desired. However, for each subsequent layer the weighting given diminishes exponentially. The standard routine available in Decision Explorer commences with a weighting of 1 for each construct directly related to the construct being evaluated, 0.5 for those two levels out, 0.33 for those three levels out and so on. Through this analysis it is possible to identify those constructs which are central to the map but may not have extensive elaboration immediately linked to them and vice versa. Comparison derives from detecting similarities and differences between the lists of central issues. The comparison is richer if the central issues for each map remain as a map which relates the issues one to another. Thus, as for the comparison of value systems, the issue systems are compared where the relationships between issues are the result of analysing the existence of paths of argument between each pair of constructs. Within Decision Explorer the network of interrelated issues can be detected easily by collapsing onto only the issues so that all other constructs are hidden but the links retained.

Clusters, emergent topics or themes

One method of exploring the complexity of the maps generated during the process of elicitation is to slice the map into chunks or clusters. This allows both the interviewer and interviewee to explore particular areas in detail to ensure verification. Furthermore these clusters are focused on a particular area and can be compared with those from other interviewees on the same topic. One form of comparison might centre on the extent of the cluster's elaboration, that is, the number of constructs captured in the cluster. Another might focus on the content and whether there is a degree of similarity between the constructs, particularly those implying possible courses of action. Any cluster tends to signify an idiographic topic, or theme, which acts as a descriptor for the whole of the content of the cluster. The theme label used for a cluster seeks to describe the emergent properties of that cluster. The sum of all the labels provides the summary statement for the map being analysed. As each cluster is typically linked to other clusters then the network of labels, as a summary, can be compared with the summaries of other maps.

Hierarchical clusters

One form of slicing is to create hierarchical clusters. 'Hierarchical systems have some common properties that are independent of the specific content' (Simon, 1981) and these properties can be used when comparing the cognitive maps of various individuals. For example, one comparison might entail examining the size of each hierarchical cluster. Another might review the extent to which each individual's hierarchical clusters relate to one another and to a common or reference value system. A third might consider the similarities and differences between the emergent themes of the various individual maps being compared. Using a seed set, often containing those constructs identified using the analyses for determining which constructs are part of the value system, the analysis explores all of the chains of argument supporting each member of the seed set, stopping only when it encounters another member. The results of this exploration are placed into hierarchical clusters. As such it produces tear-drop shaped clusters whose contents are not mutually exclusive. Each tear drop represents an integrated body of argument supporting a topic. As such comparisons can focus on differences in elaborated explanation for topics of interest to the researcher. Thus when synonyms across maps have been identified the tear drops of argument hierarchically supporting the similar verbal tags can be compared. Hierarchical clusters which contain only two or three constructs may suggest that the construct seeding that cluster is not a key construct and that it is either elaboration of an alternative key construct or requires further elaboration.

Island clusters

An alternative to creating hierarchical clusters is that of creating clusters through an examination of the link similarity of constructs. The analysis compares pairs of constructs along with their immediate context to determine link similarity using a Jaccard coefficient (Gower and Ross, 1969), a measure of the similarity of context and so meaning of each construct. If the constructs have sufficient common context they are placed in the same cluster. If not they form the basis of a new cluster, so an attempt is made to create clusters within which the constructs are highly similar. The constructs in each cluster are closely interlinked and the number of bridges between the different clusters kept to a minimum. The analysis provides a useful means of identifying emergent themes, with each cluster representing a theme. Many of the comparisons used with hierarchical clusters can be undertaken. It is possible (i) to compare the emergent themes produced by this analysis so as to distinguish whether there are similarities or differences in the themes; and (ii) to examine the network of interrelationships between the clusters to determine their complexity, and structure, in effect an analysis of the map of the clusters.

Island clusters, which rely on contextual structure rather than hierarchy, may appear in any position in the map as they have not been formed through a seed set selected by categorization. As such, clusters which have a large number of cross-links to other clusters are more critical than those on the periphery. Unlike the hierarchical analysis, this form of clustering produces mutually exclusive clusters and therefore they can be compared in a number of alternative ways. Nevertheless, as with hierarchical clusters, one difference arises through comparing the size of the clusters created across each map. Large clusters that cannot be broken down into small clusters provide an indication of the interviewee's cognitive complexity. A further measure is the degree of isolation of one cluster from another, as determined by the number of bridges between the clusters. A large number of bridges between the clusters demonstrates a higher degree of cognitive complexity than where relatively few bridges exist. On examination of island clusters it is sometimes the case that clusters emerge which do not contain one of the key constructs. In these circumstances it is useful to examine the cluster, identifying a likely candidate as a key construct which describes the content of the cluster and then return to the domain and centrality analysis to determine its position within the map.

Feedback loops as clusters

This analysis differs from the above clustering procedures as it identifies clusters containing feedback loops, both vicious and virtuous loops, if they exist. Loops may imply the existence of dynamic considerations within the cognition being mapped, the interviewee has acknowledged change or growth either implicitly or explicitly, a decline of feedback control. The nature of the loop can be determined by the number of negative links present in the loop. When there is an odd number the loop depicts stability whereas where there are only positive links or an even number of negative links then either regenerative or degenerative dynamics are indicated. One method for examining the impact and significance of any loop is to break a link in the loop (either through deletion or reversal) between what is considered to be the most hierarchically superordinate construct and the least superordinate constructs, for example, between a key construct and additional context, and then check for its impact on other analyses.

Erroneous feedback loops are often created in a large map through poor coding. It is difficult to determine the direction of the causality, so loops appear accidentally. Where such feedback loops appear it is useful for the interviewer to discuss the direction of the link with the interviewee to determine whether the construct fits into the hierarchy or forms a feedback loop. This is particularly the case where one interviewee will argue the link runs from A to B, while another favours from B to A, so demonstrating a potentially significant difference in their maps. When comparing the cognitive maps of a number of interviews, using specific word searches along with the loop analysis will help the researcher detect the loops themselves or their fragments, and this will show whether or not awareness of the loop is widespread. Further comparisons can be made when considering the linkages between the constructs appearing in the feedback loops. Interviewees may differ in how they perceive the relationships, whether they are positive or negative, which is the option and which the outcome.

Identifying significant intervention opportunities

While it is important to detect the value system, it is also worth considering those constructs which provide the means of realizing the value system. One means of determining these intervention opportunities is to analyse the map to identify which are the most subordinate constructs, the tails of the map. Where a construct appears at the bottom of the map, and it implies a potential intervention because it has an action orientation, it becomes a part of a portfolio of options which give meaning to the value system. The portfolio of options can then be compared with those of other interviewees. However, as maps frequently contain a large percentage of tails and therefore, by implication, options, some means of identifying those which represent good summary data is beneficial. One such method is to determine the composite tails and the other to distinguish the potent options and then compare across maps.

Composite tails

It is often the case that interviewees discuss some ideas in greater detail than others. In a map this may mean that one construct is elaborated through a tear drop or portfolio of other constructs that only support that one construct and no others. Thus the superordinate construct acts as a sort of summary tail for many more detailed tails. In order to make comparisons across maps it is helpful to detect these summary tails and then compare them as representing a bundle of options that have no consequences elsewhere in the map. The analysis used in identifying composite or summary options or constructs commences with an investigation of all the real tail constructs, those with no indegree. Where a tail construct has only one outcome or outdegree, then the analysis moves up the chain of argumentation until a branch point or composite construct is detected. Hence, when using Decision Explorer, the analysis is referred to as 'cotail' (composite tail). Clearly it is possible for composite tails to be detected at all levels of the map including those defined as values. These composite tails represent a summary statement of a number of potential actions, each of which are believed by the interviewee to impact only the specific cotail. The analysis for cotails is, in effect, a way of simplifying the map by taking out some of the subordinate detail. To this extent the analysis indicates the complexity of possible actions and potential dilemmas. The more a map is simplified in this way, the more the interviewee sees the range of options as simple in their consequences, compared to another where options have an impact across many values or through multiple lines of causality.

Potent constructs

To identify the potent constructs it is necessary to have first created hierarchical clusters. As mentioned earlier, the hierarchical clusters encapsulate all of the explanations of each construct which is a member of the seed set. Consequently the clusters may overlap to a greater or lesser extent. It is this overlap which produces the potent constructs. Those constructs which support more than one of the seed set members are more potent than those supporting only one, and a construct which supports three or four members of the seed set is even more potent. However, it is worth noting that the analysis not only identifies the composite potent construct but also any other supporting constructs. Therefore it is important to examine the overlap between potent and composite constructs. Also the potent constructs are totally dependent upon the seed set and the logic for identifying the seed set members. Typically these may be identified on the basis of structure through computing high totals of indegree and outdegree scores, an analysis of the domain of constructs, or using values as the seed set; or those constructs which were of emotional significance to the interviewee; or on the basis of content analysis categories. From the results yielded it is possible to gain some indication of the complex number of possible action packages which exist within the context of multiple criteria or values. Thus, for particular sorts of data, the total number of potent constructs in relation to the number of heads may provide an indication of cognitive complexity because it is one measure of the ability of the interviewee to define situations in ways that consider multiple ramifications. Additionally the composite potent constructs (cotails) can be further explored to ascertain whether dilemmas exist for them. As potent composite constructs, by definition, support more than one construct in the seed set, then there is the possibility that the potent construct may have a positive consequence for one member of the seed set while at the same time having a negative consequence for another.

The system of properties

Although each of the above analyses helps in detecting the emergent properties of a single map and thus helps in the comparison of maps, a map is more than the sum of its parts. It is important to consider maps as an holistic representation of the interview. Thus each of the analyses that reveals a single property of the map should be examined within the context of other properties. Sometimes those properties of a map which differentiate it from other maps are only revealed by considering several properties taken together as a portfolio of statistical information. Each individual analysis provides a different perspective of the model and so each analysis refines the understanding of one interviewee in relation to another, but a single analysis does not replace the need to gain an overall gestalt view of the model.

Concluding remarks

This chapter has argued that comparing cognitive maps is not easy. In particular the comparison of the maps of a number of individuals when attention has been paid to retaining the richness and idiographic nature of their thinking demands a broad approach which attempts to explore and compare both reductionist and holistic properties of the maps. We have suggested some approaches that are presented within the spirit of Simon's view that 'given the properties of the parts and the laws of their interaction, it is not a trivial matter to infer the properties of the whole . . . in the face of complexity, an in-principle reductionist may be at the same time a pragmatic holist' (Simon, 1981). In order to allow for the creative exploration of the system of properties of a map we have argued that the use of computer software is essential. The researcher needs an opportunity to play with the data and view them from as many perspectives as possible.

The type of approaches discussed in this chapter are often criticized for not providing precise enough measures that allow clear statistics to be used to make comparisons. There is, in our view, a great danger of this need for numerical measures producing a form of statistical masturbation of the kind which has developed for the analysis of repertory grids (see Eden and Jones, 1984, for a detailed discussion of grid analysis). Given the nature of the data which can be captured, it is important to avoid building spurious clarity into analysis outcomes. This may satisfy a doctoral student's need to produce extensive appendices with tables of numbers, but it does not satisfy the needs of good research. Triangulation of conclusions is important in this work and, as the paragraph above suggests, the data must be approached from as many perspectives as possible. So being able to play with the maps via computer programs is important for this reason.

Researchers must also ask who the measures are for. Do the statistics satisfy the academic community that demands measurement or do they satisfy practitioners who demand good sense? For example, when consultants are trained in interviewing they are taught to notice silences and other non-verbal communication, listening for these will be significant to success in practice. In other words, these data indicate something about the thinking and future actions of the interviewee. It might prove that analyses shaped to practitioners' needs are also more relevant to good academic research. In addition, because of the emphasis on the structure of maps, it might be argued that the comparisons focus on structure at the expense of content. Indeed some argue that most methods for the analysis of cognitive maps attend to either content or to structure, but not to both. This is a reasonable claim about those content analysis tools which ignore structure altogether. But the analyses in this chapter (see also Laukkanen, this volume) attach great importance to the interaction of content and structure. First, the structure of the maps themselves is created through a coding method which structurally relates to content, for the structure is partly a function of content. Second, the analysis of structure is undertaken so as to reveal, for example, clusters of content which are then labelled by the statistic which derives from content and structure taken together. In the end, researchers must be clear about whether the methods they use to interview, record, represent, and analyse reflect their limited resources, the researcher's need to reduce complexity rather than manage complexity, or their need to discover something new. As in business, the search for the quick buck or the quick paper may get in the way of long-term achievement.

Note

1 Design Explorer is software specially developed for working with cognitive maps. It runs under Windows and allows for flexible graphical representation of maps and all of the analysis discussed in this chapter. It also encompasses a 4GL type capability which allows users to design, and subsequently embed, their own analysis routines within the software. It is available from Scolari, Sage Publications.

References

Ackermann, F. (1991) Considerations of a specific GDS methodology in the light of the GDSS literature. PhD thesis, University of Strathclyde, Glasgow.

Ackermann, F. (1993) Using the 'domino technique' – for problem structuring. Working Paper 93/23, Department of Management Science, University of Strathclyde.

Ackermann, F., Cropper, S. and Eden, C. (1990) Cognitive mapping: a user's guide. Working Paper no. 90/2, Department of Management Science, University of Strathclyde.

Axelrod, R. (1976) *Structure of Decision*. Princeton: University of Princeton Press.

Bougon, M. (1983) Uncovering cognitive maps: the 'self-Q' technique, in G. Morgan (ed.), *Beyond Method: A Study of Organizational Research Strategies*. New York: Sage.

Brown, S. (1992) Cognitive mapping and repertory grids for qualitative survey research: some comparative observations, *Journal of Management Studies*, 29: 287–308.

Crockett, W.H. (1965) Cognitive complexity and impression formation, in B.A. Maher (ed.), *Progress in Experimental Personality Research*, vol. 2. New York: Academic Press.

Cropper, S., Eden, C. and Ackermann, F. (1990) Keeping sense of accounts using computer-based cognitive maps, *Social Science Computer Review*, 8: 345–66.

Daniels, K., De Chernatony, L. and Johnson, G. (1994) Differences in the cognitive models of buyers and sellers, *British Journal of Management*, 5: S21–S30.

Delbecq, A.L., Van de Ven, A.H. and Gustafson, D.H. (1975) *Group Techniques for Program Planning*. Glenview, IL: Scott Foresman.

Easterby-Smith, M. (1980) *How to Use Repertory Grids in HRD*. Bradford: MCB Publications.

Eden, C. (1992) On the nature of cognitive maps, *Journal of Management Studies*, 29: 261–5.

Eden, C., Ackermann, F. and Cropper, S. (1992) The analysis of cause maps, *Journal of Management Studies*, 29: 309–24.

Eden, C. and Huxham, C. (1996) Action research for the study of organizations, in S. Clegg, C. Hardy and W. Nord (eds), *Handbook of Organization Studies*. Beverly Hills, CA: Sage.

Eden, C. and Jones, S. (1984) Using repertory grids for problem construction, *Journal of the Operational Research Society*, 35: 779–90.

Eden, C., Jones, S. and Sims, D. (1979) *Thinking in Organizations*. London: Macmillan.

Eden, C. and Vangen, S. (1995) Exploring the success of collaboratives from the perspective of shared meanings. *Proceedings of the 3rd International Workshop on Managerial and Organisational Cognition*. Glasgow, June.

Fransella, F. and Bannister, D. (1977) *A Manual for Repertory Grid Technique*. London: Academic Press.

Glaser, B.G. and Strauss, A.L. (1967) *The Discovery of Grounded Theory*. Chicago: Aldine.

Gower, J.C. and Ross, G.J.S. (1969) Minimum spanning trees and single linkage cluster analysis, *Applied Statistics*, 18: 56–64.

Hinkle, D. (1965) The change of personal constructs from the viewpoint of a theory of construct implications. Unpublished PhD thesis, Ohio State University.

Holsti, O. (1976) Foreign policy formation viewed cognitively, in R. Axelrod (ed.), *Structure of Decision*. Princeton: University of Princeton Press.

Hunter, M. (1992) The essence of 'excellent' systems analysts: perceptions of five key audiences. Unpublished PhD thesis, University of Strathclyde.

Jenkins, M. (1995) Subjective strategies for small business growth: an evaluation of the causal maps of small independent retailers. Unpublished PhD Thesis, Cranfield University.

Langfield-Smith, K. and Wirth, A. (1992) Measuring differences between cognitive maps, *Journal of the Operational Society*, 43: 1135–50.

Laukkanen, M. (1989) Understanding the formation of managers' cognitive maps: a comparative case study of context in two business firm clusters. Helsinki School of Economics, A-65.

Markóczy, L. and Goldberg, J. (1993) A method for eliciting and comparing causal maps. Paper presented to The First International Workshop on Managerial and Organizational Cognition, EIASM: Brussels, 13–14 May.

Muller-Silva, K. (1988) *Beitrage zu Wirtschafts-und-Sozial-Wissenschaften*. Witterschlick, Bonn: Verlag M.Wehle.

Norris, F.M., Jones, H.G. and Norris, H. (1970) Articulation of the conceptual structure in obsessional neurosis, *British Journal of Social and Clinical Psychology*, 9: 264–74.

Nutt, P. and Backoff, R. (1992) *Strategic Management of Public and Third Sector Organizations*. San Francisco, CA: Jossey-Bass.

Pope, M. and Shaw, M. (1981) Negotiation in learning, in H. Bonarious, R. Holland and S. Rosenberg (eds), *Personal Construct Theory: Recent Advances in Theory and Practice*. London: Macmillan.

Scheper, W. (1991) *Group Decision Support Systems: An Inquiry into Theoretical and Philosophical Issues*. Thesis, Katholieke Universiteit Brabant, Tilburg.

Schnelle, E. (1979) *The Metaplan-Method: Communication Tools for Planning and Learning Groups*. Hamburg: Quickborn.

Simon, H.A. (1981) *The Sciences of the Artificial*, 2nd edn. Cambridge, MA: MIT Press.

Smit, H.J. (1991) *Consistency and Robustness of Knowledge Graphs*. Den Haag: CIP-Data Koninklijke Bibliotheek.

Smithin, T. (1988) *Argument*. Unpublished doctoral thesis, University of Bath.

Stabell, C.B. (1978) Integrative complexity of information environment perception and information use, *Organizational Behavior and Human Performance*, 22: 116–42.

Turner, W.A., Chartron, G., Laville, F. and Michelet, B. (1988) Packaging information for peer review: new co-word analysis techniques, in A.F.J. van Raan (ed.), *Handbook of Quantitative Studies of Science and Technology*. North-Holland: Elsevier.

Wacker, G.I. (1981) Toward a cognitive methodology of organizational assessment, *Journal of Applied Behavioral Science*, 17: 114–29.

Weick, K. (1979) *The Social Psychology of Organizing*, 2nd edn. Reading, MA: Addison-Wesley.

Weitzman, E.A. and Miles, M.B. (1995) *Computer Programs for Qualitative Data Analysis: A Software Sourcebook*. London: Sage.

12

CHARTING ORGANIZATIONAL LEARNING: A COMPARISON OF MULTIPLE MAPPING TECHNIQUES

Robert P. Bood

Within the last decade the notion that while individuals learn, so do groups and organizations, has gained wide acceptance among managers and researchers of management. Following a handful of publications in the 1970s, of which Argyris and Schön's (1978) contribution is by far the most cited, from the middle of the 1980s onward the number of books and articles concentrating on organizational learning has grown exponentially. Although the growth is impressive, when overlooking the field the conclusion seems justified that empirical research into organizational learning is still in its infancy. The majority of the writing on organizational learning is theoretical, while the minority based on empirical research is largely anecdotal. We see there are few empirical studies that systematically measure and register processes of organizational learning in time. One of the reasons may be the absence of applicable research methodologies since only a few authors have attempted to develop these for identifying and registering organizational learning (e.g. Schön, 1983).

This chapter develops a research methodology for charting processes of organizational learning. It does so by conceptualizing organizational learning in terms of cognitive change. Such an interpretation offers the possibility to employ techniques currently used for mapping managerial and organizational cognition for the identification and registration of organizational learning. After giving ground to the thesis of learning as cognitive change by studying both the nature of learning and organizational learning, this chapter explores and compares four such techniques: content analysis, repertory grid combined with multidimensional scaling, cause mapping with Laukkanen's CMAP2, and cognitive mapping with Eden's COPE (now known as Decision Explorer, see previous chapter).

The nature of learning

Although organizational learning is now a widely accepted notion, much confusion exists as to its meaning. Terms like organizational adaptation, change and adjustment are often used as synonyms (Fiol and Lyles, 1985). The relation between learning by individual managers and learning by organizations remains obscure and subject to an ongoing debate and investigation (Duncan and Weiss, 1979; Simon, 1991; Cowan, 1993). Finally, there seem to be more ideas on how and what organizations learn than is justified by the current narrow empirical foundation (Hedberg, 1981; Huber, 1991). Empirical studies that systematically measure and register processes of organizational learning are, if not lacking altogether, few and far between. Part of the confusion can be associated with the attention to the so-called 'learning organization' in management-oriented literature. To state that organizations only learn when they enhance the effectiveness and performance of their operations gives organizational learning a strong normative character, further reinforced by the almost metaphysical descriptions of the learning organization that can be found in some of this literature. For instance, Senge (1990: 14) defines a learning organization as 'an organization that is continually expanding its capacity to create its future'. Similarly, Pedler et al. (1991: 1) refer to the 'learning company . . . an organization that facilitates the learning of all its members and continuously transforms itself'.

Although definitions like these appeal to practising managers, they do little to enlarge our understanding of learning by organizations, apart from the suggestion that it has something to do with change. Such definitions do not give us clues to charting the organization's learning processes. What we need is a clear interpretation of organizational learning that, in line with most theories of learning, leaves room for the thought that organizations may learn whether or not they do so consciously or whether or not it enhances their performance. In the following we concentrate upon a descriptive interpretation of organizational learning, keeping in mind that our ultimate goal is to develop a research methodology for charting organizational learning. Before considering the relation between individual and organizational learning, we look at learning itself in some detail.

The cycle of learning

Within the organizational literature terms like change, adjustment, adaptation and learning relate to the interaction between the internal organization and the external environment. It is probably for this reason that they are often used interchangeably. However, as Fiol and Lyles (1985) note, these processes conceal fundamentally different processes. They capture the differences by distinguishing between cognitive development on the one hand and behavioural development on the other. The implied difference between cognition and behaviour is crucial, 'for not only do they represent two different phenomena, but also one is not necessarily an accurate reflection of the other' (Fiol and Lyles, 1985: 806). While both are change processes, cognitive development encompasses change in the interpretation of events and the development of in-depth understanding of past actions in the light of future behaviour. Behavioural development occurs if merely new responses or actions arise based on these existing interpretations and understanding. The centrality of cognitive processes distinguishes organizational learning from mere change, adjustment and adaptation.

If the two dimensions are combined and varied, four structural different situations arise. Figure 12.1 shows these four stereotypes. Learning may occur without any change visible whatsoever. For example, a boy who has learned that flames are hot will not intentionally stick his hand into a fire unless he wants to hurt himself. Vice versa, change may occur without any learning taking place. Learning reflects cognitive development whereas behavioural development reveals only the level of change. So, in a nutshell, learning equals cognitive change.

The notion of cognitive development stems from the field of cognitive psychology. Due to limited information processing capabilities, people are unable to cope adequately with the host of different stimuli and data they receive (Miller, 1956). Instead of that they construe simplified mental images of the world and impose these images upon the world around them (Kiesler and Sproull, 1982). These images function as a frame of reference for action and interpretation of the world (Weick, 1979; Gioia and Poole, 1984). In line with this view, Kelly (1955: 49) depicts people as scientists who are trying to understand the world around them in the process of developing and testing their own theories: 'Like the prototype of scientist that he is, man seeks prediction.'

Neisser (1976) has specified the way in which the cognitive processes of simplification and interpretation of information direct human action and perception. In his 'perceptual cycle' Neisser highlights cognitive structures called schemata that direct perceptual exploration and action. As a result of these experiences the schemata may be modified, which then form the basis for new explorations of the environment. Weick (1979: 154) describes a schema as 'an abridged, generalized, corrigible organization of experience that serves as an initial frame of reference for action and perception'. Weick's description indicates that schemata are embedded in the past, but possibly modified on the basis of present experiences and directed at the future. So cognitive processes link the past with the present and the future, as well as linking the internal with the external.

Based on his research among children, Piaget (1936, 1937) indicates that the relation between the past and the future is two-sided. The schemata influence what one perceives but what one sees may in turn lead to modifications of the schemata. Piaget (1936) denotes these cognitive processes as 'assimilation' and 'accommodation'. Assimilation is the process in which people impose their schemata to the world they live in. The opposite process of accommodation refers to the way in which people adapt their schemata to their environment. Assimilation and accommodation are opposite poles of the process through which people adapt themselves to

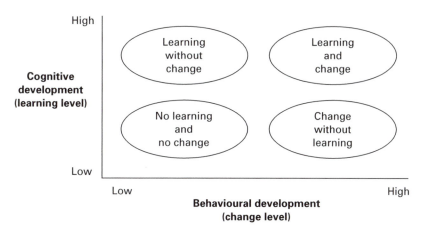

Figure 12.1   *The learning–change space (based on Fiol and Lyles, 1985: 807)*

their environment. Assimilation is a more or less conservative activity through which the environment is subjected to the perceiver, while accommodation is the source of change and bends the perceiver to the constraints imposed by the environment (Piaget, 1937).

According to Piaget (1936) schemata also tend to assimilate each other, a cognitive activity he denotes as 'reciprocal assimilation'. Reciprocal assimilation may lead to the creation of new schemata, which enables a better accommodation to novelties in the external environment. In turn, sooner or later accommodation to novelty is extended into assimilation because interest in the new is a matter of reconciling new experiences with old ones. Thus, accommodation and assimilation enter into a process of mutual interdependence. Neisser's (1976) perceptual cycle implies that the cognitive processes of reciprocal assimilation and accommodation are opposed and complementary, together forming a constructive process wherein the external and the internal are reconciled through exploration and modification.

Learning as cognitive change

Research within the area of child development indicates that as children grow older and acquire experience they are able to interpret the objects and events in their environment in more different ways and have a larger range of possibilities for action (Pervin, 1984). Moreover, they show more flexibility in doing this. These cognitive developments correspond to changes in both the content and the structure of the schemata. The former refers to the knowledge people possess and acquire, the latter to the mental organization of that knowledge. Cowan (1993), citing the *Oxford English Dictionary*, argues that experience separates knowledge from information.

Knowledge refers to some sort of awareness, consciousness or familiarity gained by experience, whereas information is merely knowledge communicated. In other words, humans only acquire knowledge through direct experience, while they can gain information without any experience at all. As Cowan (1993: 12) observes, the most important difference between information and knowledge derives from the context of reception, whether the experiences are 'within the ongoing interrelationships of their natural context'. Keeping in mind that the natural context may be simulated, for example, in a flight simulator, it seems the conditions in which the knowledge is mapped are important. The development of this process of mapping knowledge reflects the learning taking place.

Classifications of knowledge come in various shapes and sizes as several researchers have attempted to make a broad division. Ryle (1949), for example, distinguishes between 'knowing that' and 'knowing why', which he denoted as declarative and procedural knowledge respectively. This distinction is now common within the field of psychology. Paris et al. (1983) add conditional knowledge or 'knowing when' as a third kind of knowledge. While studying cultural knowledge in organizations, Sackman (1991) provides an alternative classification, consisting of four kinds of knowledge. We will follow this in the remainder of the chapter.

Sackman's (1991) first category of knowledge is 'dictionary knowledge'. This includes the definitions and classification of objects and events and more or less corresponds to directory knowledge. Directory knowledge contains information on how things are done and fits in closely with procedural knowledge. Recipe knowledge represents information on how things preferably should be done. Whereas directory knowledge is descriptive in nature, recipe knowledge has a stronger prescriptive character. Recipe knowledge partly matches with Paris et al.'s (1983) conditional knowledge, as it encloses information on when certain procedures (directory knowledge) are suitable. Finally, axiomatic knowledge encloses the fundamental beliefs or final causes that cannot be further reduced. This kind of knowledge comes closest to the notion of organization culture. Following this classification, learning involves changes in the way events and objects are described, change in the descriptive and prescriptive theories of action or changes in the fundamental beliefs.

While Sackman's classification of knowledge sheds light on the content of schemata, Kelly's (1955) Personal Construct Theory offers a deeper understanding of the structural development of schemata. Kelly (1955) sees people as construing their own theories. This view matches with the expectational nature of schemata that we identified in the foregoing section. The theories people develop consist of a finite set of constructs. With these constructs people make sense of their world by simultaneously assigning a similarity and a contrast pole to the various elements they see. These elements can be anything, ranging from people, animals and cars (see Eden and Jones, 1984) to events and processes. For example, white goes with black, guilty with innocent, fast with slow, etc. Every construct is composed of such similarity–contrast comparisons, and people use them to give meaning and structure in the world around them. Constructs have a finite range of convenience, beyond which the construct is not considered relevant. For example, the fast–slow construct which has relevance for elements like car or athlete has no meaning with respect to elements like house or sea.

In general, as a result of learning, the content and structure of people's construct system develop and their cognitive complexity increases (Bieri, 1955). Cognitive complexity can be described by (i) differentiation, the number of different constructs in a construct system; (ii) integration, which is related to the way in which the constructs are connected (Bartunek et al., 1983). According to Piaget (1937) the multiple accommodations to the diversities of reality heighten the differentiation of the schemata, while the various (reciprocal) assimilations increase the intensity of the relations between the constructs and schemata. Thus a cognitively complex construct system contains many constructs which are organized hierarchically and provides for considerable differentiation in the interpretation of objects and events. On the other hand, a cognitively simple construct system comprises a few constructs which are more loosely organized and therefore allows for only poor differentiation in interpretation. People with a cognitively more complex construct system are able to recognize subtler differences with greater accuracy and judge phenomena on the basis of several dimensions. As Neisser (1976: 93) puts it: 'The more skilled the perceiver, the more he can perceive.'

A study by Chi and Glaser (1980) may serve as illustrative evidence for this interpretation of learning as cognitive change. In a study within the field of elementary physics they found various differences between experts and novices. These differences reflect the development of various kinds of knowledge as well as changes in the organization of this knowledge. Experts knew more different domain-specific concepts and their representation of each concept contained more conceptual relations and features. Moreover, experts planned more and analysed and categorized problems thoroughly before solving them. Besides being capable of making more complex inferences and judgements, experts were able to solve new problems faster because they could retrieve from their memory procedural knowledge related to solving similar problems in the past.

The nature of organizational learning

The elementary interpretation of learning as cognitive change is on the whole consistent with most descriptions of learning that can be found in the literature on organizational learning. Argyris and Schön (1978) state that learning entails the construction, testing and restructuring of theories of action. Given their description of theories of action, this corresponds to descriptions given, for example, by Duncan and Weiss (1979), Hedberg (1981) and Fiol and Lyles (1985). These and other authors define learning, albeit in different wording, in terms of the development of knowledge about causal action–outcome relationships. Compared with Sackman's classification of knowledge, these interpretations only encompass directory and possibly recipe knowledge. Our interpretation of learning is broader. However, since it is generally accepted that organizations as entities do not learn, only their members do, we have to take a few additional steps before we can apply this interpretation to learning on an organizational level.

Organizations learn as individual members act as agents of organizational action and learn (Argyris and Schön, 1978). In the words of Hedberg (1981), individuals act on the 'stages' called organizations and learn from this acting. Organizational learning occurs as knowledge, acquired and developed by individual members, is embedded in 'organizational memory' (Argyris and Schön, 1978) or pasted into 'the organizational knowledge base' (Duncan and Weiss, 1979). The organizational knowledge that is most deeply rooted is sometimes referred to as the 'organizational paradigm' (Pfeffer, 1981; Johnson, 1987) or the 'management-orientation' (Hedberg and Jönnson, 1977). Similar to knowledge on the individual level, organizational knowledge serves as an interpretative scheme and forms the basis for managerial action (Bartunek, 1984; Daft and Weick, 1984).

Not all knowledge acquired or developed by every individual organizational member is automatically added to the organizational knowledge base. In order for newly acquired knowledge to become organizational knowledge, it first has to be exchanged and accepted by others within the organization and, besides being socially acceptable, become considered relevant knowledge for organizational activities (Duncan and Weiss, 1979). Not all individually acquired knowledge will be relevant. Besides knowledge appropriate for doing their job within the organization, individuals possess strictly private knowledge. On the other hand, knowledge relevant for organizational purposes is not limited to individually acquired knowledge. Learning within organizations is above all a social process, wherein individual members learn and develop knowledge together (see, for example, Nonaka, 1994).

Crucial in the process of organizational learning are successive rounds of dialogues wherein individual members or groups of members are involved. During these dialogues individual knowledge is exchanged and tested and new knowledge is developed. Several authors stress the importance of these dialogues. Duncan and Weiss (1979) point to this phase as 'organizational inquiry', while Schön (1983) speaks of 'rumor and conflict'. Van der Heijden and Eden (this volume) refer to it as a 'strategic conversation' which may be stimulated by several interactive modelling techniques. They argue that learning requires an effective process of conversation, through which strategic cognitions can be compared, challenged and negotiated. Metaphors play an important role in the exchange of knowledge (Nonaka, 1994). 'The essence of metaphor is understanding and experiencing one kind of thing in terms of another' (Lakoff and Johnson, 1980: 5). Metaphors allow the exchange of implicit knowledge and personal perspectives which are otherwise difficult or impossible to communicate verbally.

As individuals learn, solely or together, and not the organization to which they belong, it seems more appropriate to express the occurrence of organizational learning in terms of the degree of organizational learning taking place (see Huber, 1991). Organizational learning occurs as the members acquire chunks of knowledge and recognize it as potentially useful for organizational purposes. Huber designates the development of knowledge by individual members of an organization as the existence of organizational learning and the spread of this knowledge throughout the organization as its breadth. He distinguishes between the elaborateness and the thoroughness of the organization's learning. Elaborateness concerns the variety of organizational knowledge. Learning accelerates as the body of organizational knowledge becomes more varied or, in Huber's (1991: 90) words, 'more varied interpretations are developed'. Such development enlarges the range of possibilities for action. This attribute of organizational learning corresponds to that which Ginsberg (1990) denotes as the management team's socio-cognitive complexity, a notion that is similar to the cognitive complexity at the individual level. Finally, thoroughness pertains to the degree to which the comprehension and interpretation by the various individuals is uniform.

This attribute comes close to what Ginsberg (1990: 522) denotes as the socio-cognitive consensus of a management team and describes as 'the extent to which a diverse set of assumptions or beliefs has been synthesized into a commonly shared understanding'. According to Ginsberg (1990) the socio-cognitive complexity and consensus of a management team together give an indication of that team's socio-cognitive capacities. Although somewhat contradictory, both diversity in perspective and consensus on interpretation are necessary for teams to learn. The former is the result of a high socio-cognitive complexity and the latter is connected with a high socio-cognitive consensus. Fiol (1994) states that the socio-cognitive consensus should particularly be interpreted in terms of agreement on the frame of reference with respect to which the various interpretations are compared. This view explains why certain teams 'simultaneously agree and disagree' (Fiol, 1994: 403). The meaning attributed to objects and events is evidently related to the content of the schemata as well as to the context wherein they are employed. This indicates that, equivalent to the description of the schemata at the individual level, both the content and the structure of a management team should be described for charting organizational learning.

Charting potentialities

The most important conclusion we can draw from the preceding section is that cognition and learning are two sides of the same coin: learning entails cognitive change. Learning is a process of cognitive development during which the knowledge base of an individual or organization grows and/or is restructured. A consequence of this interpretation of learning is that insight into the development of managerial cognition over time is a prerequisite for charting processes of organizational learning. This view on organizational learning is reasonably flexible and may even be extended to the learning of networks of organizations or even an entire industry. Most importantly, it offers several clues for charting processes of organizational learning.

Changes in either the content or the structure of the knowledge held by individual organizational members may reveal organizational learning. Consequently, techniques currently employed for mapping managerial and organizational cognition can be used for identifying and registering organizational learning, known as cognitive mapping or causal mapping. By revealing the cognitive or causal maps of several important organizational members, and comparing the maps in time, it is possible to identify the degree of organizational learning that has occurred. A cognitive map is interpreted in this chapter as a knowledge representation device that contains different kinds of knowledge. Using Sackman's classification, a cognitive map consists of four different parts or submaps. This subdivision of cognitive maps is comparable to the three submaps which Fiol and Huff (1992) distinguish. The cognitive map that fits the definition of organizational learning as developed in the previous section can be expressed in terms of the degree of centrality of concepts or other chunks of knowledge. We might see circles inside circles. Those chunks of knowledge that are shared by many organizational members are closer to a centre which may be denoted as the organizational paradigm or management orientation.

A major constraint in mapping cognition and charting learning concerns the degree to which knowledge can be verbalized or made explicit. People learn both consciously and unconsciously and acquire both explicit and implicit knowledge (Polanyi, 1967; Reber, 1993; Spender, this volume). Based on an evolutionary perspective, Reber (1993) argues that explicit knowledge is only the top of an iceberg that largely consists of deeper and concealed implicit knowledge. A person's knowledge base, on the basis of which s/he perceives and acts, includes explicit and implicit elements, and the concealed nature of the latter severely complicates the charting of organizational learning. The present methods for charting cognition fall short in eliciting implicit knowledge. Currently implicit knowledge can be glimpsed in the laboratory experiments reviewed by Reber (1993), the implication being that changes in the organizational knowledge base should be mapped when they are fresh and still explicit. Anderson (1983) considers this the core of the distinction between explicit, declarative knowledge on the one hand and implicit, procedural knowledge on the other. When people learn something, the knowledge they acquire is explicit, but after a while, with practice, it becomes implicit knowledge and disappears from sight. It is essential to map during the dialogue phase, which is sometimes visible as managers attempt to solve problems of various kinds, try to close financial gaps or seek to exploit strategic opportunities (Duncan and Weiss, 1979; Hedberg, 1981; Van der Heijden and Eden, this volume) for such changes normally go hand in hand with lengthy discussions and meetings (Schön, 1983). The accompanying conflict and commotion within the organization are visible signs of organizational learning in action.

In addition to cognitive mapping and registering the rumour and conflict, changes in organizational knowledge may be revealed by studying documents. Organizational knowledge is sometimes written down in the form of procedures, plans or reports and can be withdrawn from these sources. For example, a competitor analysis may reflect, besides a classification of the firms that are seen as competitors, what management perceives as successful strategies. This in turn may provide insight into directory knowledge (the how) and recipe knowledge (the should). Finally, organizational knowledge, and thus changes in the organizational knowledge base, may be identified by the changing organizational myths, sagas, stories, although since these change slowly, this registration may take too long. Without going into this deeper, we can note strong linkages to the literature on organization culture (for example, Schein, 1985).

Four cognitive mapping techniques explored

Within the field of managerial and organizational cognition, both the term cognitive map and cause map are used. Whereas the distinction between the two is not always clear, the latter is usually limited to causality relations (Bougon, 1983) or 'phenomenological beliefs and the causal dimension in the respondents' thinking' (Laukkanen, 1992: 14). A cognitive map is a broader generic device that may contain 'all possible types of relations occurring in patterns of concepts' (Bougon, 1983: 177). Fiol and Huff (1992: 267), for example, describe cognitive maps as 'graphic representations that locate people in relation to their information environments'. A cause map is a point somewhere in the middle between maps that deal with manifest content and maps that specify underlying cognitive structures (see Huff, 1990). We follow Huff's usage of the more general term cognitive map, except when other terms provide more information.

In this section, four techniques for eliciting cognitive and causal maps are compared. These techniques have several things in common. First, each provides clear procedures for collecting data. Second, each allows for systematic analysis of that data. Third, each is supported by specialized computer software which increases the reliability of the analysis. Successively, attention will be paid to:

- content analysis;
- repertory grid technique with multidimensional scaling;

- cause mapping with Laukkanen's CMAP2;
- cognitive mapping with Eden's COPE.

In the following each technique is described, including its capacity for sys-tematic analysis and cognitive maps comparison. In the next section we try to assess when learning has occurred if the techniques are employed, which comes down to exploring what cognitive change means within the context of each technique.

Content analysis

Content analysis refers to the analysis of texts or recorded interviews that are subsequently written out. Central in a content analysis stands the grouping of (important) words into fewer content categories (Weber, 1990). Basically, content analysis can be conducted on two levels, the analysis of the manifest content or of the latent content (Erdener and Dunn, 1990). The former is sometimes described as classical while the latter is referred to as ethnographic (for example, Tesch, 1991). Analysis of the manifest content focuses on clearly discernible characteristics such as word frequency and the position of certain key words in their context. The latent context refers to the underlying meaning embodied in the text, referred to as a KWIC analysis. While both study the usage of language, the analysis of latent content attempts to capture what the writer or the interviewee actually meant when s/he used particular words in a certain combination. This can be done by mapping assertions or lines of argumentation (for example, Barr et al., 1992).

From a cognitive mapping point of view, identification of the latent content is more interesting, but relies more heavily on the subjective inter-pretation and judgement of the researcher. Weber (1990: 62) illustrates this by stating that 'the content analyst contributes factual and theoretical knowledge to the interpretation'. Because of this, latent content analysis 'introduces a tradeoff in terms of reliability' in comparison to manifest content analysis (Erdener and Dunn, 1990: 293). However, content analy-sis can also be combined with various statistical methods to analyse data based on texts (Weber, 1990). This may bypass the subjectivity problem. Simple examples include the use of descriptive statistics like word fre-quencies (for example, Winterscheid, 1994) and correlation analysis to identify which words vary together. More complex examples require mul-tivariate methods like factor analysis or LISREL. A certain combination of words or underlying themes can then be considered as a distinct organi-zational cognitive map. Subsequently, these correlations or underlying themes may form the basis for comparisons between different texts in a longitudinal study. An important advantage of the use of statistical ana-lytical methods is that they often 'reveal similarities and differences among texts that would be difficult, if not impossible, to detect other-wise' (Weber, 1990: 74). Alternatively, the use of independent coders who identify the underlying themes and lines of argumentation may improve reliability.

Repertory grid with multidimensional scaling

The Repertory Grid Technique (RGT) was developed by Kelly (1955) as a practical instrument for the application of his Personal Construct Theory. The personal theories people construe can be grasped by construing a repertory grid that relates a set of elements to a set of constructs. The RGT procedure encompasses three stages. In the first stage the elements are selected. This can be generated by the researcher, on the basis of theoretical considerations, or by the respondents themselves. During the second stage the elements are presented to the respondents together with a question to classify, rank or compare them pairwise. There is a large repertoire of different methods available for this (Fransella and Bannister, 1977; Reger, 1990). In the third stage of the procedure the grids are construed and subsequently analysed. For this an arsenal of statistical techniques is available, ranging from factor and cluster analysis to discriminant analysis and Multi-Dimensional Scaling (MDS). The latter is especially useful in combination with the RGT because it transforms non-metric input (ordinal) into metric output (distances) and allows for the construction of individual maps (Kruskal and Wish, 1991).

The input for MDS is a similarity matrix generated for each respondent, or group of respondents, during the preceding stage. The cells of a similarity matrix are filled with proximities. Each proximity indicates how similar or different two elements are perceived to be by the respondent. MDS transforms these into a spatial configuration in such a way that the spatial distance between two elements corresponds to their perceived similarity or difference. On the basis of subjective evaluation, an index of fit or stress measuring the number of dimensions underlying the non-metric data can be assessed (Hair et al., 1990). Subsequently, these dimensions are labelled, which is easier if the respondents were asked to think aloud during the ranking or comparison of the elements in stage two. As an alternative they may also be asked to do so afterwards. The combination of dimensions, reflecting the constructs used by a respondent, encloses a person's cognitive map.

When comparing different cognitive maps, respondents may be asked to identify and characterize the differences between two maps that are, for example, construed on different moments in time. In addition, maximum likelihood estimate (MLE) based MDS methods, as opposed to the more traditional MDS methods that are based on ordinary least squares like INDSCAL, allow for statistical significance testing of differences between two maps. Examples of MLE-based MDS methods are Ramsay's MULTI-SCALE and Takane's MAXSCAL. The former is limited to ratio-scaled dissimilarity data, while the latter can cope with non-metric data (Bijmolt and Wedel, 1993).

Cause mapping with Laukkanen's CMAP2

Laukkanen (1990, 1992) has developed a methodology for eliciting cause maps in combination with the accompanying software (CMAP2) to construe and analyse systematically these cause maps. The cause maps are elicited in several interview sessions, in general about three, each lasting between one and three hours. The first interview is unstructured and is used to obtain general and behavioural information. The next interviews are aimed at 'eliciting concepts and causal beliefs around anchor themes' (Laukkanen, 1990: 33). Each interview covers approximately 10 to 12 themes. Preferably notes are made in a tentative cause map format and interviews are taperecorded for reasons of backup and additional data on details. To obtain the cause maps, concepts and the cause–effect relations between concepts are fed into CMAP2 and are then available for exploration and analysis.

With CMAP2 two areas can be studied in detail: the various concepts used by the respondents and the causal assertions that relate to these concepts. Comparison can be made with other cognitive maps through the facility to translate the natural language used by respondents into a system of standard concepts. The cause maps can then be compared in terms of incidence of or links between concepts. Respondents that use similar concepts can be clustered and maps can be construed that show the cause and effect concepts around certain common concepts in each cluster. The latter are referred to as focal or domain maps. CMAP2 calculates some quantitative measures for each focal or domain map which may be of use when comparing maps of different respondents or clusters. For example, CMAP2 calculates the map's space coverage, or the degree to which it captures the maximum number of links possible between the standard terms.

Cognitive mapping with Eden's COPE

COPE (Ackerman et al., 1992) is comparable to Laukkanen's method. Like CMAP2, COPE is software for recording and analysing cognitive maps. The differences between CMAP2 and COPE originate from the different purposes for which the methods were developed. CMAP2 was developed as a research tool while COPE's roots lie in the solving of complex, strategic problems within groups (Eden, 1989). A first difference concerns the use of the software. CMAP2 is used out of sight of the respondents while COPE is preferably used together with the respondent and a cognitive map is construed during the interview in cooperation with the respondent. To facilitate smooth operations COPE has strong graphical facilities for displaying cognitive maps. CMAP2, on the other hand, is text based and not as friendly for the user. COPE builds cognitive maps of concepts linked to each other by arrows that indicate the nature of the linkage, for instance, causality. Each concept has two poles, referred to as the emergent pole and the contrasting pole. This clearly shows that COPE is based on Kelly's Personal Construct Theory (Eden, 1988). A cognitive map is built up by linking several concepts together in an hierarchical format. Next, the structure of a cognitive map can be analysed in a variety of ways. Examples include listing concepts, tracing argumentation, clustering of concepts or listing loops in argumentation. Analysis of a cognitive map may also include determining the centrality of concepts, for instance, by calculating 'the number of concepts immediately related to a concept' or by calculating 'the density of concepts surrounding the concept by weighting those closer higher than those further away on an exponentially reducing basis' (Eden, 1988: 11). These calculated derivative measures can be used as a basis for comparison.

Comparing the four techniques

Each of the cognitive mapping methods described above has its own characteristic facilities, possibilities and limitations. Table 12.1 summarizes their main characteristics and shows some differences between the four methods. Besides differences in the input data each requires, they produce cognitive maps which differ both in nature and form.

The cognitive map produced by content analysis consists in its simplest form of a combination of words. More complex maps can be generated as (for instance, with independent coders) causal maps are construed on the basis of written texts or if multivariate statistical methods are used to analyse texts. In the latter case, a cognitive map consists of underlying themes which may be graphically represented in a drawn map. The Repertory Grid Technique combined with MDS also results in such a map. The nature of the accompanying cognitive map is made up of the underlying dimensions representing the constructs used by a person. Finally, the cognitive maps produced by CMAP2 and COPE are more or less similar as both can be marked as causal maps. The former generates a text-based causal map, the latter also has the facilities to produce a graphical map. The text-based design of CMAP2 may be considered a limitation as overview is easily lost. There are however several ways to overcome this problem. For example, COPE can be used in combination with CMAP2 to produce a graphical picture of a map generated with CMAP2.

Partially as a result of these differences in the nature and format of generated maps, each of the methods compares cognitive maps in a different way. Content analysis considers either content differences in maps directly or more indirectly through comparison of the calculated statistical measures, for example, the factors and factor loadings. Similarly, using the RGT-MDS combination graphical maps can be compared directly (by sight) by the researchers or by asking respondents or more indirectly by statistical testing for differences between maps. As noted, a prerequisite for the latter is a MLE-based MDS method. In addition, there is a variety of mathematical methods available for comparison of cognitive maps (see, for example, Markóczy and Goldberg, 1995). CMAP2 allows for both comparison of the

Table 12.1 *Cognitive mapping methods compared*

	Content analysis	Repertory grid technique with MDS	Cause mapping with CMAP2	Cognitive mapping with COPE
Required data	Text	(Dis)similarity data	Cause and effect relations, lines of argumentation	Cause and effect relations, lines of argumentation
Nature of cognitive map	Combination of words Underlying dimensions Causal relations	Underlying dimensions	Concepts and relationships	Concepts and relationships
Format of cognitive map	Text Graphical map	Graphical map 2/3-dimensional map	Text-based	Text-based and graphical causal map
Nature of comparison of cognitive maps	Content Statistical measure	On sight Statistical test	Content and structure (concepts used and derivative measures)	Structure (derivative measures)
Captured type of knowledge	Dictionary Directory	Dictionary Axiomatic	Dictionary, directory and recipe	Dictionary, directory and recipe
Sign of learning	Different words used Different themes	Different dimensions Statistical difference	Change in concepts Change in linkages	Change in concepts Change in linkage Change in centrality
Disadvantage	Identification of theory-in-use difficult Texts other purpose	Comparison requires fixed pool of constructs	Influence researcher on construction of map	Comparison of content difficult
Advantage	Availability of texts	Systematic analysis and comparison	Comparison of content of cognitive maps	Interactive construction of cognitive map

content and the structure of the generated map. The former is possible due to the standardization of the concepts used by different respondents (or by the same respondent at different moments in time). Finally, comparison of cognitive maps using COPE is only possible by comparing several derivative measures.

Further differences concern the type of knowledge captured by each of the methods. Following Sackman's (1991) classification of knowledge, classical content analysis, being limited to the manifest content, mainly captures dictionary knowledge (that is, definition and labels of things). If causal maps are construed on the basis of texts and documents, directory knowledge may also be captured (see, for example, Fiol and Huff, 1992). The RGT-MDS combination is able to capture dictionary knowledge if the concepts are generated by the respondents themselves. If the concepts are generated on the basis of a theoretical study information on this type of knowledge will not be gained. Moreover, as this combination of methods digs deepest into human cognitive structures, it probably comes closest to capturing axiomatic knowledge, being the identified dimensions. CMAP2 and COPE both capture dictionary knowledge through the concepts or themes mentioned by the respondents. They also get a grip on directory and recipe knowledge. The last two mentioned reflect descriptive and prescriptive theories of action respectively. CMAP2 and COPE probably do not capture directory knowledge as completely as is possible with content analysis. However, the gap between espoused theories and theories in use may be an issue worth considering here as written text may more often reflect the former than the latter (Argyris and Schön, 1978).

Next, there are important differences between the methods regarding the signs considered as evidence of organizational learning taking place. These signs reflect significant changes on four different (partially overlapping) levels of analysis. First, changes in the words or, as Laukkanen (1992) notes, changes in the natural language used by respondents may be signs of learning by the respondents. Content analysis in particular is able to detect such changes. Second, changes in identified underlying dimensions or concepts may be indications of learning occurring. Following Barr et al. (1992) these changes may include the use of a new concept or the deletion of an old one, replacement of a specific concept by more general term or the sustained use of new variables. Both the Repertory Grid Technique and content analysis combined with a multivariate statistical technique are useful for identifying such changes. Third, changes in the linkages between concepts may be signs of learning taking place. This may involve changes in the way in which concepts are linked, changes in the clustering or centrality of concepts, as well as changes in the causality between concepts (see Barr et al., 1992). In particular both COPE and CMAP2 have facilities that enable identification of such changes, but the RGT offers probably enough possibilities for detecting such changes (see Ginsberg, 1989, for a method of calculating a map's inherent cognitive complexity). Fourth, changes in the way in which concepts are used may be indications of learning. This entails, among other things, changes in the way elements are ranked along an underlying dimension or constructs are used to judge elements. Increasing dispersion of elements along a certain dimension, that is a dimension increasingly discriminating between elements, is a sign of such changes.

Finally, Table 12.1 also lists each method's most important advantage and main disadvantage. We have already touched upon the difficulties that content analysis may have with the identification of theories in use as opposed to espoused theories. In addition, texts used for content analysis are often written with other purposes in mind. Some, for example, have a political dimension, and the content may reflect this (Huff and Fletcher, 1990). On the other hand, texts are often readily available in large quantities and over long periods of time. An important disadvantage of the Repertory Grid Technique is related to the comparison of cognitive maps. Comparison requires that the same pool of constructs is used in the construction of each of the compared cognitive maps. This need not to be a problem in certain research designs (for example, hypothesis testing), but in others it may be. If the constructs are generated by the respondents themselves, the fact that they use different constructs at different moments in time may indicate learning (see above). However, if the same pool of constructs is used, the possibilities for systematic analysis and comparison are an important advantage of the RGT-MDS combination.

Although, the disadvantages and advantages of cause mapping with CMAP2 and cognitive mapping with COPE are similar, there are some differences. The influence of the researcher in the construction process of maps may be considered to be somewhat more problematic with CMAP2 than with COPE. The excellent graphical facilities of COPE simplify constructing the final map while the respondent and the researcher interact. On the other hand, CMAP2 offers better facilities for comparing the content of cognitive maps (as construed and coded by the researcher). As both methods make use of interactively generated data, both may suffer from post hoc rationalization by respondents as they try to impose order on the past (see Huff and Fletcher, 1990). These rationalizations may reflect espoused theory (Argyris and Schön, 1978). However, this danger is reduced as cognitive mapping sessions are longer and more intensive. Moreover, as Van der Heijden and Eden (this volume) stress, we need to remember Weick's (1979: 155) saying, 'How can I know what I think until I see what I say?'. What one thinks often only becomes clear when thoughts are spoken aloud. So rationalizations may be an inextricable part of one's current thinking.

Final remarks

In this chapter we present a methodology for systematically charting processes of organizational learning. Based upon the conceptualization of learning as cognitive change, these methods offer various mapping techniques. We explore and compare four such techniques. Given the different areas in which organizations may learn, there is no sole winner. Each technique highlights different kinds of knowledge and has its own advantages and disadvantages. Consequently, depending upon the particular goals of their research projects, organizational projects studied or availability of certain kinds of data, researchers may wish to select either one or a combination of these cognitive mapping techniques. As the approach rests upon a specific conceptualization of organizational learning and is not yet used in practice, it is inevitable that it will have its own specific problems. In this context three closely related points are particularly worth considering. First, the approach concentrates on exploring the cognitive dimension and takes a pragmatic shortcut concerning the social dimension by talking about the degree of learning. More learning occurs as more organizational members obtain certain chunks of knowledge and recognize them as potentially useful for organizational purposes. By interviewing several people involved with the specific project studied and questioning them about the process in which such a project comes about, only a glimpse of the social dimension is captured. The best way to study the social dimension presumably remains the direct observation of the interaction of organizational members as they work together, discuss, argue and choose, which brings us to a second point.

The possibilities for mapping implicit knowledge are severely constrained. A large part of knowledge is tacit and taken for granted and can hardly be made explicit, if at all. This holds true for both individual and organizational knowledge, especially where it concerns the above-mentioned social dimension. For this reason, cognitive mapping techniques should preferably be used when the degree of explicitness of the knowledge is at its height. So the methodology is particularly appropriate when organizational knowledge is developed and created and topics are still hot as the possibilities of cognitive mapping techniques for elicitation of tacit knowledge are more than likely limited. This conclusion is also evident from Nonaka's (1994) model of the organizational knowledge creation processes. During this process, among other things, tacit individual knowledge is made explicit during communication, which often happens by means of metaphors. Next it can be used as an ingredient for newly created organizational knowledge, which slowly disappears from the reach of cognitive mapping techniques as it is ultimately converted into tacit knowledge.

The third point of consideration relates to the multidimensionality of knowledge of which the tacit–explicit dimension is only one aspect. Other dimensions concern the individual–collective contrast, covering the social dimension, and the differing nature of different types of knowledge (Spender, this volume). Two epistemological issues with which each researcher has to cope in one way or another are important in this respect. First, our conceptualization of knowledge and the classifications we make may not correspond to the real ones. Second, the cognitive mapping techniques applied may not be appropriate for capturing the various kinds of knowledge either used by the researcher or the manager in question. Both issues raise crucial questions about knowledge and its nature.

References

Ackerman, F., Cropper, S. and Eden, C. (1992) *Graphics COPE User Guide*. Glasgow: University of Strathclyde.

Anderson, J.R. (1983) *The Architecture of Cognition*. Harvard: Harvard University Press.

Argyris, C. and Schön, D.A. (1978) *Organizational Learning: A Theory of Action Perspective*. Reading, MA: Addison-Wesley.

Barr, P.S., Stimpert, J.L. and Huff, A.S. (1992) Cognitive change, strategic action, and organizational renewal, *Strategic Management Journal*, 13: 15–36.

Bartunek, J.M. (1984) Changing interpretive schemes and organizational restructuring: the example of a religious order, *Administrative Science Quarterly*, 29: 355–72.

Bartunek, J.M., Gordon, J.R. and Weathersby, R.P. (1983) Developing 'complicated' understanding in administrators, *Academy of Management Review*, 8 (2): 273–84.

Bieri, J. (1955) Cognitive complexity-simplicity and predictive behavior, *Journal of Abnormal and Social Psychology*, 51: 263–8.

Bijmolt, T.H.A. and Wedel, M. (1993) An investigation into multidimensional scaling: tast effects on similarity data and solutions of MAXSCAL, Institute of Economic Research, Groningen. Research Memorandum no. 547.

Bougon, M.G. (1983) Uncovering cognitive maps: the self-Q technique, in G. Morgan (ed.), *Beyond Method: Strategies for Social Research*. Beverly Hills, CA: Sage.

Chi, M.T.H. and Glaser, R. (1980) The measurement of expertise: analysis of the development of knowledge and skill as a basis for assessing achievement, in E.L. Baker and E.S. Quellmalz (eds), *Educational Testing and Evaluation: Design, Analysis and Policy*. Beverly Hills, CA: Sage.

Cowan, D.A. (1993) Rhythms and variation: patterns that integrate individual and organizational learning. Paper presented to the First International Workshop on Managerial and Organizational Cognition, EIASM, Brussels, 13–14 May.

Daft, R.L. and Weick, K.E. (1984) Toward a model of organizations as interpretation systems, *Academy of Management Review*, 9 (2): 284–95.

Duncan, R. and Weiss, A. (1979) Organizational learning: implications for organizational design, in B. Staw (ed.), *Research in Organizational Behavior*. Greenwich, CT: JAI Press: 75–123.

Eden, C. (1988) Cognitive mapping: a review. *European Journal of Operational Research*, 36: 1–13.

Eden, C. (1989) Strategic options development and analysis, in J. Rosenhead (ed.), *Rational Analysis for a Problematic World*. London: Wiley.

Eden, C., Ackerman, F. and Cropper, S. (1992) The analysis of cause maps, *Journal of Management Studies*, 29 (3): 309–24.

Eden, C. and Jones, S. (1984) Using repertory grids for problem construction, *Journal of Operational Research Society*, 3 (9): 779–90.

Eisenhardt, K.M. (1989) Building theories from case study research, *Academy of Management Review*, 14 (4): 532–50.

Erdener, C.B. and Dunn, C.P. (1990) Content analysis, in A.S. Huff (ed.), *Mapping Strategic Thought*. Chichester: John Wiley: 291–300.

Fiol, C.M. (1994) Consensus, diversity, and learning in organizations, *Organization Science*, 5 (3): 403–20.

Fiol, C.M. and Huff, A.S. (1992) Maps for managers: where are we? Where do we go from here?, *Journal of Management Studies*, 29 (3): 267–85.

Fiol, C.M. and Lyles, M.A. (1985) Organizational learning, *Academy of Management Review*, 10 (4): 803–13.

Fransella, F. and Bannister, D. (1977) *A Manual for Repertory Grid Technique*. London: Academic Press.

Ginsberg, A. (1989) Construing the business portfolio: a cognitive model of diversification, *Journal of Management Studies*, 26 (4): 417–38.

Ginsberg, A. (1990) Connecting diversification to performance: a sociocognitive approach, *Academy of Management Review*, 15 (3): 514–35.

Gioia, D.A. and Poole, P.P. (1984) Scripts in organisation behaviour, *Academy of Management Review*, 9 (3): 449–59.

Hair, J.F., Anderson, R.E. and Tatham, R.L. (1990) *Multivariate Data Analysis*, 2nd edn. New York: Macmillan.

Harrigan, K.R. (1983) Research methodologies for contingency approaches to business strategy, *Academy of Management Review*, 8 (3): 398–405.

Hedberg, B. (1981) How organizations learn and unlearn, in P.C. Nystrom and W.H. Starbuck (eds), *Handbook of Organizational Design*. London: University Press. pp. 8–27.

Hedberg, B. and Jönnson, S. (1977) Strategy making as a discontinuous process, *International Studies of Management and Organisation*, 7: 88–109.

Huber, G.P. (1991) Organizational learning: the contributing process and the literatures, *Organization Science*, 2 (1): 88–115.

Huff, A.S. (1990) Mapping strategic thought, in A.S. Huff (ed.), *Mapping Strategic Thought*. Chichester: John Wiley. pp. 11–49.

Huff, A.S. and Fletcher, K.E. (1990) Conclusion: key mapping decisions, in A.S. Huff (ed.), *Mapping Strategic Thought*, New York: John Wiley. pp. 403–12.

Johnson, G. (1987) *Strategic Management and the Management Process*. Oxford: Basil Blackwell.

Kelly, G.A. (1955) *The Psychology of Personal Constructs*, vol. 1. New York: W.W. Norton.

Kiesler, S. and Sproull, L. (1982) Managerial response to changing environments: perspectives on problem sensing from social cognition, *Administrative Science Quarterly*, 27: 548–70.

Kruskal, J.B. and Wish, M. (1991) *Multidimensional Scaling*. Newbury Park: Sage.

Lakoff, G. and Johnson, M. (1980) *Metaphors We Live By*. Chicago, IL: University of Chicago Press.

Laukkanen, M. (1990) Describing management cognition: the cause mapping approach, *Scandinavian Journal of Management*, 6 (3): 197–216.

Laukkanen, M. (1992) *Comparative Cause Mapping of Management Cognitions*. Helsinki: Helsinki School of Economics and Business Administration. Publication D-154.

Markóczy, L. and Goldberg, J. (1995) A method for eliciting and comparing causal maps, *Journal of Management*, 21 (2): 305–33.

Miller, G.A. (1956) The magic number seven plus or minus two: some limits on our capacity for processing information, *Psychological Review*, 64: 81–97.

Neisser, U. (1976) *Cognition and Reality – Principles and Implications of Cognitive Psychology*. New York: Freeman.

Nonaka, I. (1994) A dynamic theory of organizational knowledge creation, *Organization Science*, 5 (1): 14–37.

Paris, S.G., Lipson, M.Y. and Wixson, K.K. (1983) Becoming a strategic reader, *Contemporary Educational Psychology*, 8: 293–316.

Pedler, M., Burgoyne, J. and Boydell, T. (1991) *The Learning Company: A Strategy for Sustainable Development*. Maidenhead: McGraw-Hill.

Pervin, L.A. (1984) *Personality*. New York: John Wiley.

Pfeffer, J. (1981) *Power in Organizations*. Cambridge, MA: Ballinger.

Piaget, J. (1936) The origins of intelligence in children, in H.E. Gruber and J.J. Vonèche (eds), *The Essential Piaget: An Interpretive Reference and Guide*. New York: Basic Books. pp. 215–49.

Piaget, J. (1937) The construction of reality in the child, in H.E. Gruber and J.J. Vonèche (eds), *The Essential Piaget: An Interpretive Reference and Guide*, New York: Basic Books. pp. 250–94.

Polanyi, M. (1967) *The Tacit Dimension*. Garden City, NY: Anchor Books.

Prahalad, C.K. and Bettis, R.A. (1986) The dominant logic: a new linkage between diversity and performance, *Strategic Management Journal*, 7: 485–501.

Reber, A.S. (1993) *Implicit Learning and Tacit Knowledge: An Essay on the Cognitive Unconscious*. New York: Oxford University Press.

Reger, R.K. (1990) Managerial thought structures and competitive positioning, in A.S. Huff (ed.), *Mapping Strategic Thought*. Chichester: John Wiley. pp. 71–88.

Ryle, G. (1949) *The Concept of Mind*. London: Hutchinson.

Sackman, S.A. (1991) *Organizational Culture and Leadership*. San Francisco, CA: Jossey-Bass.

Schein, E.H. (1985) *Organizational Culture and Leadership*. San Francisco, CA: Jossey-Bass.

Schön, D.A. (1983) Organizational learning, in G. Morgan (ed.), *Beyond Method: Strategies for Social Research*. Beverly Hills, CA: Sage. pp. 114–28.

Senge, P. (1990) *The Fifth Discipline: The Art and Practice of the Learning Organization*. New York: Doubleday.

Simon, H.A. (1991) Bounded rationality and organizational learning, *Organization Science*, 2 (1): 125–34.

Spender, J.-C. (1998) Workplace knowledge: the individual and collective dimensions, in this volume.

Tesch, R. (1991) Software for qualitative researchers: analysis needs and program capabilities, in N.G. Fielding and R.M. Lee (eds), *Using Computers in Qualitative Research*. Newbury Park: Sage. pp. 16–37.

Van der Heijden, K. and Eden, C. (1998) Managerial cognition, organizational cognition and the practice of organizational learning, in this volume.

Weber, R.P. (1990) *Basic Content Analysis*. Newbury Park: Sage.

Weick, K.E. (1979) *The Social Psychology of Organizing*. New York: Random House.

Winterscheid, B.C. (1994) Computer-aided text analysis: are words a window to the mind?, in C. Stubbart, J.R. Meindl and J.F. Porac (eds), *Advances in Managerial Cognition and Organizational Information Processing*, vol. 5. Greenwich, CT: JAI Press.

13

THE THEORY AND PRACTICE OF COMPARING CAUSAL MAPS

Mark Jenkins

This chapter considers choosing methodologies for eliciting the causal structures which managers use to make strategic sense of their world. While such methodologies are already accepted within the strategic management literature, we focus on the issue of mapping across multiple organizations and thereby contribute to the debate on the application of such maps to strategic management research. Traditionally strategic management research has focused on the content or the 'what' aspects of strategy and has done so from a rational economic perspective (for example, Porter, 1985). Recently there has been increasing dissatisfaction with such rational, content-based approaches. In particular, criticism has focused on a general lack of understanding of the process or the 'how' aspects of strategy. This has underlined the limitations of assuming that managers are rational beings who see and act within a defined, objective environment (Mintzberg, 1978; Weick, 1990).

Stubbart (1987) refers to cognitive science as providing the missing link between environmental conditions and strategic action. The cognitive perspective redirects attention away from the objective 'out there' to the subjective way in which individuals see the world. Managerial cognition is the broad term applied to research that takes a cognitive approach to understand how individuals and organizations construe their environments. Such research has focused on issues such as: selectivity and agenda setting (Kiesler and Sproull, 1982; Dutton et al., 1983); cognitive biases in strategy formulation (Schwenk, 1984; Duhaime and Schwenk, 1985; Fletcher and Huff, 1990); information processing (Walsh, 1988; Dutton et al., 1989); strategic learning (Argyris and Schön, 1978; Fiol and Lyles, 1985); competitive structure and positioning (Reger, 1988; Porac and Thomas, 1990; Daniels et al., 1993) and managerial attribution of performance (Salancik and Meindl, 1984; Huff and Schwenk, 1990; Clapham and Schwenk, 1991). These studies have afforded new insights into strategic processes and provided empirical evidence of the non-rational phenomena to which critics of traditional strategic management research have frequently referred.

A general term for the methodologies applied in cognitive studies of strategic management is cognitive mapping. This term has been attributed to Tolman (1948) who proposed an alternative to the stimulus–response models of human behaviour based on the concept of field theory. Field theory asserts that individuals create fields or maps in order to understand and anticipate their environment. These ideas have been developed in the management context through the application of a number of cognitive theories which seek to explain how individuals make sense of their world. Causal mapping is a subset of cognitive mapping and is concerned with representing cognition as a set of causal interactions. Causal mapping studies have illuminated individual decision-making (Axelrod, 1976b), the idiosyncratic maps of individuals (Cosette and Audet, 1992), organizational change (Narayanan and Fahey, 1990) and intervention into organizational issues (Eden et al., 1979; Eden, 1988). This chapter presents a framework for evaluating mapping methodologies. We consider the critical design issues in developing a research question and methodology to undertake comparative causal mapping. We will reflect briefly on the theoretical basis for causal mapping, review the application of causal mapping in the management literature and critically discuss alternative approaches for creating causal maps.

Evaluating mapping methodologies

To establish the necessary criteria for selecting a mapping methodology we show a conceptual framework in Figure 13.1. Placed within the context of a body of theory, this takes an interpretive perspective and accepts that behaviour is modified or influenced by individual cognition. The mapping method is nested between two key dimensions, methodological issues which are concerned with the soundness of the approach based on accepted research practice and theory, and the research context which considers the specific nature of the research study. These two dimensions overlap through the concept of practicability which mediates either dimension's influence on the final selection of the mapping method. An optimal methodological solution may be too time-consuming and complex for the research context while the most appropriate approach, such as a questionnaire which can be quickly completed by a number of managers, may be inadequate from a methodological perspective.

The distinction between the three phases of surfacing, mapping and analysis contained within mapping method is fuzzy. They are bridged by many of the current mapping methodologies; for example, Jones and Eden (1981) combine surfacing, mapping and analysis in one interactive process. The purpose of identifying these phases is to assist in evaluating existing approaches using the cartographic analogy suggested by Weick (1990). Surfacing is concerned with elicitation in the same way as the cartographer collects data through surveying or from studying existing maps. Mapping

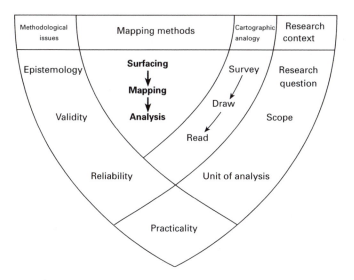

Figure 13.1   *Conceptual shield for considering mapping methodologies*

is where the raw data are combined to create the map through a particular transformation process, whether this is concerned with converting language into a mathematical matrix (Langfield-Smith and Wirth, 1992; Laukkanen, 1992), through an assessment by the respondent (Bougon et al., 1990) or through a structured coding process (Clapham and Schwenk, 1991). The final stage is analysis, where the map is actually read or interpreted, whether this be to provide further insights into the thoughts of an individual or group (Axelrod, 1976b; Cosette and Audet, 1992), to establish predictive qualities (Narayanan and Fahey, 1990) or to make comparative judgements between maps (Ware, 1978; Stubbart and Ramaprasad, 1988). In order to develop methodologies which can enhance the process of comparing causal maps it is necessary to review some of the current methods in the context of the conceptual framework. The methodological issues of epistemology, validity, reliability and practicability are of particular relevance to studies which aim to compare across multiple causal maps. The remainder of the chapter will therefore focus on these key issues.

Theories of causal mapping

Huff (1990) suggests five families of maps which cover a variety of potential relationships. A representation of these ideas is shown in Figure 13.2. As can be seen from Figure 13.2 causality is represented by the third category, although it is also included as a component in the higher levels of maps such as argument maps or schemata. Causality is one type of cognitive relationship, but has proved popular with those researching strategic

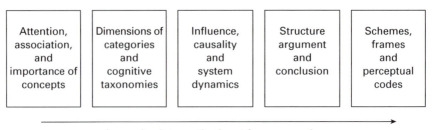

| Attention, association, and importance of concepts | Dimensions of categories and cognitive taxonomies | Influence, causality and system dynamics | Structure argument and conclusion | Schemes, frames and perceptual codes |

Increasing interpretive input from researcher

Figure 13.2   *Five families of cognitive maps (based on Huff, 1990)*

management. The reason for this is partly evident from Huff's (1990) five families. In the context of understanding decision-making, causality provides a potentially higher level of procedural knowledge (how it works or how to do it) than other sets of relationships such as association, constructs or categories. In addition its output is relatively robust and parsimonious, which is in contrast to the complex frameworks of argument maps and schemata that rely on high levels of interpretative input from the researcher in order to create the final map. The application of causal mapping in the context of strategic management is a reflection on the nature of strategic decisions. Strategic decisions involve the manager with ambiguous, unique and complex issues (Dutton et al., 1989). In addition, an implicit aspect of such decisions is their concern with future events. Strategic decisions are those which underpin long-term direction, as illustrated through the often cited strategic questions, 'Where are we now, where do we want to be in the future and how do we get there?' (Pearson, 1990: 23). This temporal element underlies all strategic management issues. We are using the past and the present to infer what will happen in the future. It is this aspect of future inference which makes causal frameworks of cognition particularly appropriate for representing strategy.

The management literature on causal mapping is fragmentary in terms of identifying a clear theoretical grounding for representing cognition as a causal structure. The published work can be divided into two groups. First, that undertaken by Eden and colleagues (Eden et al., 1979; Eden, 1992; Eden et al., 1992) and work located in the area of consumer cognition (Reynolds and Gutman, 1984). These approaches adopt Kelly's Personal Construct Theory (Kelly, 1955) as their underpinning. While Kelly provides a comprehensive basis for understanding sensemaking, there is no explicit causal platform within his theory. This omission has been corrected by Hinkle (1965) who developed Kelly's research to look at the slot change where an individual moves a stimulus along a construct due to changes along another construct. For example, to see the future as moving from fixed to uncertain (construct 1) may then change the type of planning horizon from long- to short-term (construct 2). Hinkle focuses on

explaining a change in terms of its effect on the current construct repertory, as opposed to creating new concepts through their causal interaction.
The constructs remain the focal aspect of cognition but are interlinked
through causal connections.

The second group is less cohesive and has not recognized one specific
theory but a collection of related work. In the strategic management literature it is exemplified by citations from the work of Axelrod (1976a), for
example: Bougon et al. (1977); Stubbart and Ramaprasad (1988); Cosette
and Audet (1992). Axelrod's work in the study of political elites (1976a) is
seminal in that it provides an unprecedented collection of research applying causal mapping concepts to study individual and group
decision-making. However, Axelrod's work is largely applied rather than
theoretical and draws on a number of sources for the theoretical basis of
the methodology. The work of Maruyama (1963) is presented as a theoretical basis for much of the mapping undertaken by Axelrod and his
colleagues. This work has been extended using directed graph theory
(Harary et al., 1978) to allow complex computations to be made on the
elicited maps. A concern with such an approach is that, while it offers analytical credibility, for Axelrod emphasizes the added rigour of a
mathematical system, it appears atheoretical in that these are theories of
analysis rather than theories of sensemaking. Maruyama's (1963) research
focused on causal maps related to population systems in order to explain
population movement, rather than individual sensemaking at a cognitive
level. This is in marked contrast to the comprehensive underpinning, at an
individual level, of personal construct theory (Kelly, 1955).

There is, however, a body of theory in cognitive psychology that does
provide a more direct foundation for the causal mapping approaches
which are currently being applied. Attribution theory has developed in the
area of social psychology as a way of understanding interpersonal interactions and the interpretation of actions and events (Fiske and Taylor, 1984:
20–71). The work of Heider (1944, 1958) bears similarities to that of Kelly
(1955) in that he proposes a theory to explain how individuals interpret
and predict their world. Heider uses the term 'common-sense psychology' where individuals relate their own actions through attribution and
inference as to what their causes and effects may be. This naive analysis of
action provides a basis for representing sensemaking as a series of causal
links between concepts. Heider's work has been developed by many social
psychologists, but lacked the complementary methodology which Kelly
(1955) provided with the repertory grid. More recently researchers have
applied Heider's theories and developed research frameworks for their
implementation. Kelley (1983) provides some valuable observations on
the possible nature of such causal structures including their temporal
direction or emphasis, their extent, and their structure. A number of these
concepts is already being applied in the analysis of causal maps (Eden et
al., 1992). We suggest that causal mapping has a number of theoretical
antecedents which provide a basis for maps that focus specifically on the

causal linkages between concepts, especially those related to Kelly's Personal Construct Theory and Heider's Naive Analysis of Action.

Causal mapping studies

Causal maps are created to serve a wide variety of research questions and focus at many different levels of analysis. One approach to differentiating between studies using causal mapping approaches is the type of research question which is being addressed. Causal mapping studies can be categorized as focusing on the internal dynamics of the maps, on changes in the maps over time or context, or on making comparisons across the maps of individuals or organizations. First, causal maps are constructed for the purpose of examining their own internal dynamics (Maruyama, 1963; Roberts, 1976; Bougon and Komocar, 1990; Cosette and Audet, 1992). Such studies are often conducted for the purpose of explaining and developing the methodology and involve elaborate levels of analysis to establish relationships within the maps. For example, Bougon et al. (1977) found a significant relationship between the level of influence that an individual felt they had over a concept and the number of causal inputs a concept received from other concepts within the map. This relationship has subsequently been supported by other studies (Porac, 1981; Komocar, 1985).

The second type of study is concerned with changes in the causal maps over time or in differing contexts. Such studies are often undertaken to establish the predictive qualities of causal maps. Narayanan and Fahey (1990) used documentary evidence to examine the decline of an organization during the 1960s and 1970s. Huff and Schwenk (1990) looked at how maps varied between good times and bad for particular organizations. A focus on explaining the antecedents to particular events is evident in Axelrod's (1976a) collection of causal mapping research projects (Bonham & Shapiro, 1976; Axelrod, 1976b). In the case of one particular study (Bonham and Shapiro, 1976), the researchers found themselves in a situation where the predictive qualities of a map could be assessed. The map of a government adviser had been constructed from a simulated crisis; this was then followed by an actual crisis. The original map was not able to anticipate completely the adviser's response, but a number of important aspects would have been predicted by the earlier map. In a less specific sense, Eden and colleagues have also considered the change in maps over time (Eden, 1988). In this case it is the improving utility of the maps in a consultancy situation. As the causal maps evolve they provide increasing explanation of complex problems and become adopted and utilized by the respondent group (Eden and Jones, 1980; Jones and Eden, 1981).

The third classification concerns studies which have attempted to make direct comparisons between differing causal maps at the individual, group or organizational level. Stubbart and Ramaprasad (1988) compared the maps of two executives within the US steel industry. They found these to be highly idiosyncratic but with some overlapping concepts. Researchers have also focused on managerial attribution of success and failure in order to make comparisons across industries (Bettman and Weitz, 1983) and between organizations with stable and erratic performance (Salancik and Meindl, 1984; Clapham and Schwenk, 1991). Langfield-Smith (1992) looked at a number of individual maps within an organization and attempted to define common concepts which represent the values of the organization. Hart (1976, 1977) undertook two differing studies to compare the maps of policy-makers. Ware (1978) made a comparison of the maps between two groups of students, identified as academically successful and unsuccessful, the purpose being to establish whether the causal maps could help explain the differences between these two groups.

It is perhaps surprising that there are not more studies which directly compare maps across organizations. Much of the mainstream research on strategic management is concerned with making comparisons across organizations in order to determine the issues which may explain differences in strategic behaviour (Miles and Snow, 1978; Porter, 1985). It is suggested that a possible reason for this lack of application is the difficulty in finding methodologies which are able both to capture adequately causal cognition and permit an effective basis for comparative analysis. If research in managerial cognition, as represented through causal mapping, is to develop further in offering a new perspective on strategy, then the ability effectively to compare and contrast such maps is central to this development (see Laukkanen and Eden and Ackermann, this volume).

Causal map methodologies

Research which applies causal mapping utilizes a number of distinct methodologies. Four established approaches are reviewed, all of which focus on using primary data that are gathered either through an interview or a group discussion. A number of causal mapping studies have been based on documentary, as opposed to interview, data. There are good practical reasons for this, such as the need for data spanning many years, recorded as they occurred, rather than as they were subsequently post-rationalized (Schwenk, 1985). This discussion is concerned with techniques which use primary as opposed to secondary data. Primary data collection offers greater flexibility in matching the data to the research question. It is not reliant on the availability of a particular type of data, such as letters to shareholders (Huff and Schwenk, 1990) or the minutes of meetings (Levi and Tetlock, 1980). Primary data sources therefore provide a potentially more extensive and flexible research tool for strategy research (Eden et al., 1993).

Four approaches have been selected as they represent the more dominant causal mapping methodologies. While there are others (Langfield-Smith and Wirth, 1992; Markoczy and Goldberg, 1993), the following represent the more widely developed and adopted approaches: the Self-Q technique (Bougon, 1983); the Means–End Chain Method (Reynolds and Gutman, 1984); COPE-based Cause Mapping (Eden et al., 1992); Comparative Cause Mapping (Laukkanen, 1992).

The Self-Q technique (Bougon, 1983) is an interviewing process based on self-questioning by the respondent. It is a methodology which focuses on the elicitation rather than the analysis side of the mapping activity. Originally Bougon's technique utilized four interviewing stages (1983), later to be reduced to three with the respondent completing some elements of the process away from the interviewer (Bougon et al., 1990). The stages involved the collection of the concepts (Stage 1), the verification of these concepts (Stage 2), the identification of the causal links between the concepts (Stage 3), and the verification of the map by feeding this back to the respondent (Stage 4). The advantages of such an approach are that, while it allows respondents to elicit their idiosyncratic concepts in a relatively unstructured way, it does then impose structure through a ranking exercise to focus respondents on the issues which are most relevant to the particular research question. The self-questioning approach is designed to minimize the possible bias which can be introduced by the interviewer, thereby optimizing its reliability. It does however restrict the respondent in the third stage where causal connections are only made between the concepts which have been elicited in stages one and two, rather than allowing the causal inferences to generate new concepts. In the most recent form of this approach (Bougon et al., 1990) respondents use multicoloured forms to complete the process. While there is little detail on the likely duration of the interview programme it is probable that this will run to at least three or four hours in total.

The Means–End Chain Method has been developed for eliciting and analysing consumer cognition as opposed to managerial cognition. However this approach has been applied in a managerial context (Eden et al., 1979; Jolly et al., 1988). It also introduces a number of new perspectives to the creation of causal maps. In common with Eden's work (1988) the means–end chain approach is grounded in the work of Kelly (1955) as developed by Hinkle (1965). The triadic sort technique is applied to elicit data from the respondent. This is an approach which minimizes interviewer influence over the respondent. However, it can be time-consuming and boring for the respondent, depending on the number of elements being used. The triadic sort elicits constructs which are then laddered (Reynolds and Gutman, 1988), a technique involving the interviewer establishing why the respondent prefers a particular pole of the construct. These data are then constructed into a matrix of all the constructs elicited which are then aggregated across respondents to produce a hierarchical value map (Jolly et al., 1988). The advantage of this approach is that it is relatively efficient in terms of the time commitment needed from the respondents. In the case of the management-based study (Jolly et al., 1988), the mapping exercise lasted between 45 minutes and one hour. An area of concern is the approach to aggregation which involves constructing a map from all the individual connections made between concepts by all the respondents. In terms of cognitive theory the overall map may therefore be atheoretical, in that it fails to represent any one individual's causal framework but is created by the aggregation of all the connections. For example, an aggregate map which shows A causing B which in turn causes C may be derived from half the respondents believing A causes B and half that B causes C, but no single individual holds the aggregate cognition that A causes B which then causes C.

In contrast to the alternatives discussed here, the mapping approach put forward by Eden (1988) is designed to be used as an interactive tool assisting in clarifying problems and facilitating group solutions to complex issues. The approach is grounded in personal construct theory as developed through Hinkle's implication grid (1965). In this particular context an important contribution is Graphics COPE software. This analysis package allows the visual display and analysis of causal maps in a way which permits multiple analysis and assessment. Unlike the Self-Q technique the process for eliciting maps involves relatively unstructured elicitation, thereby allowing concepts to be developed from causal links, as opposed to linking defined groups of concepts. Therefore the causal connections, as opposed to the constructs, become the focus of the mapping exercise.

Laukkanen's (1990, 1992) approach to causal mapping is of particular interest in this context, as it has been developed specifically for making comparisons across causal maps. This process involves a programme of three interviews with respondents each estimated to take three hours (nine hours per respondent). This is longer than many of the idiosyncratic studies applying techniques, such as the Self-Q methodology (Bougon et al., 1990). With Laukkanen's methodology the researcher conducts the interviews and codes all the data, which are then incorporated into maps. The process involves an unstructured interview, based around a pre-established protocol, which seeks to uncover the causal patterns that the respondent uses to make sense of a situation. The method has high content validity as the data are recorded in the form presented by the respondents, who are relatively free to introduce the concepts which they feel are salient. The data reduction is then carried out post hoc by reducing the maps to a standardized natural language in order to allow for subsequent analysis. The concern with such an approach is that, at this stage, there appears to be no attempt to ensure that the data are being transformed in a reliable way, as would be the case if this involved the content analysis of a document (Berelson, 1954). A further issue is that the focus of analysis is at the level of concepts and their links: the concept of profit can be effectively analysed across a group of respondents to evaluate its position in a cause and effect structure, rather than the focus of analysis being the individuals and the context in which they use these particular concepts. Laukkanen's (1992) CMAP2 analysis is an important contribution for it addresses the complex issues of comparing maps and introduces the notion that maps

designed for the purpose of direct comparison will be significantly different from those designed for idiosyncratic reflection.

All of these approaches bring particular strengths and weaknesses to the
researcher's dilemma of how to elicit and analyse causal maps for the purposes of comparison. The Means–End Framework (Reynolds and Gutman,
1984) offers a particularly focused interview protocol, reducing the time
needed to have access to the respondent. The Self-Q approach (Bougon et
al., 1990) provides a particularly rigorous and structured basis for ensuring
that the maps are covering the key issues as reliably as possible. The COPE
framework (Eden et al., 1992) offers a well-founded methodology with a
highly usable analysis package which allows for the detailed analysis of
individual maps and the opportunity for fast interactive mapping.
Laukkanen's comparative mapping provides a framework designed
specifically for the comparison of causal maps with an analysis packaging
for examining concepts across a population of respondents. Referring to
Figure 13.1, the methodological issues of validity, reliability and practicability need to be considered in determining the most appropriate
methodology.

Issues in comparative causal mapping: validity

The concept of validity is often expressed as a question: 'Are we measuring what we think we are measuring?' Kerlinger (1973: 457). In the
context of causal or any other form of cognitive mapping, this question is
clearly difficult to answer. Individual cognition is, at the present time,
unknowable and such maps can only be an attempt to capture a partial
structure through concepts and links. Kerlinger's question can be
regarded as a positivistic view of validity. It assumes that there is a reality which can be established and measured in some way. Easterby-Smith
et al. define the phenomenological perspective of validity as follows: 'Has
the researcher gained full access to the knowledge and meaning of infor-
mants?' (1991:41). This approach to validity is more appropriate to the
causal mapping context and leads to the question: 'Have we allowed the
respondent to respond in a way which is salient and meaningful to him or
her?' In reviewing the existing studies which have made comparisons
between individual maps there is a number of concerns highlighted by
this question.

Saliency versus comparability

Many studies have noted that the comparative analysis of causal maps is
problematic and essentially requires some level of trade-off between
saliency, capturing the variables and relationships which accurately reflect
the cognition of the individual, and comparability, ensuring that there is

sufficient commonality between the maps to make meaningful comparisons. A common approach to this problem has been to use a priori variables where all the variables in the map are presented to the respondent who is then required to make the necessary causal links. This has been used in a number of studies (Bougon et al., 1977; Roberts, 1976; Ware, 1978; Porac, 1981; Ford and Hegarty, 1984; Komocar, 1985) using various numbers of variables from a total of 5 (Porac, 1981) through to 25 (Komocar, 1985). The advantage of this approach is that the researchers can identify the total number of possible connections and are therefore working with a predefined matrix across all the maps. While there are obvious benefits in terms of analysis and reliability, the validity question is whether using these a priori variables captures individual views of the world, or whether they force the respondent to work within a set of variables which is not central to their individual cognitions of a situation. Ford and Hegarty (1984), who used a fixed set of variables to compare MBAs with practising managers, consider that one of the reasons why their maps were relatively simple (in terms of a lack of causal connections) was a lack of saliency for the respondents with the eight researcher defined variables. The danger with such an approach is that it potentially removes a key strength of mapping research: the ability to reflect the divergence of respondents' reasoning which can detect new aspects of managerial thought not yet considered in the established literature (Reger, 1988).

Atomistic versus holistic

A further characteristic of the a priori mapping studies is that they have tended to use paired comparisons for eliciting data from the respondents. This approach requires the respondent to make single causal links between the presented variables (A causes B; A does not cause C). The concern is that when the respondents are providing data in this fashion, it can lead to a highly atomistic approach to constructing a cognitive map. While this has a practical benefit, in ensuring that all possible permutations have been considered, it is inconsistent with Tolman's (1948) original concept of the cognitive map. Tolman (1948) describes pathways and landscapes as forming the map structure: the map is a gestalt or holistic set of connections which make up a coherent whole. The application of paired comparisons may potentially create maps which are atomistic and do not reflect such a holistic view. In some studies this issue has been addressed by feeding back the structure to the respondents and asking them to amend the map to provide a more coherent representation of their views (Stubbart and Ramaprasad, 1988). The issues raised in discussing the validity of comparative mapping methods all relate to the question, 'What are we actually comparing?' Cognitive mapping is essentially a qualitative research approach. It is a way of eliciting meaning and promotes our understanding of how an individual makes sense of a situation. The notion of validity as capturing individual sensemaking is therefore pre-eminent in the design and undertaking of mapping research.

Issues in comparative causal mapping: reliability

As with the concept of validity, reliability can also be viewed from a number of perspectives. Many qualitative research perspectives consider that the concept of reliability is inappropriate to this paradigm (Taylor and Bogdan, 1984). However, the general view is that reliability is concerned with replicability (Easterby-Smith et al., 1991; Gummesson, 1991): if the study is undertaken by another researcher using the same methodology with the same respondents, the results would be the same. Kerlinger (1973) provides a further dimension to this view concerning the distribution of error. In this definition the concept of reliability is concerned with ensuring that the distribution of error is as even as possible: there is no systematic bias caused by preconceptions held by the interviewers, coders or other individuals which may affect the data.

In comparative mapping studies two differing approaches to the issue of reliability have emerged. The first is to present the respondent with a set of variables which they will then link with causal connections. This process of using a priori variables has been designed to alleviate reliability and analysis problems, the respondents make the connections explicitly themselves and thereby contain any bias within their own maps. The second approach is found in studies which are concerned with the use of documentary data. In this situation there is a need for post hoc coding which is approached with differing degrees of rigour in the published studies. Several widely cited studies noted the use of multiple coders but made no mention of levels of agreement or how disagreements were resolved (Bonham and Shapiro, 1976; Hart, 1977; Levi and Tetlock, 1980; Stubbart and Ramaprasad, 1988). Others made no mention of any coding process, or what other steps may have been taken to ensure reliability (Roos and Hall, 1980; Hall, 1984; Cosette and Audet, 1992). In contrast, many provide clear accounts of the coding strategy and how disagreements were handled (Axelrod, 1976b; Bettman and Weitz; 1983; Huff and Schwenk, 1990; Narayanan and Fahey, 1990), with one study going as far as to separate out the outputs of two coders as they were not happy with their levels of agreement (Clapham and Schwenk, 1991). Overall there is a lack of consistency as to how coding issues are dealt with and reported. This is of particular concern in the context of studies which are making comparisons across multiple individuals and/or organizations. In these situations any form of systematic bias, distributed non-randomly, would have a profound effect on the output of the mapping process. This is likely in situations where the surfacing and mapping process involves high levels of interviewer input in terms of the latitude available within the protocol, this being determined by the amount of structure designed into the interview. Methodologies which allow latitude but do not address how the issue of reliability will be resolved must raise concerns as to how the cognitions of the researcher are separated from those of the respondent.

Issues in comparative causal mapping: practicability

While all management researchers strive for maximizing the validity and reliability of their research, they are ultimately governed by the nature of the management context and the disposition of their respondents: 'feasible research questions may be determined more by access possibilities than by theoretical considerations' (Easterby-Smith et al., 1991: 6). For mapping approaches to become more widely applied and therefore provide a consistent method for strategic management research, it is imperative that they are appropriate to the situation of the respondent. While many successful studies have used documentary evidence, with its attendant strengths and weaknesses, this can ultimately only provide a limited insight into organizational strategy due to the potentially wide range of research questions which need to be explored. The discussion on practicability focuses on the issues of obtaining and sustaining the cooperation of the respondents appropriate to a particular research question. Methodologies which allow the respondent to reflect their own views, in their own language, are likely to be more acceptable and therefore more successful in their application to management research.

Brown (1992) discusses the problems of rigorous methodologies which cause irritation and avoidance behaviour in the respondent. It is unacceptable in today's lean times for managers to spend up to nine hours with a researcher unless there are very clear direct benefits from this use of time. While such benefits and interest levels may exist in many research programmes, particularly those which involve in-depth studies, they are less likely to be evident in comparative studies which involve the elicitation of multiple maps to be compared across many organizations. There appears to be a view that rigorous research needs to involve the respondent in lengthy interviews to capture the requisite richness of the cognitive map. However, this is not necessarily so. For example, Daniels et al. (1993) developed a card sort technique that produces results which converge with the Repertory Grid Technique, but in a fraction of the time. It is perhaps surprising that, as this type of practicability is central to the success of management research, the issue of how acceptable methodologies are to managers themselves has not been more widely discussed. The most rigorous methodology is meaningless if you cannot get managers to take part in the research.

Summary: critical design issues and observations

This review has elicited a number of concerns over methodologies which have been applied to make comparisons across multiple causal maps. The methods currently available undoubtedly possess many strengths in terms of validity, reliability and practicability. The problem is that, dependent on the research context, these approaches do not always offer the optimal solution. The purpose of this chapter is to suggest that the elements of the mapping process need to be reviewed and reconfigured according to the question which is driving the research. We have reviewed a number of the existing causal mapping methodologies from the position of developing methods to compare maps across organizations and individuals. A number of concerns has been surfaced in terms of their suitability to become more widely applied in strategic management research. These concerns are the critical design issues which the researcher needs to consider in order to make the most appropriate choice for a particular research decision. This chapter has suggested that these design issues can be grouped into four broad categories:

- epistemology – what is the theoretical basis for representing cognition?
- validity – does the methodology capture the issues which are salient to the respondents?
- reliability – are they free from systematic bias imposed by the researcher or other individuals?
- practicability – do they allow management researchers to build the sort of relationships they need with the management community, through methodologies which are efficient and challenging, rather than time consuming and irritating?

Figure 13.1 provides a framework for considering the questions which need to be resolved in terms of defining the methodology, the scope and nature of the research question, and the practical problems of actually undertaking the research. These elements are essentially linked and iterative, a change in the methodology may involve a change in the level of analysis and scope of the research question, and vice versa.

It is suggested that a number of approaches can be taken to ensure that comparative mapping provides a valid and practical basis for researching managers and organizations. However, this development of the methodology does require researchers in being clear as to the nature and role of this methodology in the context of their research. As a methodology, cognitive mapping is concerned with eliciting the underlying sensemaking of individuals or groups. It is therefore central to the process that the respondents, rather than the comparison, remain as the central focus. This requires the application of approaches which retain the language and sensemaking of the respondent. While there is always the inevitable trade-off between individual context and the need for comparison, researchers need to ask themselves whether they have taken sufficient steps to ensure that they are as close as is practical to the respondent's view of the world. Many mapping studies are highly rigorous in terms of their adherence to conventions of analysis. It is suggested that in the context of cognitive mapping, rigour should primarily be concerned with a trail of evidence that validates the maps in terms of their saliency and relevance to the respondent.

The reporting of many mapping studies has not engendered the development of new research, as many of the processes are not explicitly identified. Whereas this may be the judgement of reviewers and/or editors, a lack of clarity over the interview and coding processes, which are fundamental to the creation of the maps, is unhelpful in terms of building a wide knowledge base on these approaches and conventions.

Finally, management researchers are dependent on the cooperation of managers for their work. In order to develop these relationships the management community needs to understand the purpose and benefit of mapping, both in terms of how it can be used within their organizations and in terms of the insights it provides to the understanding of organizational processes. A critical design issue is therefore the likely impression and benefit provided to the respondent, as well as the value to the researcher. Comparative mapping methodologies have an undoubted contribution to bring to our understanding of the strategies of managers and their organizations. The continued development of such approaches will ensure that, as researchers, we extend our understanding of the sense-making and priorities of those making strategic decisions.

References

Argyris, C. and Schön, D. A. (1978) *Organizational Learning: A Theory of Action Perspective*. Reading, MA: Addison-Wesley.

Axelrod, R. (ed.) (1976a) *Structure of Decision: The Cognitive Maps of Political Elites*. Princeton, NJ: Princeton University Press.

Axelrod R. (1976b) Decision for neoimperialism: the deliberations of the British Eastern Committee in 1918, in R. Axelrod (ed.), *The Structure of Decision: The Cognitive Maps of Political Elites*. Princeton, NJ: Princeton University Press. pp. 77–95.

Berelson, B. (1954) Content analysis, in G. Lindzey (ed.), *Handbook of Social Psychology*, vol. 1. Reading, MA: Addison-Wesley. pp. 488–522.

Bettman, J. and Weitz, B. (1983) Attributions in the boardroom: causal reasoning in corporate annual reports, *Administrative Science Quarterly*, 28: 165–83.

Bonham, G.M. and Shapiro, M.J. (1976) Explanation of the unexpected: the Syrian intervention in Jordan in 1970, in R. Axelrod (ed.), *The Structure of Decision: The Cognitive Maps of Political Elites*. Princeton, NJ: Princeton University Press. pp. 113–41.

Bougon, M.G. (1983) Uncovering cognitive maps: the self-Q technique, in G. Morgan (ed.), *Beyond Method: Strategies for Social Research*. Beverly Hills, CA: Sage. pp. 173–88.

Bougon, M.G., Baird, N., Komocar, J.M. and Ross, W. (1990) Identifying strategic loops: the self-Q interviews, in A.S. Huff (ed.), *Mapping Strategic Thought*. Chichester: John Wiley. pp. 327–54.

Bougon, M.G. and Komocar, J.M. (1990) Directing strategic change: a dynamic wholistic approach, in A.S. Huff (ed.), *Mapping Strategic Thought*. Chichester: John Wiley. pp. 135–64.

Bougon, M.G., Weick, K.E. and Binkhorst, D. (1977) Cognition in organizations: an analysis of the Utrecht Jazz Orchestra, *Administrative Science Quarterly*, 22: 606–39.

Brown, S. (1992) Cognitive mapping and repertory grids for qualitative survey research: some comparative observations, *Journal of Management Studies*, 29: 287–308.

Bryant, J. (1983) Hypermaps: a representation of perceptions in conflicts, *Omega*, 11 (6): 575–86.

Clapham, S.E. and Schwenk, C.R. (1991) Self-serving attributions, managerial cognition, and company performance, *Strategic Management Journal*, 12: 219–29.

Cosette, P. and Audet, M. (1992) Mapping of an idiosyncratic schema, *Journal of Management Studies*, 29 (3): 309–48.

Daniels, K., de Chernatony, L. and Johnson, G. (1993) Mapping managers' mental models of competitive industry structures. Paper presented at the Occupational Psychology Conference, Brighton, January.

Duhaime, I.M. and Schwenk, C.R. (1985) Conjectures on cognitive simplification in acquisition and divestment decision making, *Academy of Management Review*, 10 (2): 287–95.

Dunn, W.N. and Ginsberg, A. (1986) A sociocognitive network approach to organizational analysis, *Human Relations*, 40: 955–76.

Dutton, J.E., Fahey, L. and Narayanan, V.K. (1983) Toward understanding strategic issue diagnosis, *Strategic Management Journal*, 4: 307–24.

Dutton, J.E., Walton, E.J. and Abrahamson, E. (1989) Important dimensions of strategic issues: separating the wheat from the chaff, *Journal of Management Studies*, 26 (4), July: 379–96.

Easterby-Smith, M., Thorpe, R. and Lowe, A. (1991) *Management Research: An Introduction*. London: Sage.

Eden, C. (1988) Cognitive mapping, *European Journal of Operational Research*, 36: 1–13.

Eden, C. (1992) On the nature of cognitive maps, *Journal of Management Studies*, 29 (3): 261–5.

Eden, C., Ackermann, F. and Cropper, S. (1992) The analysis of cause maps, *Journal of Management Studies*, 29 (3): 309–24.

Eden, C., Ackermann, F. and Tait, A. (1993) Comparing cognitive maps – methodological issues. Paper presented at the International Workshop on Managerial and Organizational Cognition, Brussels, Belgium, 13–14 May.

Eden, C. and Jones, S. (1980) Publish or perish? – a case study, *Journal of the Operational Research Society*, 31: 131–9.

Eden, C., Jones, S. and Sims, D. (1979) *Thinking in Organizations*. London: Macmillan.

Fahey, L. and Narayanan, V.K. (1989) Linking changes in revealed causal maps and environment: an empirical study, *Journal of Management Studies*, 26 (4): 361–78.

Fiol, C. M. and Lyles, M.A. (1985) Organizational learning, *Academy of Management Review*, 10: 803–13.

Fiske, S.T. and Taylor, S.E. (1984) *Social Cognition*. Reading, MA: Addison-Wesley.

Fletcher, K.E. and Huff, A.S. (1990) Strategic argument mapping: reformulating strategy at AT & T, in A.S. Huff (ed.), *Mapping Strategic Thought*. Chichester: John Wiley. pp. 165–94.

Ford, J.D. and Hegarty, W.H. (1984) Decision makers' beliefs about the causes and effects of structure: an exploratory study, *Academy of Management Journal*, 27 (2): 271–91.

Gummesson, E. (1991) *Qualitative Methods in Management Research*. Newbury Park, CA: Sage.

Gutman, J. (1982) A means–end chain model based on consumer categorisation processes, *Journal of Marketing*, 46, Spring: 60–72.

Hall, R.I. (1984) The natural logic of management policy making: its implication for the survival of an organization, *Management Science*, 30: 905–27.

Harary, F., Norman, R.Z. and Cartwright, D. (1978) *Structural Models: An Introduction to the Theory of Directed Graphs*. New York: John Wiley.

Hart, J.A. (1976) Comparative cognition: politics of international control of the oceans, in R. Axelrod (ed.), *The Structure of Decision: The Cognitive Maps of Political Elites*. Princeton: Princeton University Press. pp. 18–54.

Hart, J.A. (1977) Cognitive maps of three Latin American policy makers, *World Politics*, 30: 115–40.

Heider, F. (1944) Social perception and phenomenal causality, *Psychological Review*, 51: 358–74.

Heider, F. (1958) *The Psychology of Interpersonal Relations*. New York: John Wiley.

Hinkle, D.N. (1965) The change of personal constructs from the viewpoint of a theory of construct implications. Unpublished PhD thesis, Ohio State University.

Huff, A.S. (1990) Mapping strategic thought, in A.S. Huff (ed.), *Mapping Strategic Thought*, Chichester: John Wiley. pp. 11–49.

Huff, A.S. and Fletcher, K.E. (1990) Key mapping decisions, in A.S. Huff (ed.), *Mapping Strategic Thought*. Chichester: John Wiley. pp. 403–12.

Huff, A.S., Narapareddy, V. and Fletcher, K.E. (1990) Coding the causal association of concepts, in A.S. Huff (ed.), *Mapping Strategic Thought*. Chichester: John Wiley. pp. 311–26.

Huff, A.S. and Schwenk, C.R. (1990) Bias and sensemaking in good times and bad, in A.S. Huff (ed.), *Mapping Strategic Thought*. Chichester: John Wiley. pp. 89–108.

Jackson, S.E. and Dutton, J.E. (1988) Discerning threats and opportunities, *Administrative Science Quarterly*, 33: 370–87.

Jolly, J.P., Reynolds, T.J. and Slocum, J.W. (1988) Applications of the means–end theoretic for understanding the cognitive bases of performance appraisal, *Organizational Behaviour and Human Decision Processes*, 41: 153–79.

Jones, S. and Eden, C. (1981) O.R. in the Community, *Journal of the Operational Research Society*, 32: 335–45.

Kelley, H.H. (1983) Perceived causal structures, in J. Jaspars, F.D. Fincham and M. Hewstone (eds), *Attribution Theory and Research: Conceptual Developmental and Social Dimensions*. London: Academic Press. pp. 343–69.

Kelly, G.A. (1955) *The Psychology of Personal Constructs*. New York: W.W. Norton.

Kerlinger, F.N. (1973) *Foundations of Behavioural Research*, 2nd edn. London: Holt, Rinehart and Winston.

Kiesler, S. and Sproull, L. (1982) Managerial response to changing environments: perspectives on problem sensing from social cognition, *Administrative Science Quarterly*, 27, December: 548–70.

Komocar, J.M. (1985) Participant cause maps of a work setting: an approach to cognition and behavior in organizations. Unpublished PhD thesis, University of Illinois. Ann Arbor: University Microfilm International.

Langfield-Smith, K. (1992) Exploring the need for a shared cognitive map, *Journal of Management Studies*, 29 (3): 349–68.

Langfield-Smith, K. and Wirth, A. (1992) Measuring differences between cognitive maps, *Journal of the Operational Research Society*, 43 (12): 1135–50.

Laukkanen, M. (1990) Describing management cognition: the cause mapping approach, *Scandinavian Journal of Management*, 6 (3): 197–216.

Laukkanen, M. (1992) *Comparative Cause Mapping of Management Cognitions*. Helsinki: Helsinki School of Economics and Business Administration Publications, D-154.

Levi, A. and Tetlock, P.E. (1980) A cognitive analysis of Japan's 1941 decision for war, *Journal of Conflict Resolution*, 24 (2): 195–211.

Markoczy, L. and Goldberg, J. (1993) A method for eliciting and comparing causal maps. Paper presented at the International Workshop on Managerial and Organizational Cognition, Brussels, 11–15 May.

Maruyama, M. (1963) The second cybernetics: deviation amplifying mutual causal processes, *American Scientist*, 51: 164–79.

Miles, R.E. and Snow, C.C. (1978) *Organizational Strategy, Structure and Process*. Tokyo: McGraw Hill.

Mintzberg, H. (1978) Patterns in strategy formation, *Management Science*, 24: 934–48.

Narayanan, V.K. and Fahey, L. (1990) Evolution of revealed causal maps during decline: a case study of admiral, in A.S. Huff (ed.), *Mapping Strategic Thought*. Chichester: John Wiley. pp. 109–34.

Pearson, G.J. (1990) *Strategic Thinking*. Hemel Hempstead: Prentice-Hall.

Porac, J.F. (1981) Causal loops and other intercausal perceptions in attributions for exam performance, *Journal of Education Psychology*, 73 (4): 587–601.

Porac, J.F. and Thomas, H. (1990) Taxonomic mental models in competitor definition, *Academy of Management Review*, 15 (2): 224–40.

Porter, M. (1985) *Competitive Advantage*. New York: Free Press.

Reger, R.K. (1988) Competitive positioning in the Chicago banking market: mapping the mind of the strategist. Unpublished PhD thesis, University of Illinois at Urbana-Champaign.

Reynolds T.J. and Gutman, J. (1984) Laddering: extending the repertory grid methodology to construct attribute – consequence – value hierarchies, in R.E. Pitts and A.G. Woodside (eds), *Personal Values and Consumer Psychology*. Lexington, MA: Lexington Books. pp. 155–67.

Reynolds, T.J. and Gutman, J. (1988) Laddering theory, method, analysis and interpretation, *Journal of Advertising Research*, February–March: 11–31.

Roberts, F.S. (1976) Strategy for the energy crisis: the case of commuter transport policy, in R. Axelrod (ed.), *The Structure of Decision: The Cognitive Maps of Political Elites*. Princeton, NJ: Princeton University Press. pp. 142–79.

Roos, L.L. and Hall, R.I. (1980) Influence diagrams and organizational power, *Administrative Science Quarterly*, 25 March: 57–71.

Salancik, G.R. and Meindl, J.R. (1984) Corporate attributions as strategic illusions of control, *Administrative Science Quarterly*, 29, June: 238–54.

Schwenk, C.R. (1984) Cognitive simplification processes in strategic decision making, *Strategic Management Journal*, 5: 111–28.

Schwenk, C.R. (1985) The use of participant recollection in the modelling of organizational decision processes, *Academy of Management Review*, 10: 496–503.

Stubbart, C.I. (1987) Cognitive science and strategic management theoretical and methodological issues, *Best Paper Proceedings, Forty-Seventh Annual Meeting of the Academy of Management*. New Orleans, Louisiana. pp. 46–50.

Stubbart, C.I. and Ramaprasad, A. (1988) Probing two chief executives' schematic knowledge of the US steel industry using cognitive maps, *Advances in Strategic Management*, 5: 139–64.

Taylor, S.J. and Bogdan, R. (1984) *Introduction to Qualitative Research Methods: The Search for Meanings*, 2nd edn. New York: John Wiley.

Tolman, E.C. (1948) Cognitive maps in rats and men, *Psychological Review*, 55: 189–208.

Walsh, J.P. (1988) Selectivity and selective perception: an investigation of managers' belief structures and information processing, *Academy of Management Journal*, 31 (4): 873–96.

Ware, J.P. (1978) Student perceptions of causality in the academic environment: the causal maps of successful and unsuccessful freshmen. Unpublished PhD thesis, Cornell University.

Weick, K.E. (1990) Cartographic myths in organizations, in A.S. Huff (ed.), *Mapping Strategic Thought*. Chichester: John Wiley. pp. 1–10.

Weick, K.E. and Bougon, M.G. (1986) Organizations as cognitive maps: charting ways to success and failure, in H.P. Sims and D.A. Gioia (eds), *The Thinking Organization*. San Francisco, CA: Jossey-Bass. pp. 102–35.

Wrightson, M.T. (1976) The documentary coding method, in R. Axelrod (ed.), *Structure of Decision: The Cognitive Maps of Political Elites*. Princeton, NJ: Princeton University Press. pp. 291–332.

INDEX